The Witching Way

Hill

A Sourcebook of Hidden Wisdom, Folklore, Traditional Paganism,
and Witchcraft

"Through the threads of the present do legends race
Through breath and words and desperate hearts
In the small clay cup and wooden plate
Is the antlered king, and all his court"

The Witching Way

Of The

Hollow Hill

The Gramarye of the Folk
Who Dwell Below the Mound

Robin Artisson

PENDRAIG PUBLISHING, LOS ANGELES

Third Edition: August 2009
Second Edition: 2006
First Hardcover Edition: 2006

Text Copyright © 2005-2009 by Robin Artisson

Artwork Copyright © 2005-2009 by Thorgrimr

ISBN   978-0-9820318-8-9

Contained Herein

Dedication
10

Introduction
13

Reclaiming
19

**Part I. The Witching Way:
Understanding the Worldview of Traditional Paganism and the
Old Craft**
33

What is Seen and Unseen. The River of Time and Rebirth. Body, Soul, and Spirit: The Lost Mystical Anthropology of the Ancients. Concerning the Mysteries. The Metaphysics of Rebirth and the Red Thread. The Path of Fate. The White Tree and the Horse. Fate and the Child of Truth and Beauty. The Adamantine Grip of Fate. The Doom on Man and the Hidden Wisdom-gate of Awareness. Mastery and the Timeless Self. The Strange Double-Bind of Fate. Fate and Wisdom-Awakening. The Spirits and Powers of the Old Ways. The Master of the Craft. The Native God and the Secret of the White God in the Land. Goat Master and the Stag-King. Vindonus and Janicot. Basajaun and the Goat-Master. Names and Correspondences. Apollo Vindonus. The Light Between the Horns. Witchmother: The Dark Matriarch of the Craft. The Origins of the Old Veiled Witch-queen. The Daughter of the Great Queen. The Pale People, the Good Folk, and the Master Men. The Strangers.

**Part II. The Twilight Art:
The Secret Doors of Trance and Fetch-Flight**
133

Awakening Awareness: The White Tree, the Ghost Tree, or the God Stone. Attaining the Witch-sight: Second Sight and the Great Quest of Humankind. The Quest for the Young Puck. The Key to the Quest. Dreams, Death, and Destiny. The Hissing of the Serpent. The Serpent in the Land: The Power Below and Within. The Widdershins Walk: The Left-Way Road or the Crooked Path, and the Doors in the Land.

Part III. The Secret Tradition:
The Hidden Wisdom of the Old Ways
175

Traditional Pagan Morality and the Ballad of the Cruel Mother. Eyes of Wood, Heart of Stone: The Hidden Metaphysics in the Ballad of Tam Lin. Eyes of Wood. A Heart of Stone. The Seven Year Tithe to Hell. The Challenge of the Guardian: The Key to Any Door. The False Knight on the Road. The Truth as it is Born. The Test of the Guardian. The Hard Road of Spontaneity. What is Right and What is Easy. A Final Mystery. The Tale of the White Serpent: A Hidden Wisdom Tradition. Wholeness and the Master Spirits.

Part IV. The Master Keys of the Craft:
Four Roads to Mastery
227

The Path of Initiation: The Fivefold Pattern of the Witching Way. The Secret Under the Mounds: The Origins of the Old Rite, and the True Meaning of Sacrifice. The Funeral Cult. "The Passage Between" and the Key. The Phantom of the Slain. Poor John Barleycorn. Gods of the Dead. Straw and Twig Body of the Lord of the Land: The Rite of the Wake-Fire and the Funeral Mound. Three Rites of Mastery. Witch Consecrations and Dedications. The Grand Rite of Elemental Regency.

Part V. Ritual Book:
The Craft of the Hidden People
269

Echoes in the Unseen. Two Things that must be Remembered. The Missing Element. The Red Meal: The Housle, or the Sacrament of Bread and Wine. Concerning the use of the Bell. "Killing the Red Meal". The Witch-Ring: Drawing the Witches' Compass. The "Going Forth" Declaration. The Spell of the Road. The Spell for the Water and the Four Roads. The Spell for the Fire. River's Edge Incantations. The Ring of Art Invocation. The Art of Spell-making, Invocation, and Incantations. Invoking and Calling the Old Powers. The Petition Charm. Making objects "Red." Ash-protection charm. Exorcising the Restless Dead. The Thorn Tree by the Crossroads. The Induction Charm and the Initiation. The Four-Sided Shrine and the Offering Well. The "Two Trees" working for entering the Spirit World. The Rite of Arriving: Guardianship and the Old Persuasion.

List of Essential Books and Works
353

Index
357

About the Author
367

List of Illustrations

Plate 1: "Haunted Earth"
12

Plate 2: "The Master Andras"
91

Plate 3: "The White King"
99

Plate 4: "Hulda the Queen of Elfhame"
113

Plate 5: "Fair Queen of Elfland"
123

Plate 6: "White Body of the Lord in the Land"
163

Plate 7: "Under the Mound"
239

Plate 8: "White Body Inverse"
253

Plate 9: "The Goat Ring"
259

Plate 10: "The Matrones"
297

Plate 11: "Great Inheritance"
303

Plate 12: "Serpent Stone"
337

Dedications

A work such as this is the product of a massive chain of forces- but chief among those forces is the love, dedication, and effort of many, many people and spiritual powers. I have to try to thank them now:

To Jennifer Postler: You are living proof that when the Powers who watch over us decide to send their blessings, they don't hold back- your tireless devotion to the Old Ways, and your generosity is the reason why this book finally saw print. You have let flow an ocean of love and sharing, and no dedication or gratitude will ever be enough to repay you. As long as the worlds endure, I and those closest to me will love you.

To the people at the Hollow Hill: Robin Artisson lovingly dedicates this book to you, and hopes that you can help him to take it to the next place.

To my fetch-beast, my Familiar spirit, the very wise and watchful Owl: allow me to quote the master poet Rumi in your praise: "In your light I learn how to love; in your beauty, how to make poems. You dance inside my chest, where no one sees you. But sometimes I do, and that sight becomes this art."

To the Pale Lady who lives in the Land, the Mother of my Spirit, She who holds the dead inside Her- and to Her Lord, the White Horned One of great knowledge, teacher of the Art: Do not see only this mortal effort, but see the great love and spirit behind it. I am your devoted servant and son, and I place myself in your hands, now and always.

And to my wife, Sara- the finest and the most beautiful that Ireland ever produced: Your love is the heart and soul of everything I do; there is no Son of Art without you. Thank you for being my strength and my all.

To Michael Quirke, woodcarver of Sligo Town and guardian of the hidden doors of Wisdom in the Land of Eire, to T.L., R.B., and to the other gentleman who wishes to remain unnamed; you are the guardians of the true Old Ways, and your Wisdom can now be partly expressed in this book, even if a book cannot do it full justice.

Finally, I want to thank all the people out there who, when they saw a good thing, *knew* it was a good thing- and were not afraid to say so.

Introduction: The Lasting Path

The book you hold in your hands is the culmination of 11 years of reading, research, travel, spiritual questing, and Fate. I am Robin Artisson, called "Son of Art" because I feel myself to be a son of this Art- the Art, worldview, and Craft of the Old Ways.

This "Art" is an art of the spirit; this worldview is a "way of seeing" that places the power of the Land, and the unseen places within the Land, first in all a person thinks and feels; and this "Craft" is the Craft of living in accordance with the Land, with the source of dreams, and the deeper urgings of Fate.

"The Old Ways" is a rather broad term that really just refers to the non-Christian and pre-Christian way of thinking, which was so vital a part of the lives of many peoples all over the world. In the sense I use it, it refers to my European ancestors particularly; however, the path I discuss in this book is not limited to people of European ancestry only. This is because the powers I believe in, the things I have experienced, and the values I treasure, are human powers, human experiences, and human values, before they ever were "European."

This book is a record of my journey into Traditional Paganism and craft- and it is not offered as a book of "scholarship," but a book of spirituality, born in some scholarly research, but mostly rooting from personal experience, interviews with people I have met, personal meditations and considerations, and, finally, strong intuitions.

The usage of the term "Traditional" causes quite an amount of confusion on the part of some people, and quite a rebuke from others. I began to use the term when I realized it stood for something very important- it stands for a perspective on the Old Ways, and a perspective on modern-day revivals of things such as Paganism and Pagan sorcery or witchcraft, that is not an outgrowth of the "new age" movement.

Traditional Paganism, and traditional forms of "power manipulation" or sorcery, or pre-Christian spiritual ecstasies, is "traditional" precisely because it is not born from the cradle of the New Age- it is not born from Theosophy, from selective aspects of liberal Christianity, from ceremonial magic, from Kabbalism, or the other "aspects" of the New Age mixture, including historical revisionist feminism, Eastern religion, Yoga, or any of the like.

These paths, like ceremonial magic or Kabbalism, or Eastern religions, are all useful and powerful paths for those that utilize them with seriousness and with an eye for cultural context, but the watered-down and haphazard mixtures that they normally appear in, in the "new age" movement, are actually quite insulting both to them and to the other traditions they are oftentimes entangled with.

The traditional path includes the legendary "family traditions" of people who claim to have kept a "pre-Christian" tradition of some form of veneration or systematic manipulation of older powers and virtues, and it includes all the people out there who are alone, or just with a few close spiritual friends, living on the Land, and who see the Land as a holy power that contains the memory of mankind.

It includes people who keep a "ground-level" moral and ethical code, and who understand where the true "Paganism" of the past vanished off to- it vanished off into the souls of men and women and into the Land. It re-emerged constantly through folk songs, folktales, faery tales, and ballads- all of these things, as we shall see in this work, are the true wellsprings of the hidden tradition or the secret tradition of the true Old Ways.

Traditional forms of Paganism and traditional worldviews are not flashy, not structured to the nth degree. They are as old as the ground under us, and they are as old as the souls within us. They have no appeal to those who are looking for flashy names, ceremonial robes, and titles. They are not a fast road to having sex or orgies, nor are they a place that offers comfort to the rebellious ego, that only exists to please itself.

The traditional path is one of quiet immediacy and deep seriousness, and it offers no great and simple code for you to thrust in the faces of other people during debates. It offers no great assurances past the greatest assurance of all: "You are one with the Land, and all is as it must be."

The "magic" of the traditional path is the magic of the heart of the Land and the unseen spirit of mankind and nature- and its metaphysics are not simple to grasp, nor do they come easily to those who have their understandings of "magic" tainted by the new-age. All the same, those who can master the traditional path's many tests and trials can come to a destiny that humans can scarce dream about or comprehend- the unfolding of the human being into the fulfillment of Fate herself. But this is not possible without the "ground level" work of coming into a true and consciously reciprocal relationship with the Land and the Old Powers that dwell within. This is the first work of the essential human, and when this work is accomplished, the other will be, as well.

Traditional Paganism, in common with many traditional "folk" religions around the world, is a spiritual path that deals with the Land itself as the most sacred manifestation of a timeless reality, which is full of many great powers, including those worshipped as Gods by our ancestors, and the spirits of the dead, who forever fill nature and make her the repository of all the Wisdom and power of our shared past.

Any path that deals with direct, simple experience of the "gateways" between the human consciousness and the immense, eldritch powers and spaces that exist within the body of the Land all around us, and any path that can approach these powers with a respect born out of spontaneous and genuine love, can claim to be "traditional," on some level.

The human mind can experience many things, and the language of symbol is the key to unlocking the latent power in the mind. Traditional Paganism, like all traditional spiritual paths, relies on symbols found in myths, folktales and folksongs, and in oral lore, which lead the mind into the right "place" to undergo a transformative and rather indescribable experience, which is the heart of true initiation.

In the British Isles, which is the cradle of my own traditional path and all of my most crucial understandings, balladry and myth- coupled with the stories and talks I've gotten from local traditional Pagans- include within them symbols that cause a person's mind and soul and spirit to enter into a communion with the Land, and with all things seen and unseen. This is the art of the seer, this is the meeting in which the human being enters into a wordless "depth" experience and becomes a familiar power to the Land and to the powers within it. They return the favor and come to the person, becoming Familiar to them, and becoming the teachers and protectors of the human who has the mental strength and devotion to respond to them, without fear or hesitation.

The traditional path is like a dusty antique shop full of forgotten things, thousands of old shapes and lumps and hollow-eyed dolls, old cups and bowls, and clocks that stopped working a long time ago... but underneath them all is a great void full of noise, color, and Mystery, just waiting to pour out and frighten and enlighten.... it is a path for people who can understand and appreciate the ambiance of ruined cottages with just the chimney stones standing, and autumn woods after rain, or the power of the sky at night, in the middle of a field. There's really no other way to express the essence of it. It's a path for people who can see folklore and old stories as not "just stories," but timeless realities all unto themselves, pieces of an eldritch puzzle that unlocks a door into what we are inside, unseen but potent.

There's something going on... something happening, hidden from most people, but right below the surface for a person who can understand what I just said. For those who wish to gain a few hints and pointers to awakening this within themselves, I confidently point you to the huge body of folk-tales and myth that exists as a record of the beauty and spiritual power of our Pagan past- but also to your own heart, which forever speaks words you need to hear.

Second to those things, I offer you this book, and wish you all the best of luck. I hope my words can help you, in some small way, to experience a path to Wisdom and peace that is as lasting as the Land itself.

Let us live and love in Wisdom, in day and in darkness.

Robin Artisson
Lammas 2005

"They cast about the trunks of Elf-Trees
They flew with abandon through the countryside
They drank from sacred wells
And climbed into the sky

In all this time, the wind was watching
Blowing from its home in the north
Towards the east, where the fire burns
And the white tree grows unseen forth

See owls or geese in the sky
And the changing, unchanged Land below
New days perhaps have come
But the old days do not go..."

Reclaiming

The Reclaiming of The Pagan Worldview and The Heart of Mysticism

In my way of thinking, what makes a person a "Pagan" is not adherence to the surface beliefs of a Pagan religion, nor some strongly individualistic way of challenging the status quo, nor even embracing an antique religious model- in the modern day, what pass for "Pagan" religious models tend to be created by certain left-wing people to bolster some equally-as-left-wing ideologies. True and honest "Paganism" is hard to come by.

In my opinion, being "Pagan" is far from any of that- it is a matter of changing your worldview to an older way of seeing and being, giving reconsideration to older Wisdoms, and making them relevant to you today. There is a struggle of spirit going on- people are looking for Wisdom and peace, and some look back to the past for hints about how others once found it. This is a good impulse- the past has much to teach us. But it is still a struggle, because mainstream religions strongly disapprove of people looking too far back.

Modern mainstream religions "win" the struggle of the spirit in a new way- they win when people have no awareness of the subtle power of worldview, and when people do not question where the features of their worldviews come from. In the old days, the *modus operandi* was for the Church to convert kings and rulers, get influence over the laws, and kill the heretics and dissenters. But organizations like the Church couldn't do what they were trying so hard to do, which was change the basic worldview of the people they converted. That took centuries.

Conversion in name is not enough- to become a true follower of a religion, you have to embrace the worldview associated with the religion completely; and that normally only happens when you are raised from an early age surrounded by a culture that espouses and demonstrates the features of that worldview. Christianity took generations to "set in" properly and fully. In the modern day, Pagans have a lot of "unlearning" to do, before they can really say, "We are Pagan."

A Matter of Worldview

Nowadays, people can believe whatever they want. There is no locked, enforced way of believing. But there IS a worldview that most people in the west accept, people who are Pagan and Christian alike, without even realizing they accept it. Many people today feel and want so much to be "Pagan" again and to escape the dominant Judeo-Christian paradigmatic worldview, but it doesn't happen overnight, just like it didn't grow overnight.

Some people don't understand this- they think that being Pagan is a matter of reading some books, of making a blanket rejection of their original religious beliefs, and taking part in "Pagan" rites or even "doing their own thing"- and nothing could be further from the truth.

The essence of Paganism is found in the worldview. Worldview is a matter of how you feel and think about things, on a deep, mostly pre-conscious level. Worldview is normally tied up in culture, and it is a matter of how you were raised, from day one, to think about things and see them. "To be Pagan" is to alter or change these deep patterns in your mind, to be more in alignment with a genuine Pagan worldview- and a "genuine" Pagan worldview should be based on older Pagan ideas and ideals. Hopefully, if any "modern Paganism" is worth its salt, it will be inspired by older Pagan ideas that still have importance and relevance for us today- and many do. Some features of older worldviews can be interpreted in new ways to make them relevant. We are dealing with organic features that changed to suit the times and needs of long ago, so this is not odd in the least.

Part and parcel of the standard "Pagan" worldview, ancient or modern, is a sense of the sacredness of the Land; that the Sacred Land is alive and inhabited by spiritual forces ranging from Godly spirits to the souls of the dead, that all life emerged from the Land or from nature, and that all will return to it cyclically, on the tides of birth and death.

The relationship between men and women is vital to the modern Pagan worldview- the rather destructive imbalances of the past, evidenced in antique (and in some places, persistent) social orders between men and women, fill most modern Pagans with a desire to find a healthier way for men and women to relate.

Pagan mythologies present men and women as being created simultaneously, not one before the other, or one for the other, as Eve seems to have been a device created from Adam to alleviate Adam's boredom or loneliness; in ancient Germania we have Woden creating a man and a woman at the same time from trees; the same story gets told in a different form in other places- and even the Greeks, before the late-breaking "Pandora" myth, had man and woman springing up simultaneously from the Earth itself, or from the humus and trunks of ash trees.

Men and women have different biological functions with respect to reproduction, but no spiritual, mental, or any other ontological inequalities. If men can offer women the gift of physical fertility, women, and the feminine, offer to men the no less vital gift of emotional and spiritual fertility. Man's strength is not there to hold down and control the feminine, but to protect it and support it, for she is the source of his life and his generations, and the secret heart of his honor and joy- the very form of his deepest spiritual yearnings. There is a great and holy reciprocity between the sexes, they are needful to each other, and modern Pagans tend to stand strongly on this issue, as well they should.

The very basic Pagan worldview- in common with the ancient beliefs of all Indo-European Pagans- is one of animistic fullness, with a simple, earthy, "ground level" emphasis on the idea of all things having a spiritual dimension, and on the value of life and of human cooperative well-being.

With the possible exception of the belief in the all-important value of life and the Truth, there is no sense of "hard absolutes;" there is an ambiguity at the heart of all things, for Nature Herself is nowhere clean and clear-cut, on any expressed level. Humans must decide, within the context of every situation, what actions are proper and try to bring their actions into alignment with whatever course brings about a greater harmony. This worldview requires humans to be flexible, brave and responsible.

This worldview has no sense of human moral depravity; no sense of guilt or loathing for the basic organic realities of human life; it has a basic trust in the dignity and goodness of mankind. Most scandalously, there is no sense of the necessity of salvific revelations or the prophets and saviors of revealed religions. "Revelations" for those who live on the Land, and who live as parts of the Land, are ongoing. "Revelations" can be heard by anyone who listens in the wind or to the Land, and can be heard daily in the interior of the heart.

The Pagan worldview also has no sense of linear "salvation history;" the world is not going to suddenly end one day at the behest of a heavenly judge who will then dole out rewards and punishments. Responsibility for making this world a better place is squarely on humans and the community of life. "Meaning" in life is not to be found at life's end, or at the end of the world, but in every day, in every action and breath.

The end of the world-cycle or this era will come naturally, organically, just as it started; it is not a heavenly catastrophe, but a natural reality, and the coming of this end- which is itself a pre-cursor to a rebirth for the world- is not the primary concern of humans, as much as *living this present moment* with Wisdom and peace.

Finally, and most importantly, the Pagan worldview has a strong emphasis on the surreal, supra-rational presence of the Otherworld, the immense reality that lies beyond the boundaries of our own human perceptions and preconceived notions, and which occasionally breaks through into our "world" and perceptions in mysterious, exhilarating, or frightening ways.

This great presence, this extra-sensory reality, is the force behind Pagan myths and legends; it is the animating principle of Pagan mythology, and the single, pervasive and omnipresent principle by which otherwise inexpressible universal Truths can penetrate the world and mind of man or woman. This reality is the home of the Gods, the source of divine inspiration. Mythology is the presence of the Otherworld in the form of ancient stories; mythology- any mythology- can be thought of as its manifestation.

Any mythology can be thought of as a gateway to a truly mystical experience of timeless truth. Though the mythical stories themselves don't tend to be literally "true", they are nonetheless still "true", all being expressions of great Truth. The ancients had no problems with their myths not being literal. It was the symbolic and metaphorical nature of these holy stories and lore that gave them power; they spoke in the language of the Otherworld.

With the World or Against It

Having made this simple outline of a general "Pagan" worldview, it seems pretty straightforward. But modern neo-Pagans tend to help preserve a very non-Pagan and decidedly non-traditional worldview, even when they are in the grip of what they so fervently think is "Paganism."

And the problems of reclaiming a true Pagan worldview today are not just consequences of religious oppression, or the history of religion in the West; even our modern materialistic sciences have problems. As much as modern people (and even modern Pagans) think that the sciences are positive forces that are "against fundamentalist superstition and ignorance," it is a sad fact that many scientific paradigms aren't any more healthy than fundamentalist Christianity- the sciences, too, can be based on firmly non-spiritual and totally "we are automatically right and you are automatically an ignorant, superstitious person for not accepting our math and theories" attitudes. Sadly, science for many becomes a new form of elitism, with its own dogmas and faith in its ability to answer the Mysteries of the universe.

But many Pagans, thinking that science is a firmly non-Christian and totally positive advancement, walk around trying to make our ancestors' lore and ancient spiritual notions "fit in" with scientific-sounding explanations; I have heard such horrid things, ranging from "the trance state is really just an alpha state of consciousness" to "Paganism and Wicca are just quantum physics mixed with the ancient Mysteries."

I've heard neo-Pagans actually trying to explain how their "law of return" was firmly based on physics, and I've even heard neo-Pagans trying to "prove" that there is an "afterlife" with the rather tired, pseudo-scientific anecdote that goes something like this: "Hey man, we're all just energy...electricity, and according to physics, energy can't be destroyed or created, it just changes form...so when we die, our energy just changes form..."

I can't tell you how depressing it looks when someone takes the most precious gift of our ancestors- mythology- and all the lore and power it contains- and tries to explain it all away in these analytical terms, to make it more palatable to the science-dazed masses who think that things can't be "real" unless you can explain them in mathematical terms or demonstrate them in a lab.

What is real and important in life cannot be so explained. A person who thinks they can, will never reach the promise of the spiritual worldview, nor achieve Wisdom. They will join the endless mental paper chase, which only ends in new questions, new debates, and never in peace. They are swept away with the tools of dissection, and can chop things into eternally smaller pieces, but never reach the bottom; they can analyze, over-analyze, discover possible explanations, but never find meaning.

An Older Wisdom

Our ancestors were very wise; they knew secrets to reality and about reality that we can still access today, but only when we understand that we need our ancestors and their legacy more than they need us- because they weren't savages who needed Christianity and rationalistic science to save them from their errors; the "old days" didn't need our ultra-enlightened "modern day" to "fix" its superstitious mistakes. I'm not saying the old days were perfect, but they did have access to a source of Wisdom that we have mostly grown unconscious to. And this source of Wisdom can spell the difference between life and death.

Let's have a look at our ultra-enlightened modern day! Look at how we Europeans, and to an extent, Africans and Asians, are all suffering from spiritual amnesia, all of us, with lost memories of our ancestors, and of who we are, and where we come from- replacing our wise Pagan heritage with foreign cultural beliefs based on guilt and misogynistic, spiritually elitist hallucinations- look at how we have bathed this world in blood; look at how we waste without shame; look at how we degrade the world and environment!

And look at how our new "champion" science has produced just enough miracle technology to give us guided missiles and monstrous weapons that could destroy the entire planet, and how it has gifted us with just enough technology to keep most of the poor world under the oppression of a small majority of the rich world, and just enough technology to improve the "quality" and length of life- so that we can each have 90-100 year life spans, all the more time to feel alienated from each other and confused, more years to suffer under the oppression of other countries and corporations (if we happen to be born in the non-technologically advanced world), and more hollow years of doubting the existence of anything that we can't see and hear and feel.

This is the curse of losing who we were and who we are. Wisdom was lost with those things. Science would be a beautiful, wonderful tool, if we had Wisdom to temper it. But we don't, and so science is abused and it has become another monster, just like the old church.

I'm not saying we should destroy science; I'm saying we should restore Wisdom. Wisdom is to be found in the heart, in the fetch, in the soul, in the feeling self- and the keys and gates to Wisdom are encoded in Mythology, and in the actual blood and spirit of each human being. What allows access to this Wisdom is trust in the self, trust for the basic goodness and capability of humankind, and honesty to the deepest emotions. Religions or philosophies that tell people not to trust their own hearts are poison, designed to shackle humans in slavery.

It's all there for the taking. It's there for the re-remembering. I can't say where the road lies for each individual, because only each person can discover that; but I can say where it certainly doesn't lie:

1. It doesn't lie in trying to make Paganism and old religions "fit in" with the Judeo-Christian worldview or any of the monotheistic religions, who, chiefly by denying the true and full power of the divine feminine, and the ancestrally held truth of the multiplicity of divine beings, were lacking Wisdom from day one. Trying to make ourselves "fit in" with them is already death to our cause. Modern neo-Pagans who walk around with their well-meaning "all Gods are one God" idea are doing nothing but sealing up the victory of the monotheistic machine over our wise ancestors, who believed in many Gods. Gods are individuals, not "aspects" of "one God."

2. It doesn't lie in trying to make our ancestors' mythologies and Wisdoms "fit in" with a modern scientific worldview. Our ancestors were deeper than the modern world tends to give them credit for; they had mystical contacts with states of awareness that were and are above and beyond any limited left-brained equation or logic pattern; the Gods dwell in

states that even the most brilliant human mind cannot perfectly explain or express, and which does not need to be "expressed scientifically" to make the presence of the Gods a transformative, real presence in our lives.

We can all experience what we need to experience, if we let go of our "need to know," realize that some things defy the "knowing" of mortals and their brains, and cast ourselves into the Infinite, leap without fear into the fearsome-seeming "unknown" and go with bravery towards the unknowable.

There, in the strange shower and whirlpool of mythological images, of strange symbols, and of ancestral stories, a miracle happens- the symbols and images and words all start to make a deeper sense; the mind goes into some "new mode." It's rather impossible to explain, but you reach a "new place," which is actually a very old place, wherein you commune wordlessly with what is real, with the reality under and within the words and symbols.

You experience yourself again, but not a self you ever guessed or knew was "you." You meet the Gods. You suddenly understand, in a way that you cannot easily explain, HOW they exist and work in the world, and how your existence ties in to the World-Fate.

You learn how to sense your actions, what your actions "mean," what they will accomplish, from whence they spring, and how much power you have to tremble the threads of Fate to seemingly create your own destiny, which is (and always was) a greater destiny. And the whole time, you will be mystified at the whole process, unable to really explain it, and beyond that, not feeling the overpowering need to explain it.

A person who has gone through this experience is changed forever; they have become (as our northern ancestors said) a Wyrd-worker. They become a Witch; a Pagan mystic whose awakening was not possible without the older worldview of wonder and Mystery, where Wisdom is supreme.

The Sleeper Has Awakened

That awakened person understands the role of Wisdom in everyday life. That person can then be a scientist, without his creations turning on him, and on others. That person can then be religious, without his words and deeds tarnishing what our ancestors' "religions" were intended to communicate to mankind. That person can then be human, and be completely and totally satisfied with that. That person can be himself or herself, and that is enough.

We have all experienced upbringing in a Judeo-Christian world, even if we weren't brought up as a monotheist; the unspoken yet real influence of this worldview permeates all aspects of our lives. Even people far from the West have elements of monotheistic culture that permeate their existence. Christian and Muslim missionaries pick away at the bowels of Eastern nations, trying their hardest to turn those people away from their traditional religions and spiritual paths, and for the largest Eastern Land- China- the scourge of atheistic communism has plundered its majestic spiritual heritage.

India, the last home of true polytheism, has begun to succumb to the monotheistic battering of Islam and Christianity, and to this day, when Hindu religion is taught to westerners, the "acceptable" form is to tell everyone that the Hindus ALWAYS believed in "one God"- Brahman- and how all the other Gods were mere aspects of "Him." The obvious polytheism of the Vedas is ignored, in favor of monotheistic re-interpretation, and many Hindus themselves see monism and monotheism as acceptable paths to finding acceptance in the "new" world.

This monotheistic homogenization, this sadly narrow way of seeing the world, and the rationalistic curse of the brilliant yet unwise sciences, have an affect on people from all over, consciously and subconsciously.

Changing the deepest programming, the deep and essential assumptions that were put there by the simple fact of how and where we were raised, is the first and greatest task of liberation, and of the modern Pagan, of any stripe or predilection, and it makes no difference where that Pagan might be from. I speak mostly to an audience of western Pagans, descendants of European peoples- but I also mean these words for all Pagans.

We can be free to revive the Wisdom of the past, and the key is in having the bravery to part ways with the "modern assumptions"- the many modern myths that we are all exposed to from an early age.

These myths include the myth of religious and cultural homogenization, the killing need to mutilate the Truth by forcing it into a simple, unitary mold, and the myth of "rationality"- the myth that tells us that all of reality can be explained and understood by the human mind coupled with enough education and scientific endeavor. These myths serve the human ego, serve our need to think that life is at heart simple, predictable, and explainable. Life, as the wise of all eras have known, is anything but.

Forget about explaining everything. What we have to do is learn to FEEL again, without having to rationalize every feeling; we must learn to DIVE INTO the symbols and images of ancestral mythology, without trying to "explain it all," and letting these symbols and myths reveal their hidden meanings to you- you must submerge yourself, and let the feelings and insights rise.

This is intuitive work; modern people's difficulty in learning how to do this is a direct consequence of the loss of Pagan Mysteries; a direct consequence of the demonizing of the divine feminine, Dame Wisdom herself, a programmed mistrust of the feeling, intuitive aspect of our natures. Dominant religions are oriented around a basic mistrust of the human heart and feelings- the heart is corrupt with sin, even according to the Bible. At this point, we must make a stand, and part ways with the human-hating religions that turn people against themselves, all to better force them into reliance on dogma, and into reliance on religious leaders and institutions.

A person, at some point, has to stop fighting to make every aspect of their experience "conform" with some notion of how things "have to be," and let the great web of Fate be what it is, because nothing can change how Fate is, or how things "are" on the deepest levels. Luckily, it's not Fate we have to change, but how we experience it.

You "let it all be" and go still and totally open- you let yourself feel love, real love for the grandmothers and grandfathers who passed their Wisdom down, and for the Gods and spirits that they loved- and what is *real*, what is immortal and precious, what does not come nor go- will rise into your awareness, because it is the basic reality of *you*.

This is the promise of the Old Ways, and it shall be, for what is immortal and real is an inseparable part of us, and we can allow it back into our conscious reality, at any time, so long as our hearts are given over with consent, trust, and total honesty.

What is precious- the very heart of the old worldview, that Mystery which filled our ancestors with peace as they sat around hearths or fires listening to old stories, or when they gazed upon the natural world at certain striking times- that precious "way of engaging" the world will certainly rise in you, once your awareness is not clouded with modern mythology, nor with constant mental grasping.

With love, devour the images and symbols of true and holy ancestral mythology- go into them, and take them into you; be an idolater! Love the idols, the symbols, the non-linear and mad-seeming stories! Surely they seem strange, for the path to the Otherworld is strange- realize that each one is a door into you, and through you, through your soul, for they are things of the Gods.

Mythology was born in the experience of ancient people, experiences they had of Nature and Divinity. These stories are not merely "made up" or foolish; they encapsulate Mysteries and their symbols are an Otherworldly language, waiting to reveal a special Truth to you. They will forever flow with Truth, if you will forever go deeper into them.

The true myths are the footprints of the Ancients, the marks of Divinity on the world, and on the human mind and heart. Welcome to our Faery Tale! As it turns out, there is no such thing as "just a made up story" after all. If you want peace, and insight, then be what these sacred stories and images call you to be, and be it with all your heart.

When you have done this, you will find that the rites, beliefs, and ideas of whatever Pagan religious expression or tradition you feel drawn to come naturally and with total, elegant ease, in a way that they didn't come before this deep change. They come with a satisfaction they didn't bring before, even if they did feel satisfying before.

The human spirit is a deep layer of Fate, an ever-moving and yet ever-still thread of Fate. This is its identity. It touches the spirits and Gods, who are also a part of the web of Fate or Wyrd, in a very profound way. Let your soul be what it already is- a sorcerer's soul, one that touches and communes with the divine forces that rule over this world and every other. This is the work of the True Pagan mystic.

The Witching Way:
The Worldview of Traditional Paganism and the Old Craft

The Old Way of Seeing

The path begins with worldview. The true power and depth of the Old Ways cannot be internalized and experienced without understanding the basic "way of seeing the world" that leads us to find the Land sacred, and to seek the unseen powers within it, and within ourselves.

The following writings present a particular "way of seeing" that I have become familiar with, from traveling around Britain and Ireland, journeying through the Land I live on, interviewing people who embody this path, and from my own spiritual experiences and researches.

With some variation, all practitioners of Land-based Paganism understand and embody the following concepts and teachings. These perspectives are quite vital to understanding and awakening the potential that is found the rest of this book.

This worldview portion of the book is the foundation of all the rest- and it includes detailed discussions about the Land-centered spiritual perspective, the notion of rebirth, and many thought-provoking perspectives on the all-important idea of Fate. After these three topics, there will be an exploration of the inner realities of the powers and spirits that exist within the metaphysical current of traditional craft and Paganism. Consider all these things carefully, for as you come to understand this book in its fullness, they will begin to make more sense, to fall into place.

But these words and understandings are not ends in and of themselves- they are meant to point you to the door into yourself. In time, you will see how learning about the Land, and the doors into it, and about Fate, in all Her implacable seeming Mystery, is really a discussion about you, in the greatest sense. And through all that, the Land and Fate and spirits and lost histories all still exist as we know them, seemingly apart from us- and you must approach them with a deeper understanding. That road starts the moment you are born, and with luck, ends in a far deeper place.

What is Seen and Unseen

The true worldview of "Old Ways" is not outwardly complex. It lives inside of the Land, and inside human hearts and minds, as an organic and mystical vision of wholeness. It includes intuitive and secret methods of achieving union between what is seen and what is unseen.

The primary metaphysic of the Old Way is strongly focused around the reality which is at the heart of all things, metaphorically pictured as "below" everything; the eternally renewing and expressive "power" of Elfhame, or the Underworld, sometimes called the "White Under-Wood."There is what is seen: the Land that you walk on, your own body, and the physical forms of others and all things- and there is what is unseen: the "inner" mystical dimension of things; the timeless "internal" reality within the Land, which the ancients called "the Underworld." This distinction can be called "this world" and "the Otherworld," if you like- but in the current I operate in, we say "the Land" or "that which is seen" and "the Underworld" or "that which is within, hidden, deep below, or unseen."

All of these descriptions- "within," "deep below" or "unseen" all refer to the same thing- the timeless and eternal dimension of great and mysterious power that exists at the heart of all things. This great hidden power is the source, the origin and sustaining power of all things that are seen.

The Underworld is a timeless pool of potentials that exists at the heart of all things- and from this dark pool, all things "express" or come to birth or creation; they rise into what we call "manifestation," and eventually, as Fate weaves reality onward, they return to the dark unexpression, to sleep or wait in potential again, for their renewal or regeneration- and, as Fate is always in motion, always birthing, destroying, and renewing everything, regeneration on every level always comes to pass.

The craft of the wise is about joining together the two realities, using the medium of the conscious human mind and body; it is about bringing together what is seen, with what is unseen. It is about wholeness. In that wholeness is power and Wisdom.

This entire process is about the growth of a mortal being into a being of fullness, or an immortal being. The natural processes of life show us the pattern- we watch children grow into self-awareness from the dark nourishment of the womb, into full adults, and on (it is said) to greater things, to the Truth, through cycles of life and death. All living beings follow this great path.

The unseen world is a terrifying one to most people, for it contains not only the grim reaches of the shadowy world of the dead, but all the interior and deeply-buried things within yourself that you don't wish to face. The key to true Wisdom would be found in the last place you wish to look- what better place to hide such a treasure as Wisdom? What you do not wish to see inevitably becomes what you must see, what you most need to see, for your completion as a being.

Remember- the deep places within yourself and the "deep Underworld" are the same spiritual location or "place"- this is a great Mystery, and an important one. The Necromantic workings of the craft, the traffic with the dead and spectral intercourse with spirits in the unseen is a reality; but it is not a reality that stands apart or separate from the deeper metaphysic- that of wholeness.

The spirits in the unseen world and the dead themselves act as guardians of certain places, certain experiences, certain powers; some of them can even act as guides and initiators into Wisdom. Whether you see working with spirits and the unseen as dealing with your "deep self," or another world, you are right.

But you should believe both, for both are true- you are dealing with real spirits that have their own existence- and you are dealing with the common reality that unites all, and which holds the contents of what you call "yourself." For the sake of sanity and tradition, you must realize that both are true- spirits are not simply "parts of your mind"- they are also individual beings with motivations and powers, and not all are friendly. It just so happens that the reality we call "our minds," on the deepest level, shares a singular reality with the essence of all places and things.

The craft is about "crossing the boundary" between this world and the other, of crossing between the seen and the unseen. The unseen world contains the secret, the ultimate source of all conditions and events and beings- and thus, anything that occurs in the "seen" world has its ultimate "reason" in the unseen world.

The unseen world contains the master key to understanding, but that understanding means nothing unless it is united with this world, and thereby brought to full conscious expression- for what the unseen world contains is truly beyond a human being to understand or express; but when the unseen and the seen are brought together as one through the body and mind of a human being, suddenly everything is "understood" in a directly experienced, and very mysterious way.

The meaning behind Fate, the hidden Law of creation, cannot be "known" in terms of thoughts and words and numbers- but it can be experienced, in a wordless, yet clear and powerful manner, by an individual. We call this the "genuine experience," the supreme mystical experience. It is what occurs in the "Hour of God," the thirteenth hour that exists timelessly outside of time.

This experience is the height, depth, and the point of each being's existence. This is the culmination-point of Fate and Reality, and when a being has undergone this experience, their Fate is "changed"- the supreme transformation occurs, the "Wisdom-Metamorphosis," or the "'Faery-Metamorphosis" or the "Grand Initiation"- and the being's future is now a part of a mysterious order of being that non-transformed humans can only whisper about and guess at.

The human being can enter into a new condition of being, joining the "'Grand Array" or the communion of the Master-souls. The "Master Men" or "Justified Ones" are among the ancient spirits who dwell in the wholeness of Reality, emerging through natural phenomenon and the Landscape itself at certain times and places, on behalf of Fate, to help others to fulfill their destinies. They even sometimes take part in the events that deal with the destinies of nations.

All is connected. The system of Fate, expressed as Nature or Reality is one, whole, and undivided- All contents of the deep mind are shared- in deep trances and dreams, the boundless contents and Wisdom of all reality is available to you. Jung knew of this reality, and approached it as a "collective unconsciousness"- which was not only a mind-state, but a reality that all things shared.

It is this connection that makes contact with spirits and the powers in the Land possible. This connection makes the transference of Wisdom possible; it makes change and growth and learning possible. Nothing is separate; all things flow into others, affect others, create others; all things change, become aware; all things are alive. Nothing, not even one tiny thing, is static and cut off from the web of Fate which is Reality.

Now, we know what is seen: the Land that you walk on, your own body, the physical forms of others and all things- and we know that there is an unseen: an "inner" dimension of things; the "internal" reality within the Land, which the ancients called "the Underworld."

The Queen of Elfhame, the Great Soul of the Land and what is within the Land- Old Fate, or the Great Queen, aside from her existence as a divine being, represents the exchange that occurs between what we call "this side of life" and the source of life, the mysterious "other reality" that is such an essential part of this one- indeed, this other reality is the sustenance and the seed of eternity of "this reality" or our mortal world.

The Great Queen is the "source and sustainer," the "Lasting One"- the Witchmother or Bloodmother of all strands of existence; in one manner of thinking, Her great power and being, and what we call the "Otherworld," are the same. The Great Spirit or God that dwells in the Land (and indeed, all powers dwell in the Land), He who is called the White King or the Ancient White One, the God of both the sorcerous light of Wisdom and the dark reaches within the Land, acts as the power who rules over the "transition" between the two perceptual ways of being- he rules over the "paths" that connect the seen and the unseen.

His appearance in both myth and legend, as well as in the mind and lives of modern adherents of the Old Ways, signals the gateway or transition between the mortal world and the numinous world that lies only a heartbeat beyond the veil of sight and thought. In this capacity, he is not only initiator of the living and wise, but the guide of the dead into the unseen.

What the True Beings, the Master-Spirits or "'Gods" desire of human beings is that we become more like them- beings of wholeness, and not beings who dwell in a perceptually "cut-off" or limited condition, wherein we experience only one portion of reality.

Beings who are not conscious of the wholeness, beings who do not dwell in the clear light of true Wisdom, live in a narrow range of experience and in a narrow range of reality, and their decisions and actions reflect this lack- every angst, emotional disturbance, violent outburst, fear, or problem in the human world is born of the inability to see the fullness of things. In other words, there is no peace or true and lasting happiness without Wisdom- Wisdom being the power to see what is real, to see the totality of things as they are, as opposed to the lack of sight, or the ability to see only what we wish to see.

The greatest Beings in reality are not only the bodies of reality itself- Fate and the messengers of Fate- but teachers, initiators or guides towards realization as well. While some forces and spirits in Pagan mythologies were blind and greedy and destructive, the "Gods" always acted in a capacity of supporting and protecting the world from those powers, those titanic powers of destruction, and also acted as teachers to mankind, teachers of both culture and law, as well as the eldritch Mysteries of the unseen, Mysteries by which humans could come to full Wisdom.

All "gifts" of the Gods or spirits were gateways to a mystical realization, no matter how mundane we may have come to think of them; all cultural features like crafts, blacksmithing, technologies and even systems of scientific thinking and laws, are disguised forms of mysticism, that lead people who understand the truth behind them towards realization. But throughout the entire human experience, we have been involved in a deeper reality- the motion of Fate, which leads us to merge and transform constantly from day to day and life to life.

The Fate of all beings who live perceptually "on the Land" or "above ground" is one of merging. The living who have gone before, the Ancestors, have died and entered into full perceptual oneness with the eternal reality at the heart of all things. They have merged with the ground, the trees, and all that you see. The body of Nature is the body of both the living and the dead.

These beings, these merged beings, appear as the souls of the Ancestral dead, as well as the spiritual forces of nature. Some are cyclically reborn into our perceptual "human" state; some are born as animals, spirits, or natural phenomenon; others remain deep within all things, moving towards some other mysterious Fate. In traditional witchcraft and Paganism, it is sometimes said that "the Landscape is haunted"- and this is why: the Land is full of spiritual forces, who move within it and manifest through it. Sensitive individuals who wander the Land during the day or night often become aware of this.

The Mother who stands behind and within the entire process of Fate, emergence, re-integration, and rebirth, is the great being who is the Mother and key of the craft. The life that is exchanged is Her life; Her gift is Truth, though Her soul is change and transformation.

The sacredness of the "Land" as the "ground level concept" cannot be understated. The merging process, as well as transformation both here and now and beyond, is the only sacred reality, and all beings, whether seen or unseen, are undergoing it.

Part and parcel of the attainment of the craft is to extend your awareness to those who are in different stages of this reality; the dead still live- they have just come into strange new relationships with the Land and with perceptual reality. These Pagan "necromantic" workings are as old as the hills.

This is the heart and core of the true Old Ways. To learn to integrate ourselves into this process in new ways, to gain Wisdom and insight, is the method of the craft's path to realization. This is a very earthy and simple way of approaching the Mysteries of life. There are no complex and foreign Gods and pantheons, no over-ceremonialism; just an intuitive, organic approach to the realities within, realities which have the "feel" of the quiet dark ground and creaking trees, and silent stones.

There is a great power in silence; a great power in the Land and in the simple moments of peace amid the power of Nature. The Old Ways teach that this silence and natural power is a gateway to an indescribable fullness of being.

The River of Time and Rebirth

We humans experience what we call "subjectivity" daily and nightly; always we experience inner thoughts and feelings, calling these things the activity of "our minds." Some mistakenly believe that the "mind" is a phenomenon caused by the brain, but this is not totally true- during a human life, the brain acts as a "cooperative factor" along with the mind to create human consciousness.

The "mind" is actually a greater, stranger thing- a timeless activity that springs from the timeless heart of all things- and it is not limited to just your head or body. We normally experience it as such, but at times, we drift into strange places within where we seem to share in experiences that are not entirely our own.

The reality is that the "mind" in the greatest sense is the experience of the internal, omnipresent, and eternal reality of all things. Yes- the Land itself has the substance of "mind;" all things are aware- though all things are not conscious in the same manner as a human being or an animal with a brain is conscious.

But all things and beings, whether we call them animate or "inanimate", are centers of experience, because *all reality* is a great awareness, a great center of experience. This is the most ancient religious truth known to mankind- the truth of animism.

We naturally think of ourselves as "separate" from the Land and the world around us, but the truth is that we are only experiencing a sense of separation. There is no true, ultimate separation, only a relative, conditional one. Most people dislike this idea, feeling that it threatens the truth of their individuality, but it does not; the conditional separation is not something that ever ends; it changes, but continually arises in many different forms. To be a "being" of any kind (even an immortal being) is to be a conditional phenomenon, not ultimately different from reality, but relatively different from it, and perceptually different on some level. Ultimate conditions and relative conditions arise simultaneously and continually; there never is one without the other.

The strange, invisible or "clear" reality that is the substance of our minds is the same substance that flows through the Land, stones, trees, and everything. To be an individual means to have a sense of separation from things, while simultaneously being one with all things. It is a strange paradox, but it is the truth of the human condition, to be neither one nor the other, but "both and neither."

As Fate or Nature has sent all beings and things forth from the deep, all beings and things will continually exist in some fashion through many cycles of transformation. A being can seem to be many things, and undergo many transformations and exist in many conditions. In all of these conditions, however, the "being" will in some manner be aware of itself, though again, not necessarily as a human being is consciously aware.

We are one with all, so in the great weaving of Fate, we have not always been as we are now, and will not always be as we are now. Some of the conditions Fate weaves for beings are painful; others frightening or dull; some are pleasurable and peaceful. The Great Dark Mother that stands behind Fate has a half-dark and half-bright face; she is the source of life and death, the truth of any painful situation, and any peaceful one.

Her power, which is the power of the Underworld, Hell, and death, as well as life and birth and Wisdom, is an all-encompassing power. Her servants, the powers in the Land, and the beautiful and terrifying beings of the Underworld, fill the mythologies of the modern world with fearful things labeled "demons" and "devils," and other sinister spirits. They are not "evil" in the usual sense of the word; they are servants of What Must Be; they are instruments of Fate who weaves out Wisdom, eventually, through all experiences.

In the power of the Great One, and under the power of Fate and the Underworld, many states and conditions arise, some painful and harrowing, others beautiful and tranquil.

No state remains the same, however, and so no mortal pain or peace lasts forever. Some states- like the human condition- are a great mixture of joy and sorrow, of intrigues and boredom. Wisdom is the key to the entire system; to have Wisdom is to understand ultimately "who" and "what" you are- and thereby no longer having to flow ceaselessly through states of pain and pleasure in search of peace… and no longer having to flow through states that begin and end and begin again, wherein you eventually lose your mortal memories.

To have true Wisdom means that you no longer have to endure being separated from the others you have come to love and cherish, by death and other changes- the truly Wise have defeated the unconsciousness and lack of self-knowledge that most beings within the system of Fate have to endure. They have realized a greater reality wherein a timeless, changeless condition is triumphant, and nothing is lost or forgotten.

The neverending river of time and transformation, the dynamic yet largely unconscious transformations of mind and body that the half-wise must undergo, the Fated flow between states of mind, states of being, and between different forms or bodies after death, is what is called "rebirth."

Body, Soul, and Spirit: The Lost Mystical Anthropology of the Ancients

Dr. Claude LeCouteux has done more than any other modern writer to reveal the lost understanding of the ancient Pagan European anthropology, or the truth about the Pagan idea of the "soul."

Much of mythology, as well as folklore that has its roots in pre-Christian European Pagan culture, is not understandable without first understanding how the ancients viewed the issue of the "soul." Once the European Pagan notion of the "soul-complex" is understood, a great amount of clarity is achieved. For the witch, understanding this most important of topics is a key to greater Wisdom.

In the modern day, the Christian notion of the "soul" is radically different from what Pagans believed. The Pagans I am referring to are the Pagans of Northern and Eastern Europe, the Celts, the Germanic peoples, and the Slavic peoples. However, the "soul" explanation given here, drawn from experience with traditional Pagans, the work of great scholars like Dr. LeCouteux, and other historical research, fits into the ancient Greek model of post-mortem realities as well, though it takes a tiny bit more effort to see how.

The notion that the human being is comprised of a "body," which is mortal, and a"soul," which is eternal, is flawed. It is a very Christian model. To Christians, the "soul" is the seat of personality, thoughts, feelings, and memory. It is eternal; it outlasts the body, carrying the personality and memories of the human being, as well as the person's ability to perceive themselves as a separate being.

But this is not how the human being was understood in most Indo-European Pagan anthropologies. Instead, Pagan peoples had a complex of forces and "beings" that came together, to allow for the "life" of a human being to manifest. At death, when these forces diverged, it was not a mortal "personality" that continued on unhampered, but something else, something more mysterious.

Death is a great Mystery, and hard for living humans, chained by rationality and limited to their own memory of previous sensory inputs, to truly comprehend. What we end up saying about the dead and their condition usually says more about us and our condition.

But if we trust in the ancestral gnosis of our ancient foremothers and forefathers, we can grasp at a vision of the truth about life, which reveals its own message to us, internally, by correlating many streams of mythology and intuition, and by refusing to fully give us the egoistical pleasure and "certainty" that modern religions give people regarding death and the afterlife. The ancients looked to death as a challenge, a Mystery, and a passage to another world, and the passage to a new condition of being.

Pagans believed that the human being was comprised of a body, a "life force" and a mysterious "other" being, a divine being that acted as a "follower" or "double" to the living human being; a spiritual entity that was tied somehow to the destiny of the human being, but, from the perspective of the living human, seemed to be an autonomous, independent being. All the same, this "follower" or "guardian" spirit was vital to the life of the human being; for without it, the human would die.

The "life force" that animated the body also acted as the seat of most of what we call "personality"- for it was the force that made intellect and memory possible. The life force was what maintained the body, and the body, in turn, provided the physical means for the consciousness and the attendant memory and intellect to continue to function.

The life force was also called the "shadow soul" or the "body soul." At death, the body died, and the life force returned into the ground itself, or was dispersed back into Nature, from which it was originally drawn. The only immortal part of the human being was the spirit, the spiritual double, or the "follower," which we talked about a moment ago. This "double" is none other than the daimon of the Greeks and the genius of the Romans. This double is the "Fetch" of the old craft.

The life force or body soul IS the soul, which is a different thing from the double or the spirit. Many people today, thanks to the degeneration of subtle understandings, consider soul and spirit to be the same, but they certainly are not, and from the northernmost reaches of old Europe, to Plato's academy, the soul and spirit were always seen as distinct. The body is what is seen; the spirit is of the unseen. The soul is part of the "mortal world," but still unseen- it is physical and mortal, but acts as a medium through which spirit communicates with body, and as the sustaining force of the body.

From this point, we have to venture a bit into a philosophical understanding of what it really means to be a "being" of any kind, before we see how the ancients understood the point of human life, and the destiny of any human.

What does it mean to be a "being?" It's an odd question, but a very important one. The entire concept of the human being, and the destiny of the human being, is tied into the all-important concept of "Fate." To Pagans, Fate was the supreme "reason" why anything at all happened- why any event occurred. It was not only the reason for all events coming to pass, but also what Must occur.

Reality, the entire cosmos, was a grand occurrence- a great, multi-layered and multi-leveled event. This is very important to understand. Fate was depicted as a feminine being (or a trinity of feminine beings) that weaved or spun all things into existence. To get a good lock on that image is important- it announces the fact that existence, the cosmos or reality, was an event; a great thing that was always in motion, always changing. Spinning, weaving- eternally.

What we call a "being" is not a thing that exists somehow in an eternal, unchanging manner. Nothing exists in that way. Anything that exists is an event- a motion of Fate and power, not a metaphysical lump of some unchanging "stuff."

A being is an event. That is a very hard concept for a lot of people, who have (thanks to Christianity) an idea that the soul is "eternal"- and by "eternal," they think "always existing as it is, no matter what."

Nothing that we experience or have knowledge of exists "as it is, unchanging, no matter what." Fate is a process. And there is nothing that is not part of the process of Fate. Even the Gods are part of Fate's spinning. To be immortal, as spirits or even Gods are, from the human perspective, is not to be unchanging. It is another matter entirely. It shall be discussed more later.

Fate is a web, a weave. Events "occur," and must occur, as a part of that weave, on one of the countless metaphysical "strands" which make up the fabric of Reality.

I say that events occur "on" a strand of Fate, but it is useful to think of the event, and the strand of Fate that it occurs "on" as the same thing, in a way. The strands are like potential. The event that occurs is a potential made manifest. Then the event is over- however, the strand, the "field of potential," is still there. Further events, related to the event that manifested and passed away, usually follow on that "strand," from that strand.

Please, consider this carefully. Fate is, as a whole, the great "Field of Reality" that makes anything possible, a great and infinite well of potentials. From it, all things occur, and "on" it, "within" it, "as" it, and because of it, things CAN occur. The dark interior of this "Field of Reality", this great pool of sleeping potentials, is what the ancients called "the Underworld".

Our ancestors were animists- that is, they believed that everything, from stones to trees to animals to people, and even things like winds or fire (any physical phenomenon or occurrence), had a spirit, or a living principle that co-existed somehow with the physical phenomenon. Everything, in a strange way, was a "being"- a combination of seen and unseen forces-you couldn't separate a tree or a stone from the spirit that was attached to it- but how and why was a "spirit" attached to these things?

It was the same for humans- the "follower" that moved about and around each human was the spirit of that human being. It was not a "soul" as Christians thought; and yet, it was immortal and necessary to the human. But this Mystery requires further exploration.

The "spirit" principle that accompanied every manifest thing, was key to the Mystery of Fate. The "spirit" principle was responsible for actively helping to manifest the occurrences or potentials that brought about the form of any phenomenon or "thing" on that strand of Fate. An example may be in order.

Let us look at a stone, with the eyes of an animist who happens to believe in Fate. A stone- like everything else- is part of the weave of reality, the weave of Fate. The stone is an event- it is firstly a manifestation of a strand of Fate; it is the most recent in a long chain of occurrences that finally manifested as a stone, in this strand of Fate.

So, Fate gives (or acts as) what I call a "being principle," and this principle is the simple possibility that a thing can physically "be" at all, and exist as seemingly separate from other things. Notice that I said *seemingly* separate, for the seeming does not imply that things are ultimately separate at all; it only seems so, from the lesser perspective of perceivers within the web of Fate. Remember that Fate is ONE great weave- one great event, with many seemingly separate parts. Many, yet one.

At any rate, the "being principle" is *always* and necessarily accompanied by, or paired with, another principle- a "life principle" or a "spirit principle," and this spiritual force manifests the occurrences or events that make this particular being principle into what we see or experience as a "stone." Remember that the stone is not sitting still- it is always changing.

Events are continually occurring even inside the stone, and it is gradually changing into something else- Fate is always weaving it, always weaving its strand, always moving, and the spirit of the stone (which is the spirit of anything that ever was or is or ever will manifest on that strand of

Fate) is doing what Fate requires to the rock, seeing that what must occur to the rock comes about.

A point may come when it is no longer classified by us as a "stone" at all. But the strand of Fate, the being principle, and the spirit principle, will still be there, for Fate's weave is indestructible. The physical matter of what we once called "a stone" will still exist, even if it is in a radical new form, like dust. A chain of cause-and-effect, or physical events, will always be occurring on the strand that the "stone" once occupied.

Yes, the spirit or spiritual force that acted as the "other half" of the equation, to bring about the occurrence of the stone, will also exist- but its existence is mysterious, and its true task, its origin and purpose, belongs to a realm that is very hard for mortals to understand. At any rate, the spirit itself is beyond the scope of this short essay. The spirit comes from an eternal place, to manifest occurrences needful to a given strand of Fate, and when its task is done, it returns to that place.

But if something, anything, appears or occurs in our experience, whether it is a mountain, a stone, a river, a person, an animal, the body or form of that thing is coupled with a Spirit. The being principle and the spirit principle are never found apart, ever. They could not be, for the being principle requires the spirit to manifest, and without the being principle, the spirit could not actualize itself.

Human beings are (in some ways) no different when it comes to the example of the stone. A spiritual being- our Fetch-Mate, our double, also called our "follower," or our "Fylgja" as the Norse said, the daimon as the Greeks said, or the spirit- the personal Fate or personal God of what we call a "human being," comes from a timeless, divine realm, to mediate the will of the Gods to mortals. They are mediators of Fate, the supreme power that reigns over all, and the messengers of divinity to us.

They are the far-seeing guardians of each person, the being that passes down clannic or family memory, and mediates the power or luck-force of each family to its members who are alive.

These spirits often appear as women and are the source of the Pagan "Clan Mothers"- the Collective feminine divine-ancestor women that appear in all Northern Indo-European cultures- the Fylgjas, the Dises, the Family Norns, or the Destiny Mothers- the Rozenhitsye of the Slavs. Doubtless, the ancestral cults among the Greeks and Romans gave honor to the very same powers- the Matrones, Genii and spirits of families.

Dr. LeCouteux says: "The Otherworld appears like a reservoir of (spirit) Doubles- Time there is nonexistent, and everything coexists at the same moment. The other part of ourselves (the Otherworldly double) which comes from this other world without totally detaching itself from it, materializes our potentialities and our destiny."

Some people are suspicious of talk of spirits- or even of the need for a separate life principle to exist alongside the manifestation of anything physical. The truth is that Fate is a unitive system; spirit or life and physical matter or manifestations are not truly alien substances, ultimately separate from each other. They are complementary, necessary to each other. They are both inter-active and co-creative with each other. Both are "real things;" one is not "more real" than the other. Both are events; both are always in motion.

It just so happens that we do not dwell in a world of only physical things, nor do we dwell in a world of pure spirit. We dwell in a world that is the manifestation of these two things working together, or the combined occurrence of these principles. That is Fate. That is how all strands of Fate come to manifest as they do.

The idea of a life principle manifesting needfully alongside ALL physical things, is found in the Taoist tradition as well- and in a show of harmony, the idea that there is a "form principle" and a co- existing life principle for all things, is a perfect manifestation of the Way, or the Tao- the Way of All Things, the hidden law behind Reality, or Fate.

The two simultaneously arising principles are therefore, ironically, how the Wholeness of Reality arises. The two principles are not two realities; they are two manifestations of one Wholeness, one perfect thing.

I always turn to Indo-European mythology for illumination, and in this case, I wish to examine the Slavic myth of the creation of human beings. This myth shares a lot in common with Greek and Norse ideas, and the Celts (though their myth is lost to us) no doubt had a similar one.

Anyone who reads Ivan Hudec, Carl Kerenyi, or any copy of the Eddas, can see some version of this myth mentioned or recounted.

It is said that the Earth Mother, Pripelaga (or whatever name she was known by to the culture that created the myth), gave birth to the first humans, from within herself. The Gods saw the seed of Chaos searching within the empty bodies of these beings, and breathed a tiny portion of what the Gods call "eternity" into these beings- thus granting them a spirit.

This story is detailing the primal makeup of human beings- it shows that humans are a composite of physical bodies and physical life force (born from the Earth) and a spiritual, eternal principle, which came from the world of the Gods, at the will of the Gods. It is merely recounting what I have been discussing- the two principles uniting to show a human being.

Of course, Chrisitan translators often change the language of the story and call the eternal portion of the human a soul, but spirit is more appropriate, for the soul (and some people use the terms interchangeably) usually refers to the life-force that makes intellect, reason, memory, and personality possible- the same life force that is "between" the body and the spirit.

What are we? We are human beings. We are each the expression of a strand of Fate- a being principle, strange "portions" of reality, metaphysical "locations" at which Fated events and potentialities can manifest or occur- and we are joined with a spirit, which itself is the manifestor of the events that lead up to the form each of us currently manifests- including the form of your body, your personality, your intellect, your likes and dislikes, what have you.

A chain of events occupies the "strand" that you currently manifest, which stretches back to the womb of the Earth Mother Herself, eons ago. That womb is the dark void of the Underworld, or Fate- Old Fate was your true Mother; we all came out from the timeless deep.

The mortal personality that you have has never existed before now. What you call your "self," your ego, your mind, your memories- all of these things are events. They are very recent events on the strand of Fate that "you" occupy, and they are limited in time- they will all pass away soon. This is what it means to be mortal.

But as a "being," you will always exist. You have no choice; the Earth Mother birthed human beings. The strands of Fate that she set into motion are beings. A Spirit is joined to your strand, to your being principle. It manifests what destiny or Fate requires within each of these strands.

Oddly enough, what seems to be occurring is that a spiritual being is finding its destiny through what you call "you"- not the other way around. The occurrence of your personality, ego, feelings, memories, these are not the primary event, nor the peak event of your Fate. They are only really side-effects, but important ones.

Your personality and memories- mortal things that they are- die with you. This fact bothers many people, but hear me out! There is a bit more to it than you may imagine.

"You" die. But Fate persists; a spirit/being union cannot die. Fate is still there; the strand or being principle is there; the chain of events manifesting as that strand is still there. The spirit is always there, manifesting destiny or Fate. But where are "you" in all this?

"You" as you know yourself are a matter of a collection of memories from one mortal life. Those things fade when the life-force or body soul fades.

But the life principle or spirit, which always remains, is the reason why you "perceive" anything at all, or why this entire process is "experiencing" itself as something. This is a very subtle but important point, and must be understood if you wish to understand what will become of you after death.

A being principle or "form" by itself has no possibility of subjectivity. But as we have seen, there is no such thing as a being principle or a form that lacks the spirit or life principle; as was said above, these two things are only found together; they arise simultaneously. They are never apart.

It is the spirit or life principle that makes subjectivity possible; it is the "perceiver," the root of perception, the event of perception within the entire system of Fate or cosmos.

If body and the vital force of soul allow for your brain and consiousness to arise and be sustained during life, the spirit is the "awareness" within you that is more essential than consciousness- the invisible and silent perceiver that seems to be "inside" you, that hears your thoughts, that "knows" what you experience at any moment. Even when you are unconscious, you are still aware, on a deep level. This essential awareness is of spirit; it is timeless and deathless.

This awareness permeates the entire web of Fate; all things- ALL things- have a share of awareness and eternity. Even if you lose consciousness at death, and memories fade, the basic, primordial root-awareness that you experience right now continues, and moves on in accord with your Fate, into involvement with another form. However, there are certain powers in our lives that can affect this transformation in many ways.

In Slavic myths, a great ancestor of humanity made a dangerous voyage into the Underworld, to find a miraculous plant for humanity, for his people. He went to find the wheat plant- to alleviate the hunger of his people.

This plant, with its nourishing, sweet seeds, was in the Underworld, the world of the dead- and when he reached his destination, he was in danger, for he had forgotten practically everything- why he had come, and who his family and people were. It was the intervention of one of the Fates that reminded him- and She did this in a special way. When this man was shown the faces of his family, all hungry and pleading, he did not remember any of them; but when shown the face of his true love, he remembered.

Love was a force strong enough to overcome the forgetfulness of death. Death is, in fact, the forgetfulness that occurs naturally through the process of change. We can look to the holy myth of Orpheus' own journey into the Underworld, where love led him even to overcome the hard heart of the Lord of the Dead, and nearly reclaim his love.

It is interesting that Love was able to overcome this death-fugue; but even more interesting is the fact that all Indo-European Pagans had a God or Goddess- a divine being- that represented memory. In Slavic myths, the God Pereplut was the God of memory- He remembered everything that happened. Among the Greeks, the memory of the Lord of the Gods was eternal; as were the others.

Thus, even at your death, a God, an immortal being who is not vulnerable to forgetfulness, though He (like all beings) has to change, will remember everything. If true love was yours, you may be able to overcome the forgetfulness as well- but here is the forecast for your mortal self at death:

The body dies, and the life force or soul eventually fades back into Nature; but the spirit manifests further changes, in accordance with Fate (and according to some, in accordance with events that had occurred in the life that just ended) to manifest a new order of life- another being who, while lacking most of your memories and personality, is still "you" in the sense that it occupies the same strand of Fate. As I said above, we are all events. You and I are strands of Fate, being principles that are always changing in accordance with the events which are from our Fated destiny, and which are brought about by our spirit, daimon, or personal mediator and Fate-being.

The being that follows your death will dwell in another world, usually- normally the Underworld of the "Dead"- but largely without your passions or memories. However, the same seed of "perception" or "awareness" in you will experience that world, though not really "as" you, in terms of your current personality. Taking rebirth as a spirit in the Underworld- becoming Sidhe or Fae or Feeorin- the Fate of most of the dead- is depicted in the folklore and folk-beliefs as a mysterious state of being, but the experience of the Underworldly beings is exhiliarating as well as strange- the "people under the mound" were often seen by living humans as being engaged in feasting and merriment.

This is why the Celts believed that death here was a rebirth into another world; and they were quite right. However, the rebirth was not necessarily "yours" as you know yourself now; each being was a great shape-shifter and could become many things after death; aside from just going on to take a rebirth as a being in the Land of the Dead, it could become another spirit, in another world, including this one (a concept which was important to Pagan people, who made actual attempts to "create" guardian spirits or beings by sacrificing people at times and burying them in the foundations of buildings, for example, or who buried certain dead people in certain places and in certain ways); or the soul could become even an animal or some other natural phenomenon.

A person's strand of Fate was intimately involved in all forms and all lives within the entire tapestry- the Druids called this "the circle of the spirit."

Most people, according to Pagan beliefs, seemed to "journey" on to the Land of the Dead, wherever it was; there it usually enjoyed either dim, quiet darkness, or many joys, depending. Virtue or bravery in life was sometimes thought to condition the existence of the dead being into a greater condition, but this is far from universal. On the whole, the notion that a "good" man would not be abandoned by the Gods, even in death, is a useful one to consider, as it was a genuine Pagan belief.

Clearly, the beginning of the journey of the death-transition was something that happened at the moment of death, and in the short period that followed it; to some, there was a seven or nine-day period in which the life force, not yet fully dissolved, yet apart from the body, still housed the identity (the intellect and memory) of the deceased, and, in this period, the spirit or follower had to "guide" the dead away- interestingly, this experience of the journey would be a "vision" granted by the spirit, to explain to the released soul or psyche what was occurring, and what had to occur; a revelation of destiny.

At the end of this "revelation," the being (from its perspective) would lose consciousness, to "awaken" embodied as a new being altogether, in another world or form, with little or no memory of its past existence. In the British Tradition, this transitional period was symbolized by the "Mothers" or the Maidens ferrying the person/being/soul to Avalon, where it was to be healed and regenerated, for a "return" one day.

This is captured in the classical world with the journey to the realm of Hades. The newly released life force, along with the psyche (the personality, intellect, and memories) journeyed (normally guided by Hermes or another psychopomp representing the force of guidance from the divine world, or the spirit-guardian of the dead person) down to the Underworld- where, after crossing into that realm, they eventually came to drink from the well or spring of Lethe- forgetfulness.

This is symbolic of the transformation of death causing a fading of the intellect and memories with the final fading of the released life-force. What remains is only a shade, an imprint of a former life with little connection to the memories or passions of that life- but according to some legends, offerings to the dead (especially of blood) could revive the shade temporarily, restoring some of those things, like memory. This only makes sense as blood carried with it vital life force.

This is also why many Pagans made food and drink and even blood sacrifices to the shades of their ancestors, so that their ancestors could remember them and "be fed"- the "Alfablot," or the sacrifice to the elves of a bull at burial mounds, done in the northlands, was a good example of this. To the Northmen, the dead became "alfar" or elves.

Overall, the Fate of the vast majority of dead persons is to be found in a transition into the Underworld, where a new "being" converges; death here is a transition below and a rebirth into the World of the Dead, the dark and mysterious (yet wondrous) world of hidden potentials and regeneration- though the rebirth takes place minus most of the mortal passions, memories and identity- so the destiny of the dead is to live on in another world, but with an identity that (after a point) is not "just as it was" during its life. In some cases, or over long periods of time, it may be lost pretty much completely. This is why it is said the dead "cross the river of time"- they gradually transform fully away from the life they led, maintaining only the Wisdom they acquired in that life, as well as- perhaps- the bonds of real Love they experienced.

Lacking the source of life force to maintain the body or the psyche's intellect and memories, the shades or new beings of the Land of the Dead were now "nourished" in a new way by the Powers of the Underworld- where Zeus and the Gods of the Heavens and Earth (especially Demeter) nourished living mortals, it was Hades and the Kore who now became the sources of whatever power sustains the shades in their new existence.

The resident in the realm of the Underworld, as has been said, is only an echo of their former self and life; not the same being that died, but another being in that chain of Fate, a new convergence through transformation and passage between worlds.

The dead are not simply stuck in the Underworld, unchanging and forever- even that stage of existence, that development of Fate is dynamic. At some point, the King and Queen of the Underworld would usually allow beings to leave their kindgom and take rebirth elsewhere; all things that go into the Underworld will be regenerated, eventually, and re-emerge into a new state of being, whether in this world or in another condition. That is the nature of the Underworld- but what goes below is not purely and precisely the same as what emerges; never forget that.

But from the mortal perspective, a dead person or being *as it was known* in its life, is done dealing with the mortal world; the dead shade is an image of the realization that the living human that was once alive has moved beyond the era of their participation in the human community that they once occupied.

What developments of Fate await the dead is a sacred and unspeakable topic, known only to the Fates, the daimon or spirit of that being, and the spirits of the Deep. What you can be sure of is that existence has no beginning or end, and the spirit or daimon is truly undying, and all beings in any world have a destiny which stretches beyond the parameters of mortal participation in family or community.

Many people are bothered by the notion of their personality and memories being lost- which is of course, the curse of mortals and the curse of mortal death. It's not easy being mortal, and all Indo-European Pagans admitted this, mythologically and in their own day-to-day lives.

As I said, nothing is "lost"- the memory of the cosmos, the Gods, will not forget who you were, what you felt, or what events occurred in your life; perhaps the "follower" or "spirit" that acts as our mysterious personal immortal likewise "remembers" the many events and beings that it has manifested throughout time. The spring of memory in the Underworld is the Greek manifestation of this same Wisdom.

But do not forget love's power to make even an Underworldly being remember what he had "known" before- love is truly a force above all forces, in that respect.

To some Indo-Europeans, the Otherworld was pictured in less dark terms- the Irish Celts had their Western Isles and Tir nan oc- and this is something that needs to be remembered: the journey into the Land of the Dead, the journey back to the deep, to the other side of life, is a highly personal experience, and it is not all dark- the real darkness of it lies in our lack of understanding. Wondrous events or things may occur, both in the Otherworld, and during the journey there, for a dead person.
Terrible, terrifying events may occur as well. There may be a mixture of both. What is important to remember is that the Otherworld or the Unseen is a great Mystery, and instead of seeing it as very good or very dangerous, one should see it as very mysterious and fascinating. That is the balanced view.

For those who live in love and honesty, and who trust in their spiritual guardians and ancestors, and who trust in the Gods or the powers that be, few things need be worried over, in life or in death. Death is another journey to the Truth, to the timeless, and all people have many stops to make in that journey, many beings to encounter and learn from in various ways; many forms to inhabit and many motions of Fate to fulfill before true Wisdom is gained, and Fate culminates.

But the culmination of Fate is just the point- for those mortals who will go on to become witches, or mystics, and who will attempt to unite the soul to the spirit *while* alive- those who will attempt to cross the boundaries between the seen and the unseen, the living and the dead, *while* still alive, the experience and Fate of death can be transformed completely; the spirit/soul/body experience can fulfill what Fate is driving it to fulfill, here and now.

The average man or woman will die, without ever consciously experiencing what was real and crucial, here and now, in life- without ever experiencing the Wisdom and experience of the timeless that transforms the Fate of death into something very different- the Fate of the timeless.

This is the secret- that the Fate of death is also not unchanging. You do not have to live life being cut off from the reality of spirit and the deeper Wisdoms beyond. You do not have to live life everyday, waiting for death to come- you can choose to die before you die, and thereby alter your Fate forever, and perhaps escape the Fate of forgetfulness that awaits most mortals.

You can choose to walk the path to experiencing wholeness and free yourself from the lack of full consciousness that drives beings from form to form, from darkness to darkness, and from world to world, in a great flowing, Fate-ordained chase for Wisdom and peace. The Mysteries of the craft, as well as the Mysteries of Pagan antiquity, offered a means by which a person could transform their Fate after "death."

Concerning the Mysteries

The Mysteries were there for the purpose of transforming our destiny or Fate into a "better" one- or perhaps for fulfilling what we call "destiny." Can a mortal become an immortal? Can we escape from the cycle of death and forgetfulness?

Yes. The Gods can grant immortality to mortals- and to our ancestors, doing glorious deeds was a real method of gaining the Gods' favor just to that end. But, sadly, the Gods seem to be pretty hard to impress! Even some great heroes vanish off at death into the Underworld, or into the worlds beyond, never to be heard from again- but they do live on in the memories of people, which is its own sort of immortality.

But the Mysteries are actual methods- rites, rituals, meditations, initiations- designed to transform a mortal's destiny into one that is more than one of death and forgetfulness.

It's really quite simple; the Mysteries are events that transform the strand of Fate which is you, into something immortal, something that is no longer vulnerable to forgetfulness. All of the Mysteries involve shifting your focus of "self" off of your ego and memories, and realizing that the root of your perception is in fact something that is timeless and divine.

This "root or quality of your perception that is timeless and divine" is nothing other than the "follower" or spirit that acts in such a mysterious capacity to the mortal mind. Yes- the Mysteries are about the union of the mortal self to the divine self, or the spirit.

Woden, in the Germanic Mysteries, sacrifices himself "to HimSelf"-while he is alive, he slays his ego-self. What does this mean? It means that he did not wait for death to slay his ego-self; he voluntarily "died" while he was still alive; he died to his limited notion of self and awakened to the true "self" that was at the heart of his strand of Fate.

By doing this, the mortal and the immortal merge on a conscious level-for this can only be done by a human being who is alive in the flesh. Woden, like all Mystery initiates, became consciously aware of the timeless. This transformed him; he was now one with his spirit; he had "become" or rejoined his own personal Fate.

He could not die, even if his body then died; for his ego-self was radically transformed, the light of immortality had "glorified" his conscious mind, his being principle, and he had permanent continuity of consciousness, no submergence in forgetfulness, from that day on, and to this day now, he exists, an immortal "stream" of awareness, unbroken by forgetfulness, acting as a guide to those who believe in him.

He returned to the timeless, to gain all knowledge from the place where all things exist simultaneously; he gained the sight of the wholeness of things, all things, the perfect circle of Fate, beyond the beginning and the end, or all notions of linearity. His strand of Fate is still there- of course. He, like any being, is a manifestation of a being principle, joined with spirit. He is an immortal, however.

And thus we see why these "spirits" or followers are working- perhaps all events that they materialize in our Fate, all occurrences, lead up to this peak experience for us all, eventually- thus making these spirits whole. Through mortality, their own immortality is assured, through their immortality, our mortality comes to be, and "our" immortality is assured, for we are truly mortal and immortal at the same time.

The Wodenic Mysteries (or the Mysteries of Lugh, his counterpart to the Celts, who also dies to be transformed) or the Mysteries of Veles, the Slavic counterpart to Woden, and the Mysteries of the Greek God of the occult rite- Apollon- (yet another God of light and serpents, ravens, and wolves) are about the individual mortal causing this radical transformation in themselves, to gain Wisdom and immortality.

These Mysteries are dangerous, however; they are occult and quite demanding.

Other Mysteries are more suited for the majority of people; these are the Mysteries of Yarilo, the Slavic Dionysos; the Mysteries of the dying and resurrected son of God. Of course, "God" here is referring to the true God- the Indo-European supreme being "Deus" (from whence we get Zeus) or Dyeus, or Deiwas, or Dievs, or Deuos, or Tiwaz, Tyr, Termagant, Zyaus-Piter, or the Great Svarog in Slavic myth. The term "Deus" or "Deiwas" originally meant "bright" or "clear" and refers to the "Bright One" or the "God of light"- the Indo-European sky father who was the father (in almost all pantheons) of a special God- one who had a human mother, like Dionysos, son of Zeus.

The idea that the greatest being in the cosmos could have a son or child with a mortal mother is another echo of the idea that within each human being is the spirit of the Great God or Gods. The figure of Dionysos or Yarilo (or any of the Godly children come to mortal flesh, such as the Sacred King of traditional Paganism, the Horn Child of the craft) is the image of the spirit of each of us.

This God usually is attacked by his enemies and torn to pieces, crucified, or otherwise killed- only to be resurrected or regenerated to new life, risen from death.

Of course, in the myth, these enemies are the forces of life itself- old age, disease, what have you, and the myths are telling the story of each of us- we are all clothed in flesh, yet within us is the spirit of the Great Gods- and we are all "dismembered" by the forces of life.

And from that death- new life! But this is sadly, not enough. These Mysteries require a person to actually enact the death of the God, to experience what he experienced- and to do so *before* your natural life ended. Again, you must die before you die.

As an interesting side note, in the Dionysian frenzy, perhaps the purpose of the "enthusiasmos" was for the daimon or spirit to be liberated and consciously merged with the soul, to take the mortal consciousness among the Gods, to immortality- to literally merge with and "contain a God."

Overall, however, unlike the Mysteries of Apollon, or Woden or Veles, these Mysteries of the dying and resurrected God were more "passive"- they are based more on hope for resurrection, or the conscious experience of the timeless after death, than they are on the direct experience here and now of it.

As mentioned above, the Dionysian frenzy was a good example of a divergent strand of mystical practice that aimed at a direct experience in the here and now, among the rebirthing God cult, and should still be sought after today.

Typically, the dying and resurrected God cult works like this: The image of the dying and resurrected God is worshipped, of course, and one has to understand that this being is also the spirit of yourself; your true self.

In ritual, this God is united to your mortal self, normally by eating the body and drinking the blood of the God- and from that mystical meal, that union, a promise is made- at your own death, the spirit of you will unite with the mortal memories and personality and endow them with immortality- in other words, the union of mortal self to immortal will occur after death, but only to the extent that the mortal- *in this life-* truly gave up on living for the ego or the self, and lived for the God, and in the promise and joy of the God's eternal life, outside of time and death.

We must end this portion of our talk on the Mysteries now, to continue on with our discussions of the mystical worldview in general. The work you hold in your hands is an expression of the Mysteries of the beyond, of the union of the seen to the unseen, the mortal to the immortal. If you desire these Mysteries, and if your Fate is such, you can walk the path to the Great Inheritance, which is everything.

The Metaphysics of Rebirth and the Red Thread

Despite the fantastic claims of elitists and charlatans, there is no physical difference between witches and non-witches. The idea of a "mystical gene" has a basis in a very subtle reality- but it is not a physical genetic bit of material.

There is a thread of Fate- the "thread" here referring to a particular dynamic aspect of reality itself- that gives rise to what we call "mystical" occurrences or propensities to mystical activity within the people who go on to express it in their life. This "Red Thread" of Fate is woven into the tapestry of humanity, and the Land itself.

Some people are born, develop and express mystical leanings and even abilities or insights. Some physical locations on the Land seem to have a numina about them that gives "entrance" into an experience that can only be described as "Otherworldly" or mystical, so long as a mystic interacts with them- although entire human populations,mystics and non-mystics, often express feelings of awe and wonder and even dread around these places.

The deep Mysteries of rebirth are not easy to understand by mortals, much less codify or discuss- all we have are the basics: ancestral and mystical ideas about what forces and overlaps exist between this world and the next, and how these things and their associated events and realities affect the greater reality of life, death and rebirth.

Fate is the power behind the process, just as She is beyond all processes- and you might say, that She is the process, as well. The process of life, death, and regeneration is the process of Reality.

A person dies; the body decays and the soul makes the transition into the Underworld. After the metaphorical "Nine Nights" is over, the soul itself is no longer a concern, for the spirit is off to its Fate or destiny beyond- and that destiny is known only to Fate and that being. And of the diminished vital body-soul, at times, it is said, a "shade" remains, suspended in the timeless dusk that borders the mortal "way of being" from the timeless way.

The spirit or timeless Mystery of the being dwells afterwards in the inner dimension of Reality; the source of all potentials, the great Mystery from which all things manifest and eventually return. In this ever-renewing and fertile, dark Mystery within all phenomenon (It is pictured as being within the Land, or the Underworld in most traditional Paganism.), the being waits for the cyclic "turning" of Fate to make conditions right for its rebirth into another state.

What those conditions are, what those states may be, is a deep, nearly impenetrable Mystery. The wisest can claim to know, and highly realized people can sometimes "know" what forms, realities, and experiences "they" have had in their timeless existence above and below the sacred land. But for most of us, these sorts of guessing games are a touch dangerous, and perhaps even spiritually irrelevant.

What *is* relevant is that we see the Land for what it is- the container of this sacred Reality- even if the Land does not literally have an "Underworld" under it, the Land and the inner, spiritual dimension of the Land *are one*. And thus, the Land and the ancestors are one. The Land *is* our source. The Land *is* our home, the Land *is* our destiny, the gateway through which we will all walk, moving to and fro, through its many gateways and paths.

We have to reverence the Land, and the powers it "contains," or we fail in our most important duty as Pagans, or as just human beings who wish to be in contact with the wholeness of our being- the Land is another part of our being. A person who cannot or will not see it this way is cut off from the great regenerating and Wisdom-granting powers that the Land mediates and contains; that person is cut away from the Wisdom of the ancestors, which lives in both ourselves and in the Land which we cannot be separated from; that person is cut off from a most precious thing.

From this point, I can draw on the Wisdom of our ancestors, and what other writers whom I embrace as being "in the spirit" of the Old Ways have said and recorded.

Until we are illuminated, we cannot know the ins and outs of rebirth, or of the full story behind these "family lines" and what compels whom to take rebirth and where. But these things I do believe, in line with folklore and history:

1. The mother's line (called "the Distaff Line") seems to be of vital importance to the rebirth. When the Fated conditions are right, the rebirth occurs through a female relative- a female member of the mother's family, or a matrilineal relative. This is the foundation of the original "clan" system, and goes back to the "Clan Mothers" idea so prevalent in

Northern Europe, the Disir of the Germanic peoples and the Matronaes of the Celts.

2. Spiritual reality cannot be considered apart from physical reality, even if they are not *precisely* the same- the system of Fate is interlocked, interwoven. When a person's ancestors *live* in a physical location, when they lay the bones of their ancestors *in* the Land of that place, when they love that place, interact as a culture and as individuals with the numina or spiritual power of that place, a *bond* is made between the people and those powers, and rebirth would necessarily be influenced by this bond.

3. A person's love for a place or a people, if that love is real and powerful- soul-felt, literally would also have to influence the conditions of a coming rebirth.

4. Even though Land and ancestral connection with certain Lands is an influence on rebirth, the Land itself cannot be so easily divided. The "Earth Mother" is the Earth Mother, whether the Land is called "Thailand" or "North Dakota." What the cultures who dwell in these places love and connect with is the particular numina or spiritual presence of that place. The Earth Mother or soul of Nature itself can and will manifest to all peoples, in terms of that area- she is the White Lady who appears in Wales, next to wells, certain tress, and caves- but also the same White Lady in other parts of England or the British Isles or France, or what have you. Your ancestors can travel from their traditional homelands, and still expect to have beings from their own "ancestral stream" born to them, even on another Land.

5. The ancient metaphysic of matrilineal line-keeping and the primacy of the matrilineal line regarding descent and spiritual identity is not an invitation to ignore the contributions of the Father. The mother's womb is the vehicle of rebirth, the "womb-door," and she, as a woman, has a connection to the source in the Underworld that men lack- however, men are the "key" to the door, as it were- and their vital power passes into the mother and thence into the child, coloring many things about the child.

A man cannot change the spiritual force that will be "with" the child; but he can and does affect the body and vital soul of the child. Plus, the spiritual protectors of his clan or spiritual family can and will protect and inform his sons and daughters, helping them chiefly to go towards places and experiences and understandings that will inevitably lead them to "where they need to be"- usually back in line with the Fate deriving from the Distaff Line.

Beyond these five points, the Mysteries of rebirth are just that- Mysteries. However, in this life, a person who gains true Wisdom and wholeness of awareness from the union of the seen with the unseen, the mortal self with the immortal, comes to understand all the Mysteries of rebirth- if not through rational knowledge, then through direct experience of the wholeness as it relates to their spiritual involvement with all things, times, and places.

At heart, the truth of rebirth and of spiritual involvement with all things and times and places is one of the most powerful truths of the Old Ways- for it is a very immense, humbling and amazing thought, a sublime thought that brings great peace and a sense of deep concern. The greatest of insights can be born in you, when you realize that all human events are intimately connected with you, and you with them- that there is no place where you are "alien," not ultimately. There is no situation that does not impact you on some level, and no form of life that you do not have a kinship to.

Mystics from places as far apart as Ireland and Greece have reported, when seeing with recall of spirit, being a wind, a boar, a salmon, a tree, a person, a stone, and a great variety of forms and beings, in the great *fullness* of their being- or what people who are trapped at the linear perspective always call "past lives."

Caitlin Matthews, in her excellent book of meditations entitled "The Celtic Spirit," has an interesting entry on "The Circuit of Births," which I need to mention here. She discusses the ancient Druidic concept of the "Tuirigin," and she gives a definition of it found in Cormac's glossary, which reads:

"Tuirigin is a successive birth that passes from every nature into another... flowing through all time from beginning to end."

She goes on to mention that "Tuirigin (one might assume) is the same as reincarnation, but this is not so. In Tuirigin, the soul (more properly "spirit") moves between the Otherworld and this world in a series of journeys."

The legendary being Fintan, whom I will discuss in detail soon, had complete recall of the "circle" of his "rebirths"- and he said "A continuity of existence remained in me, which I do not deny."

Caitlin goes on to say "Tuirigin is nothing less than the birth of the true nature, for it is not until the soul (meaning spirit, here) has been fused with everything else that it assumes its true nature; the soul's (or spirit's) many turnings bring about its Wisdom. The Celtic Tuirigin is about fusion- not the refining of the soul until it reaches nirvana, but a profound communion with everything that brings authenticity to the soul."

I don't think I've ever heard it stated better.

Now, we must discuss the Mysteries of Fate, for they are the heart and soul of all genuine understandings of both the dominant pre-Christian metaphysical worldview, and the heart of the path to Wisdom that the Old Way forever offers to mankind. We study Fate and strive to understand its Mystery, primarily because it is the Truth about our condition, but also because it is a path to great Wisdom.

As you will see, the Truth about Fate, as our ancestors understood it, is not generous to the egoistic desires and expectations of most people, and is a difficult path for any to follow- and thus, it shows itself to be a legitimate and true path to Wisdom, which never comes cheaply or easily, and never comes to many at any given time. But "time" in the deepest sense means nothing- for the current conditions that any being may be experiencing, whether you call it "this life" or whatever, do not represent all that a being "has"- all beings will eventually come to Wisdom and realization, for Wisdom or realization represents the culmination and destiny of all things. In the most timeless or Otherworldly sense, this has already occurred.

Understanding Fate, as discussed below, requires you to begin to lay aside the compulsions and dreams of the mortal ego and put aside the fixed, dualistic tendencies you have built up in your mind, separating yourself from the world and beings around you. When you put aside these things, you become a field fertile for the growth and blossoming of Wisdom. This makes you capable of clearly experiencing Truth, instead of falsehood; it makes possible the most sublime of insights that are themselves the true passages from a destiny of death to one of True Life.

Fate, also called "Wyrd," is the occurrence of Reality, at this moment. Fate refers to the great web or weave of Reality, being woven "at every moment," by the Three Spinners or the great Mystery of Old Fate, who is pictured as the great dark Goddess or Spinner, or as the Three Sisters or Mothers.

In the great tapestry of Fate, all the great Mysteries of Reality express themselves together, and all of the further "offspring occurrences" that come from the appearance and interaction of these Mysteries also occur, all simultaneously, all constantly appearing and "moving" in a never-ending, dynamic configuration and motion. Everything that occurs affects everything else.

When something occurs, it occurred because it had to occur, based on "previous" events; effects rise from causes, and the kind of effect is directly related to the kind of cause. Fate can be called the power of "What Must Be" at this moment, based on what causes and effects have manifested "before."

Reality is a dynamic whole in which change (or motion) is constant; although paradoxically, Reality or Nature, the total expression of the web of Fate, stays what it is in essence, always. The more it seems to change… the more it stays what it is.

The White Tree and the Horse

The Great Reality which is "All That Is" was pictured by our ancestors in many ways, using symbols aside from just a great tapestry- it was most often pictured as a great tree, which had roots in the Underworld, (the origin-point of all things) with its trunk representing our world, and the branches reaching the great worlds above.

The "center symbol," or the Great Tree that stands at the center of all worlds, supporting all times, places, and beings, is a crucial and universal concept to all ancient mystical systems, and it is a venerable symbol of the wholeness of Reality, of All That Is.

Other symbols have been used to represent the "center force" or the thing which embodies the "totality"- a mountain, a standing stone (sometimes called a Godstone) the form of a God or a man, a pole, a sacred fire, and even a great river that flows from above, through this world, and finally down below. This ghostly river, or the "White Tree" or sacred fire or Godstone, or whatever symbol was used, all have the same purpose and meaning.

The various worlds, and the beings within them, and all forces in reality, were not separate from the "center power," or the Great Tree. This Tree-

"Ygdrasil"- was called by the ancient Germanic peoples the "Steed of Woden", Woden being the great heathen All-Father who metaphorically hung himself on this tree to attain true Wisdom. Sacrificing yourself in reality as a whole, to reality as a whole, (for you, in actuality, are not apart from reality as a whole) is a profound statement.

The All-Father's association with horses, including his magical eight-legged horse, shows us that the horse was also a symbol for reality as a whole, and for all of Fate- this is important, as many of the Great Queen-Goddesses, as well as the Great "Father" Gods of the Indo-European peoples were associated with horses, showing their great power and connection with all- but also their ability to interact with Reality or Fate in such a way as to be omnipresent and all-knowing; to "climb the tree" of Reality or the worlds and enter any of them; to "ride" into all places, worlds, and experiences.

This all ties in with the practices of the human witch or sorcerer who, like the sorcerous Gods, has a similar relationship with Reality or an inner passage into any aspect of Reality, gained through the symbols and actual bodies of trees and horses, among others. The "riding pole" or gand-rade of the witches is itself a symbolic "horse ride" into the unseen world- for the flying pole or gand/wand hearkens back to the mystical or shamanic steed, and witches themselves descend from the old Wyrd-workers or workers with Fate.

Fate and the Child of Truth and Beauty

When the primal motions of the cosmos interacted with the dark stillness of the Mystery of Fate- (and never forget, these primal motions themselves were not separate from Fate) all of what we experience as "reality" or "nature" came into expression, and that was the "beginning" of the great universal chain of manifestation, of weaving, of cause and effect. But in reality, it was not the ultimate "beginning"- for there is no beginning, nor end, to Fate or Reality.

The timeless Mystery (which includes the dark stillness of Fate and the power of motion) is just that- timeless- and it acts as an Otherworldly, perpetual "cause" to what we experience as "this world," or "temporality," or "measurable cause and effect." The Otherworld, the dark void of the

Underworld, doesn't begin or end, it exists every moment, acting as the perpetual "cause" upholding every manifest thing.

You can see the dark stillness of the Mystery of Fate, and the primal motions, as a mated pair. Some see the dark Mystery of Fate as the Great Queen, and its manifestation as the Land and waters, and the primal motions as the King of Life and Death, and associate it with Eros- Love; the force of motion, the fiery motion-energy within all, and the airs. Of course, fire and air have the dark Mystery of Fate at their heart, as their ultimate reality as well, just as the primal motions are themselves born of Fate.

There is a "child" born of the Dark Mystery of Fate and motion- and this child is the world itself, or manifestation; it is indestructible life; it is all of us, and everything. This "child" is the Horn Child of the craft, the child of the Mystery night, Iakkos, or the Mabon of Britain. This is the child born of Truth and beauty.

Fate or Nature is Truth; the basis of what is real, and what forever manifests. The motion that "mates" with the dark Mystery of Fate or Truth is Beauty; it acts as the agent that helps bring about the manifestation of Truth, or manifest Reality- and that is beautiful. Beauty is the power (appearing to humans as a great, sublime feeling) of Truth coming into triumphant manifestation. Beauty has a great, outward majesty, which echoes back to its ultimate mysterious origins in the darkest depths of reality. There is a King of Life and Death, and life and death both share in their own sort of beauty.

The follower of the Old Ways thinks of Truth, Beauty, and the Land, (or manifest Nature) as the greatest powers, most worthy of respect and contemplation in all things. They are the highest forces, the highest causes, the first, final, eternal, and greatest powers.

"Love" is the experience of the great bond between all manifest beings and the great Reality ("Reality" here referring to Truth, Beauty and the Land or Nature) from whence they arise. Each being is a child of Reality, not separate from Reality, and forever timelessly embraced by Reality, by Nature or the Land. The bond between beings and the Land, between beings and Reality, cannot be severed; it is all-powerful and all-encompassing. Love is the secret "principle of unity" for all things.

Love cannot be fully described to anyone's satisfaction, but it can be felt or experienced in this manner, and it is an all-encompassing force, experienced by all. Love is no mere sentimental, cheap thing, such as we have been taught to think by movie companies, or wedding industries and greeting card companies; true Love is far more essential, far more demanding and transformative than that. Understanding Love is a key to understanding the self, reality, and to shattering many dearly held delusions about things. Love, as the bond between all things, has as much a share in what is harrowing about life, as it does what is blissful or beautiful.

When true Love occurs between two people, it is for no other reason than the fact that they have had a deep, internal, and sometimes even unconscious recognition or experience of the truth of unity, but glimpsed it and experienced it through the personhood of another. Any glimpse of this unity, this wholeness, is blissful, and empowers a relationship with another person with an immense feeling of "rightness"- and a true satisfaction and peace that exists around spending your life and times with that person or near them.

The truly wise have developed this same feeling for the whole of Reality itself and all its forms and manifestations- they have a conscious and perpetual experience of love for Truth, Beauty, the Land (or Nature, all things that come to exist), and all beings.

Again- you must discard any shallow notion of love here; this is not meant to imply that a wise person's love makes them tolerant and accepting of killers or rapists, or other harmful people or spirits; what it does is endow the wise with understanding and peace, despite what they experience, and allows the wise to know how best to handle any situation that presents itself to them. It endows them with peace and insight that cannot be overcome by the fiercest crashing waves of dark Fate. "Light and Dark by turns, but Love Always," the sundial says.

All people are as much a part of the all-encompassing unity of Reality as any other person. As such, true Love is possible for all people and all things. It is possible between all people and things, but it happens that Fate normally seems to limit the means or methods by which most people will experience love in their mortal lives. People who are lucky enough to experience true love will normally only experience it a few times in life, with one or a few people, or for a special cause or some other aspect of Fate that manifests in their lives, such as Love for other creatures or Love for a special place.

The Adamantine Grip of Fate

Much ado has been made about "overcoming Fate" as the goal of the craft, or of the mystical life in general. What people seldom understand is that "overcoming Fate" is a disguised way of saying "gaining true Wisdom." Throughout the process of gaining Wisdom, Fate is, Fate remains, and Fate will always remain. Fate is Truth; it is the root of Nature; there is no escaping or leaving Fate; that would be like leaving or escaping Reality- and such a thing is not possible. There is no other reality to escape to; Reality is a singular, all-encompassing, and whole thing.

As I said above, all events that follow in the inescapable motion of Fate or Reality **must** occur as they do. It's fine and well to say "at any moment, many possibilities exist"- this is true, at any moment, infinite possibilities do "exist" in a strange, unexpressed yet potential way. However, which possibility or set of possibilities will manifest is not arbitrary or random- it is directly based on forces and causes and effects that have manifested "before," and only what manifests is "tangible" to our human senses.

We do not create Fate; we do not influence it; it creates us; it influences us. Our moment-to-moment memory of *Fate's movements through us and around us* gives rise to our mortal sense of "involvement" in things.

There is no way to guess out the complete picture of the unfolding of the cosmos, or of measuring out every corner of the immense chain of cause and effect, so what we call "the future"- or "what will be"- remains unclear to even the most wise- but some people will tell you (rightly) that this physical universe is a universe of "hard" determinism.

Only effects that *had* to come of past causes, and the causes that must come of those effects exist, and that chain cannot be broken- it even echoes down to the human neurological level, conditioning our every action and thought. This is the truth of Fate's expression in the physical world. This is another part of the omnipresent tapestry.

This tapestry of Reality is being continuously woven by the Three Matres or Mothers- the Hooded Ones, the Wyrd Sisters or Norns- the Fates. Our ancestors pictured the immense and unknowable forces that expressed Fate as a trinity of old women, weaving- but when you examine the word "Wyrd," you also find that it is cognate with "Urd" or Earth- the Great Earth Mother is the source of the image of the Three Old Women- once, before there were three Fates, there was likely one- Urd, the Eldest- for the Earth Mother represents the "all-encompassing expressed nature" through which all motions of Fate come to express themselves. The body of Nature, the ground, the waters, the sky- this is Fate in expression.

All the things that our ancestors saw came in origin from nature or the land, sea, and sky; all things returned to the same nature or earth which was seen as divine; She, originally, was the Goddess of Fate and life and death, as we will see later.

The Doom on Man and the Hidden Wisdom-gate of Awareness

I talked above about the unbreakable chain of cause and effect and the power of determinism in the cosmos as we know it. As a consequence of this reality, this mechanism of Fate, we do not have "free will" as we normally think of it- though we are all Fated to feel as though we do, and *experience reality as though we do*. That feeling of freedom is another Fated effect of Fate's manifestation in living beings and in human minds.

Fate is not predetermination; the future is all potential; it does not exist in any expression. Only the moment of Fate *now* exists. As new moments arise, the configuration of the great tapestry of forces and beings- which is itself a singular thing- "weaves" and changes, only ever existing as what is *now*, though having the potential to weave itself into amazing and limitless new combinations. Those who know and are powerfully aware of the fabric of the weave of *now* are very able, with cunning, to divine what very probably shall be. Where science cannot measure the wholeness of the tapestry, the mystic may have a means to know it in other ways- through the awareness of spirit.

Of course, just because the future has yet to emerge from potentials into expressed reality does not mean that we have a "clean slate" to decide what we want to make arise. Fate is not up to you. You do not weave the web of Fate; you are a strand in it.

You are not separate from the actions and occurrences that occur through your mind and body, and you are also not ultimately the author of the universal chain of cause and effect that stretches back to the timeless beginning, and which conditions everything that happens, at any point in space and time- a chain of cause and effect that you are a part of.

You didn't weave the strands of Fate; you *are* a strand. As the web moves, you move. It is only egocentrism and selfishness- a great denial of Reality- that leads people to believe that "they" are somehow "apart" from the web of Reality, and able to "choose" to make things happen independently of everything else, and independently of Fate, as though they were exempt from Fate. Vanity is the real reason for the belief in the illusion of "free will."

What we must learn from Fate is that everything we say, do, or feel is not only a manifestation of Fate, a force, but that force becomes a new thread which leads to a new weaving, or reality. You do not ultimately make decisions; ultimately, you *are* your decisions- they make you- they, and you, are the same- a great strand of Fate, a multi-layered chain of cause and effect, stretching back to the timeless.

Our every thought or word or deed manifests through what we call "ourselves," and affects everything else, on deep, deep levels that we cannot normally see or sense; but Reality is one, whole, and undivided thing- only our minds divide up the reality of Nature or Wyrd into "parts" and label them as different.

This intimate, undivided oneness of Reality is why the forces or events we experience as "our" words and actions are consequential to the rest of reality, to the rest of the world.

We must realize that when one strand in the web shakes, the whole thing shakes, and- insofar as we feel we have the power to- try to live in a respectful manner, seeking Wisdom and insight- for Fate or Wyrd has only left us with one actual decision to make, at any given moment- to choose to be aware of what is occurring, or to ignore it in favor of our ego-centered fantasies.

We have this power because our *essential awareness* of reality is not a choice; it needs no decision, for it is an eternal quality of reality and all things sprung from reality- whether tree, stone, water, animal, human, or God.

The Mystery of primordial awareness seems to constantly draw all beings to it, draw us back through layers of Fate and consciousness to the "root," as it were, and enables us, for one moment, to remain in the clarity of awareness, or, if our luck-force and willpower strains away, lured by other aspects of Fate, to turn back to our mortal ways of half-Wisdom.

In this place of Mystery, this silent space of awareness, we face our one and only test as human beings. This is the test of tests; to join the Hidden Ones or True Beings in wholeness of awareness, to know the All, or to remain in the fragmented awareness of mortal beings.

As the universe grows and changes with Fate's mighty unfolding, it is gradually being shredded, torn, coming apart, and the powerful, chaotic beings and forces who appeared at time's first dawn (and who appear in our ancestor's mythology as Underworldly monsters, giants or titans) are slowly gaining power, the same power that they will one day use to reduce the cosmos back to fire and embers and water and ice; it will all be reduced back to chaos and dark formlessness.

The power of chaos is growing stronger, higher, and the divide between the undying wholeness of awareness, and the many pools of mortal, fragmented awareness, is likewise growing thin. All worlds, and all beings within them, are moving towards a spiritual destiny that cannot be avoided, a "personal" consummation of experience that likewise parallels the creation of all worlds and the consummation of All worlds- for the beginning and the end are one, tied together in the unbroken weave of Fate, the perfect circle of Reality.

Awareness is indeed a great Mystery; somehow, by its power, when we humans become "aware" of the nature of Reality, we enter into a new experience of Reality, in which what we once felt to be our "personal decisions" are now perceived differently. Instead of feeling isolated or cut away from the web of fate and cause-and-effect, and in isolation choosing to make decisions of "our own accord," we now realize with more consciousness how our decisions actually make us.

We realize our connection to all, which cannot be broken or changed. We realize the divine and the timeless, directly and wordlessly. The isolated mortal ego is stilled, silenced, and transformed (though not obliterated out of existence as some think), and we begin to live in a greater reality of "self," which is certainly not "self" as we once thought or named it.

And, with some awe, we then realize and experience ourselves as no longer expressing confused decisions and deeds that shock and harm the parts of the web; it is as though those who are truly Wise or aware cease to be expressers of unconscious, harmful churnings of Fate and become heirs to a "second destiny" of mystical clarity.

They become fully "what they are"- full and true beings that are free to experience reality (and themselves, which are not separate from reality) as it truly is and as they truly are, without false hopes, blinders or regrets based on thwarted dreams and fantasies. A lasting peace is born, for the timeless majesty of Fate and Reality.

In a mysterious way that lacks a satisfactory mortal explanation, True Wisdom changes everything about the character of a human being, and how that being experiences and expresses further developments of Fate. And again, that this should be an affect of True Wisdom on mortals, is a Fated reality.

Real freedom is a paradox to mortals- it is by giving up on our vain notions of "freedom" that, ironically, a greater freedom emerges- Fate will not allow mortals to achieve freedom in any other way than the Truth; if you spend your life declaring what great "free will" or "freedom" you have, and have not yet seen the Truth, you will declare your way into the grave, demanding that you have "freedom," even though you have none, and are still subject to every unconscious force and factor in the web- and from the darkness and oblivion of your grave, eventually join rebirth to move on to another branch of the quest for Truth and actual freedom.

If mortals got what they, in their mortal half-Wisdom, call "freedom," they would find it a nightmare. As has been said before, mortals have a way of loving their fictions- they paint their prison cells many different colors, and declare that they are "free."

The "Wisdom" of mortals is foolishness to Fate; the same might be said if you compared mortal Wisdom to the perfect Wisdom of the True Beings, spirits, or Gods. Mortal Wisdom has uses- but it has limits, as well. All our clever ideas and rational, logical theories and self-serving ideas about "salvation" and "heaven" and "free will" and "righteousness" all crumble to dust in the great night of time and in the sweep of Fate.

When mortals look to Fate and to the divine world for Wisdom, they begin to find the keys to unlocking the mortal dilemma, the paradox of mortality, the way from death to life. What is found- those keys- seem paradoxical, too- but that is because they are things from another world, a world that is timeless and strange to mortal minds.

Fate restrains our every egocentric ignorance, firmly holding us in place, holding us back from the various dead-end paths that we may wish to invest our minds into, allowing us to beat our heads against Fated walls and Fate-closed doors, until we finally see the Truth.

In this way, Her restrictions are actually blessings, showing us what way is useless and unrealistic, and simultaneously showing us what way *is* useful and realistic. By surrendering your notions of absolute mortal free will, you are opening up to the greater Will of Spirit, which is Fate.

That way begins when you give up on mortal half-Wisdom and release yourself from egocentric illusions of "free will." Sadly, most people will continue smashing their heads against Fated walls and Fate-closed doors, and calling this drama their "lives." They will define themselves by their limitations, miscall their limitations "freedoms," and eventually perish and come to dust. That is what it means to be mortal. And, adding a great and ancient weight to this truth about mankind, the people that spend their lives in this manner are Fated to do so!

This is not as grim as it sounds- Old Fate is not ultimately unfair; She is what She is, and What She Is, is What Things Are; She is Truth.

If She has ordained it, through expression, it is so, and could not be otherwise; and thus, as frustrating as it may seem to our human minds, it is "fair." But the real reason for its fairness is simple- because while the system of cause and effect is locked, the presence of awareness, the great divine silence of invisible awareness within the entire system, is a great and constantly open way to freedom and Wisdom.

Wisdom is salvation; Wisdom and the presence of awareness, and the spiritual beings who initiate mankind into the Mysteries, all seem to "impinge" on the locked-seeming system of Fate, in a Fateful "Red Thread" that runs through all reality, on all levels, liberating beings by allowing Wisdom to arise.

Fate, by keeping the system as it is, deterministic and solidly bound, is actually creating the needed conditions for true Wisdom to arise. Fate's limitations are, as said before, ultimately liberating factors, not lasting limitations.

The truly Wise enter into a spiritual condition that does not take any mortal definition, and thus, is boundless. These beings undergo the Wisdom-metamorphosis, and become "justified" beings, authentic beings, made whole through Fate, the Master-Men or Master-Spirits of the craft, who work to guide the destiny of others in the craft, and all peoples besides-sometimes even helping to shape the destiny of nations.

Mastery and the Timeless Self

The Grand Seal- Mastery- this is the goal of the path of the Witch, and the attainment of the Elder Rite: to be not only a Fate-Worker, but a being with Fate-Wisdom; Wisdom of Reality, which carries a person (now transformed) beyond the boundaries of the experience of everyday mortals. It is the experience of actual freedom, a freedom that is beyond what most half-wise mortals imagine "freedom" to be.

This is the fulfillment of what the True Beings, or what the ancients called "Gods" intended for mankind when they endowed us with spirit and the glowing seed of imagination and inspiration. This is the Red Thread of Urd coming to fulfillment.

Fate makes us what we are. Fate brought you here; Fate makes you feel love for what you identify in your mind as the Old Ways.

Fate is the reason for everything. You are here because being here is what you are, it is Fate. You love what you love because loving what you love is what you are, and you didn't choose to be those things or love those things. See before you and inside you the power of Fate.

Fate has implanted a feeling in you, and it says "I want peace." It may have put others- "I want Wisdom" or "I want Truth" or "I want power." It may say "I want a lover, a husband, a family" or "I want money, success."

The Threads of Fate are twisted in the configuration that is YOU. And you didn't choose for those threads to exist, nor for any weaving to twist in the way it went. Your job is simply to be aware of what Fate has wrought. "I" want. But what is "I?" It's the world talking- an expression of Fate- not just a single, isolated person. The longer you talk *as* a person, the more cut off you will become as power and understanding starts to strain at your limitations of speech and thought. Power and understanding is not just for a person. They are part of Fate, part of the world, and the life of the world, the power of the world.

Accept power and understanding on behalf of the world, on behalf of the Greater Self that is everywhere and everything- the timeless Master Spirit that has a secret relationship with your soul- and you will have the strength to wield it properly. Do it not, and you will rot in dissolution in the deeps of the Underworld, after a lifetime of being trapped in a narrow mortal definition of "body" and "personality".

The Strange Double-Bind of Fate

It is Fated that humans should feel like they have free will, and have to experience our various life-situations as though we had choice, but that, ultimately, everything is governed by absolute laws, many of which are beyond us, and some of which are able to be measured by us.

The emotions that occur in us as we flow, unstoppably, from life-situation to life-situation are unique to us- this is our test; our Fated experiences as human beings. We have to suffer in our own heads over hard decisions, even though, ultimately, there is no real decision.

We are trapped chiefly by the illusion that we are free- an interesting kind of paradox, but it is a very realistic statement about the heart of the human condition.

Our only hope is in understanding the human condition- not seeing it as bad, and being guilty, not seeing it as empty of meaning, and not seeing it as good and a force for change- a human life is not a force for change- a human life is a part of the greater process of the world. We are not masters of the world, we are parts of the world, parts that can be very aware of themselves as though they were different from the world, but ultimately, we are not different. We are all parts of the Web of Fate.

To many, this sounds grim; from the perspective of the mortal ego, it sounds very grim. But freedom- the freedom that we long for at our deepest levels, and the resolution to life's puzzle, is found in awareness-understanding- of the way things are. You "miss the mark" everyday you think of yourself as an individual with "free will," and label yourself as "this or that," apart from the world around you- even though you have no choice at this point but to do so. It is true that life, for mortals, is a Fated double-bind.

We can agonize over what we experience as "our decisions," without ever realizing that the decisions are already made- the chain of cause and effect that will lead to what you will call "your decision" began eons ago, and "you" as a mortal had nothing to do with its beginning or the shape it is taking. When we feel that we "finally make the decisions," the reality is that they are making us- not the other way around. We are them; we are the decisions; they are not ours, nor separate from us- all people are known by what they say and do and express.

No one ultimately chooses to be what they are, where they are, or the way things are- Fate does that. You can say you "chose" to read this book right now, but did you choose to make that choice? If a person had to made choices, or make decisions, a strange problem would occur- they would never be able to choose or decide. This is because the decision to make a decision is never made- you felt an unconscious impulse to pick up this book and read- but did you, two hours before you picked up this book, consciously decide, "In two hours, I am going to make the choice to read The Witching Way of the Hollow Hill"?

No, you didn't. It happened; the decision or choice emerged spontaneously from within you, and you acted on it- and, in your memory, when you look back, you think "I decided to pick up that book and read"- and thus, limited by the only linguistic way you can express what occurred, you lay claim to what seem to be "your" actions. Then, if you are like most people, you will fight to the death defending the idea that "you" decided, of your own free will, to get the book and read.

But is that what happened? Clearly not- because the ultimate decision to read was made somewhere else, in a place you normally have no conscious awareness of. If you had to consciously choose to do things, you could never choose- because before you can choose, you'd have to choose to choose, and before you could choose to choose, you'd have to choose to choose to choose... ad infinitum. This infinite regression would never reach a "first choice," so you'd find yourself unable to act.

This doesn't happen, however. The "spontaneous decision" to act arises unconsciously from within you- you don't consciously make the impulse arise- but you then consciously act on it. It arises from the great chain of cause and effect that stretches back to the timeless- the chain of Fate. This is how we express the chain of Fate; we ARE the expression of Fate; we do not make it; it makes us.

Does this mean that people are not ultimately responsible for their actions? People ARE their actions. We ARE our Fate. On the relative level of everyday expression, actions have consequences, and we must endure them. It is again part of the double-bind of Fate that we did not ask to be what we are, and yet, we are chained to the consequences of being what we are. This is all the more reason to seek insight and true freedom through Wisdom, which is the only way to not fall constant prey to seemingly blind Fate. Without Wisdom, Fated life or mortal life contains a degree of pain, of blindness and helplessness, and the double-bind of Fate oppresses our egos with its seeming "unfairness."

This double-bind does not mean that we are the cause of it, nor that we are "flawed"- only that this is what it means to be mortal. Mortality is bittersweet, and yet, perfect for what it is, for it (like everything else in the system of Fate) is just as it should be.

Becoming aware of the timeless is the only way to render the chain of Fate meaningful, and give you the true freedom you deeply desire, but which you have pursued in the wrong places- chiefly by looking into the expression of Fate for freedom, but never into the source of Fate, which is also the true source of YOU. Freedom is never found in turning "outside" and trying to force the world into shapes of our own shallow and illusionary egoistic choosing- it is found by going radically within- within ourselves, and within the depths of reality, which are the same place.

Acquiring this Wisdom found within is the only true "self improvement," and ironically, it is not improvement of "self" at all, but a thing that goes beyond definitions of "self."

Some people feel the reality of Fate, but are still prey to the strong egocentric desire to feel "free" on levels that they are not, and they try to say that "Fate controls the greater reality, but in lesser reality, I have choices to make"- that is to say, they try to say that they have "free will within the system of Fate." But this is another ego-centered mistake. The system of Fate is singular; it is one system. It operates on all levels, with equal force. We are another link in the chain of Fate, and no amount of rationalizing it will change that- we are not "sort of separate" from it on "some level." We are not consciously choosing and willing for the chain of cause and effect to affect us like it does, nor do we choose the ultimate impulses that lead to the expressions we call our "actions."

Fate has left mankind with one majestic freedom- one only. That freedom is involved with being aware of what was just said, and accepting your true place in things. This great possibility of freedom sounds simple on the surface, but it is a gateway to the greatest and most unlimited experience of reality possible. You don't just accept your place and stop changing or growing; you begin changing and growing into a new perspective, a deeper one.

When you do that, stop fighting Fate and let yourself **consciously** "become one" with Fate- a mystical transformation occurs; you are for the first time free to perfectly and effortlessly be whatever and wherever you happen to be, and in that freedom, that great realization of the great Fated flow of all things, you cease to be harmful to yourself or others. The Fated chain of events that you go on to manifest lacks harmful intent or harmful fantasies, and you become a whole person.

You can be aware of the reality of Fate, or ignore it, and continue on with the fiction that we've invented for what we "are"- and the suffering that ceaselessly and unavoidably goes along with that fiction.

It's easy to go on thinking that you have "free will" and that you can change the world of your own power- that is a very pleasing fiction. But in life, on all levels, we are faced with the same basic choice, the one choice that says everything about us: the choice between doing what is right, or doing what is easy.

We've created quite a fantasy world in our minds, and we have quite a fantasy-scheme for what it means to be "human" in our heads. This is a natural consequence of the Fate of mortality.

But the parallel Fate of awareness changes that, and Fate sends "wake up calls" to us, deep into our daily fiction, all the time. The unseen world sends these "wake up calls"- events, feelings, strange dreams, insights- things meant to wake us up... they all resonate with the feeling of the disturbing, the eldritch, the surreal, or the peaceful- "Look!" they seem to say- "You are not what you think you are, and neither is the world!"

People ignore these things all the time; nothing could be more human than doing so. Many people who read this book may ignore what I've said here. Whether people ignore this all or not, all is as it should be. An old saying goes:

"There is good, and there is bad, and that is good…there is perfect and there is imperfect, *and that is perfect.*"

This sort of calmness and peace, and acceptance of Fate, while still being aware that freedom and Truth are out there, beyond challenge, is part and parcel of the Older Way of thinking- all Pagan cultures had a strong sense of Fate. Even though the early Christians came with their ego-salving teachings about "free will," and accused Pagans of being "fatalistic," the time has come to realize the difference between these two worldviews, and for modern Pagans to realize that by spouting "free will" talk, they are only accepting and continuing a very Christian worldview-feature.

In some ways, denying Fate in favor of absolute free will is a denial of the divine Feminine, She who is Fate, the most ancient Fate Mother and power, in favor of the "will"- the consciously commanding masculine. It is another means of putting the masculine dominant to the feminine, within a person's way of thinking and seeing, and thus very well suited to Christians, now and then.

The Fate-oriented perspective is one of passivity, seeking Wisdom; the will-oriented perspective is one of activity, of seeking to change and shape and force and dominate things in accordance with human desires. The trouble begins when the "will" loses its connection to its own dark source- the source that endows the will with knowledge and awareness of its own origins, of the meaning behind things, and which gives it the Wisdom to act in accordance with harmony.

The will that becomes so isolated becomes, quite frankly, the root of the travesties that you see today- patriarchal religions, sciences, governments, moralities, and theologies that are all quite clearly unwise and ultimately destructive to themselves and others.

Thus, fatalism, or the belief in Fate, is not necessarily a bad thing, insofar as it puts a person to peace in regards to what we cannot change, or what must be. It allows a person to direct their power and awareness to places where true transformation *is* possible, as opposed to places where it is not, and it gives rise to an attitude that is far more oriented around contemplation and passivity- of watching life and learning subtle Wisdoms from "the way of things," as opposed to rushing out and vandalizing the world with a half-wise mind that ignores its own Mother-Source, and which ignores its connection to all other things. It is the will moving in full conscious awareness of Fate that creates the perfect being, the truly Wise.

This is how and why the great Master of the craft, who is the active will of reality itself, the world-shaper, moves in Wisdom; He knows his source; He is of Her, loves Her, wordlessly "knows" Her, and dies into Her, to be reborn from Her, timelessly. He is truly free to be precisely what Fate has made him. We are all invited to be the same, and we must be the same.

Fate and the Final Word, the Final Obstacle- the Ruthless Power of Wisdom-Awakening

One of the main "obstacles" that people must eventually face, in any aspect of life, but most certainly in the spiritual life, is the fact that mortal life as we experience it simply will not conform to our mortal notions of "fairness."

I will freely admit that when you approach Fate, you are approaching a concept that is hard on you- what the ego most dearly wants to hear, Fate denies it. She is the ruthless initiatrix that demands everything. Fate isn't "fair" by mortal standards. It IS fair, but according to its own reality. It is an immense system, a deep and ruthless system- it has no room for egocentric mortal ideas about "fairness."

There is simply no satisfying way to say it or explain it, on final analysis- that's because your mortal identity and ideas about the way things SHOULD be, are not necessarily the way things are, ultimately.

Fate demands that you accept what most people fiercely struggle against- it demands that you realize that "free will" is a dream, a way of experiencing a system, a life, that is not free. Ironically, what traps mortals the most is the belief that they are already free- what better way to trap people who are literally bound and unfree, than to convince them that they are free?

You can't, with your own mortal power and mind, master Fate or the world, can't make it conform to your notions of fairness and justice. You didn't ask to be here, to be a human, and your ego and your personality and your memories- the seat of what you call "you"- is not the agency that has the power to make "choices" independently and freely with "will." It is merely an observer of what Fate is "doing" at any moment.

Accepting that is hard, because you want desperately to feel that life is more predictable and free, that you can "make choices" that will "improve" your situation in life, and that humans can always- one day- rally to make the world better. But it simply can't be done... never has been, never will be. That's because egocentric joy and satisfaction is not the path to true Wisdom and freedom. Ironically, giving up those things, and undergoing a transformation into something radically different is the path to that true satisfaction and completion.

No, you didn't ask to be here, having this mortal experience, and you don't ultimately make choices and decisions- and yet, you must suffer the consequences of them. Consequence is a part of Hard Fate. It isn't "fair," and that is precisely the point.

Fate demands that we look to a radically new place to find freedom in the only true place it is found- what seems to us to be "outside" this mortal life. True freedom is not the power to make choices and decisions; true freedom is awareness of what is real, awareness of the timeless; an awareness that transcends all the entanglements and egocentric struggles of mankind. This is not something you have to "do," as much as something that you already are, something that already is- you need an awareness-shift.

The fact that Fate is so hard on us, so unfair seeming and even threatening to the ego that dearly wants to be independent and free, is a sign of its great power. It is making demands on you, that will carry you beyond the mortal, after you have stopped struggling *to be* a mortal in a "fair" mortal world- a world that was never meant to be "the point" of your spiritual fulfillment; a mortal experience that is only a tiny portion of the fullness of your being; a world full of mortal cleverness and ideas and desires that are NOT the point of your existence, only small portions of it.

The point of "Witch-sight" is to see wholeness, to see beyond the limitations. Fate requires that; Fate requires that you give up on what mortals dearly want; that you DIE, literally, to your "self" and to mortality and ego, that you be reborn in a greater, more complete way, with full awareness of Reality. From that perfect perspective, you find the Truth about things.

No matter how gentle and joyful your Fate may manifest, it is an invitation to you to "wake up," to be aware. No matter how dark or awful it may manifest for you or others, that, too, is an invitation to be aware. The wise consider every situation, with an eye of true discrimination, and do not let themselves be shaken and disturbed- they are engaging reality in a deeper way; they are looking to the deeper awareness beyond the wild crashing waves of Fate, seeing what it all points to- and it points to the timeless, far beyond our mortal experiences, and yet, never apart from them.

The Spirits and Powers of the Old Ways

Now we must take a look at the chief powers and spiritual forces that inhabit the "current" of the Old Ways, those ancient and perpetually existing forces that mediate its power to people alive here and now, in serial time. They are the active agents of the transmission and survival of the Old Ways, as well as the spiritual guardians of the true initiation into its Mysteries.

The Master of the Craft

This Lordly spirit, has been called by some the "God" of Witchcraft and sorcery. He is the spiritual being to whom witches pray and from whom they receive guidance and teachings that lead them to the source from which insights and mystical powers derive; if a person were to look with a discriminating eye at the hints provided by history and mythology, one can see that this great and universal power is He who was called the "All Father" by the Pagan peoples of Northern Europe. He came forth from the darkness of the beginning as Light and the Shaper of all things, and his life came to rest within Nature and in all living things, which he motivates and inspires, his Godly essence coiled like a serpent within each.

He is the intelligible manifestation of a deeper divine reality, and his ancient association with serpents and other creatures that took on a dark and devilish reputation after the dominance of Christianity brings him into association with the serpent of the primal Eden myth- and, to Christians, with the devil.

He was the primal teacher of mankind, the one who gave to earliest man the gift of conscious self-awareness and kindled the fire of cunning or imagination in us- in this capacity, He is called the Cunning Serpent, as the most ancient being born from his mighty Father and from Nature or Fate, He is the **Old One** or the **Ancient Wise One**. It is He whom men call the devil, and He is also addressed as "**Master.**" As the passionate life-force and coursing knowledge within each being and within Nature, he is associated with the fertile emblem of the Goat, and is seen by some as the lusty **Goat Horned One**, the lord of nature and fertility; he is also called the **Goat-Footed**, the **Black Satyr**, the Goat-buck, Master Puck, Pouck, or the **King of the Buxen**. In Wales, the Master was called **Andras.** In the golden goat's horns, and in the tutelary function that He is often associated with, He is the **Azael** of the fire-rite.

His "Father", the older, dark and "originating" power that He springs from, is captured in myth and lore as the sorcerous and terrifying Lord of the dead and the chthonic regions. This figure was called the **Horseman** or the **Hunter**; He was also called **Hob-th'rus**, but among His more inner names are **Sator** and **Conal Cernac**.

It is my intention to present the Master and the darker, more titanic figure of the chthonic "Father" as two distinct but related spirital presences, important to the Old Ways and the craft. Modern pagans can see this distinction mythologically between Odin in his most chthonic aspects and in his mercurial aspects, or even between Frey and Odin; between Dagda and Lugh, or between Zeus and his sons Hermes, Apollon, and Dionysos.

Regarding the great Fore-Father of the mercurial Master, his name "Conal Cernac" contains many Mysteries- the name is normally mistranslated to mean "Victorious Conal," but in reality it means "horned wolfish (one)"- Conal Cernac is the "Horned Wolf." This ancient and primal symbol shows Him to be the balancer and ruler of all creation, for He is part predator, part prey- but also the one who holds the balance between life and death, creation and destruction; He is the active force within Nature which is found within death and life, inside of creation and destruction, but also in a "third" mysterious condition, transcending all opposites. That "third" face of transcendence is precisely the Master Himself.

The concept of Three was tied to the Master, for symbolically, all three-faced beings see the beginning, the middle, and end- they have the omniscient sight of wholeness. The Master, like His Father, saw into the celestial regions, the world of mortals, and the deep Underworld; He saw both the world without and the unseen world, or the world within, but He also "saw" the Truth, or the transcendent Mystery that we mortals describe as "Wisdom." Communion with the omnipresent numinous being of the Master is a road to the perfection of a being, to

Hob th'ras Buc~Andras

the perfection of consciousness and the unlocking of many sorcerous insights and abilities.

Communion with the Master through the agency of the rites of the craft causes transformations to occur on all levels within a human being, starting at the deepest, most unconscious levels, and gradually arising into the consciousness, before exalting the consciousness into a direct communion with the Old One- this is how the "Great Inheritance" or the Wisdom that recognizes reality is brought forth into the minds of mortals, thus changing their destiny forever. It is the Grand Seal of the Master, His promise and gift to mankind.

The Master was pictured as a brilliant spirit of light, and His Father as a hard-hoofed and dark horned or darkly-clad figure, on a great dark steed and with the hounds of hell in His hunt. Sometimes the Master was seen as a goat horned angel of light, or a rustic wooded satyr, oak-clad and goat-horned. This is the Lord of the World, the Word of Creation, the Spirit of All. Wolves also accompanied the Master of light in many mythologies, just as the hounds and wolves accompanied His Father, the Horned Wolf.

The wolves represent the primal canine force of both "Otherworldliness" and dark Wisdom-Chaos, and they go on to appear as the Cwn Annwn, or the hounds of hell. They connect any being that is associated with them with the Underworld and the sorcerous or transcendent realities, in the same manner that the antlers or horns of animals connect beings with this world, and the chthonic Mysteries of nature and life. The Master is Lord of life and death, guide of souls, and He resonates throughout the human consciousness with very mysterious aspects, as well as very earthy aspects.

All of the symbols, times, seasons, and implements "northwards" of the Compass are connected with these beings, as well as southwards, for as mentioned (and as shall be discussed in greater detail), the Master and His father mediate the powers of life and death, ruling over life and death, ruling over the seen world and the unseen alike, with living faces and dead faces, and keeping the portal-ways between the seen and the unseen worlds.

The Native God and the Secret of the White God in the Land:
The True Lord Standing Near

When I visited the Land of Britain, I asked the God of the Land to reveal Himself to me through that Land. I gradually became aware of His presence as I traveled from Wales to Northern England, in a manner that revealed His nature with a clarity that I had only gained hints of in other places. I came into the presence of the true chief native God of Britain, and the spiritual presence that reigns over all places in the natural world.

I came to understand that the Master and His Great "Father" (that great reality that is his origin) were complimentary- one a great force of light and awakening, a force that was responsible for laying the bonds of Fate upon all shaped things- things that He had shaped and that He was called upon to consciously bind in accordance with a darker, deeper law of Fate, and the other the "shadow" of supreme Godly power, contrasted with the manifest light of the Shaper- the deeper, darker power of conscious divinity that hovers over all things as a timeless fore-parent.

The bright Master was the great teacher and shaper, Lord of the world and the world-law, a figure who was master of the motions of sky and heaven, shaper and mover of sun and rain, but without understanding His origin, one could not understand Him. He was sprung from a deeper, more "earthy" manifest presence- which I metaphorically call His Great Father- a wild, powerful, and primordial presence that was older than the world-order, and which still resided within the body of Nature and the Land itself. This was the "Ancient Whiteness," the force of origins, and a force that was the root of fertility, and forever inseperable from the Land.

Interestingly, "Frey" among the northern heathens was that God of the Land and fertility, as well as the fertility of the sky and sun- the boar that was sacred to Him was linked to both sun and Land. I realized that reports of Witches in the middle ages calling upon their "devil" for rain was due to the fact that the Lord in the Land, the Horned Master of the Witch-coven, (seen in my model as the Father of the goatish master) was the "God of Nature" in the broadest sense; He bridged all realms of nature, from the order of binding and cosmos, to the wild force of nature which emerged in the time of chaos, and which persists in darker seasons, and in the deepest places of the Land.

The "wild" aspect was the Great God within all things, the face peering out from the flora and fauna of the world, and the White Horned King inside of the body of Nature itself, the King of the Sacred Land.

The White Horned King was that presence- a manifestation that was older than old, older than the world-order, coeval with the uroboric darkness of chaos, and which was the older and chief root of the "Horned God" mythos so beloved in the ancient world, and by modern Pagans. In some ways, this Great God could represent the ultimate Mystery of all origins, or the primary "Godly" force inherent in the body of Nature.

It made sense to me that a movement in the modern day, such as Paganism, which tried to return to spiritual roots in Nature Herself, would bring this power into the forefront of the consciousness of the members. This "Horned King" or great chthonic power was attested to in all Pagan Religions of the ancient world. Time and time again, this presence would appear in mythologies, forever connected with horned and antlered beasts, and the body of Nature, the source of life, and the Underworld.

The presence of this great power was "marked" by His association with antlered creatures, horned creatures, serpents or snakes, boars, and, when He made His appearance as a hunter, with the hounds of the Underworld and horses.

His connections were not only with the darkness of the Underworld, but the light of the sun and stars, but also the more mysterious "transcendent" light of transformed consciousness. The instruments of the hunter, like bows and arrows, were not missing in His historical associations; His connection with the archers and the Gods of light (to whom He was sometimes seen as Father, or as the Light-God Himself) were not absent, either. Ravens were His messengers, and it is telling that ravens were the messengers of more than one God of light, occultism, and archery/ spear-wielding/hunting in the various Indo-European pantheons.

I began to receive indirect manifestations of His presence years ago, but when I visited the holy isle of Britain, I began to gain direct insights into

His nature, as the Land of Britain itself could and would transmit to me in trance.

It began in Wales, when I made contact with Him via the names Pwyll and Gwyn- the "Penannwn" or "head of Annwn," the ruler of the Underworld, alongside the ages-old presence of the Great Queen- the powers of the Land of Wales seemed to respond with great force to these names. I was searching for a forked-wood or a stang at the time, and I asked Him to deliver one into my hands, as I was having trouble finding one. A day later, a gentleman I met at a farm I was staying at gave me a long piece of forked hazel wood that he happened to have in his shed. I have that forked wood staff now, and to this day, it acts as a conduit to that time and place, where the White Lady that dwelled in that holy Land, and the White Horned King spoke so clearly.

The finding of this hazel-wood stang was key to understanding what I later came to understand about the Master in the Land. It was given to me by Him so that I would recognize a vital clue, later.

But what stood out in His contact, more than the strong reactions I could feel the power of the Land having, was His "Whiteness"- the immensity of it, the pervasiveness of it. It wasn't just white as the snow is white; it was a great clarity within all, and a savage one that moved like the wind at times. It moved my heart as much as the trees of that Land.

The name "Gwyn" comes from the word VINDOS, which means "white" or refers to "the white one." The Celtic root-word *wid, which means to know, leads us to widtos, meaning knowledge; the term *windo means "white," or clearly seen. There is an association between "white" and "clear"- the Proto-Indo-European words WEI and HWIT, from which Vindos can be traced, mean "clear" and "white," but bear in mind that this "clear whiteness" also refers to "knowing" and "knowledge."

This is an important hint regarding the nature of the Great Being of which we speak; He is the son of Old Fate, Fate being the same as the Uroboric Darkness that preceded light. As the light, He is the clear "whiteness" or light of knowledge, the undifferentiated consciousness that arises from the primordial darkness.

Vindos, Vin- or Gwyn, becomes Finn in Irish- Finn Macool, whose name conceals the entire truth- the "cool" in his name comes from the Proto-Indo-European "Kolyo," which as we shall see, is the root-name for the Great dark Goddess of the Indo-European peoples, Old Fate, the Most Ancient One; Finn Macool is the "clear white knowing one, son of the Concealed or dark one; poetically "clear light, son of darkness." Old Irish associates the word Finn with "vision," the word "find" which means "white," and "fiuss" which means "knowledge."

In Welsh, this takes us to "Gwyn," meaning "white," and the Gaulish "Vindos," also meaning "white." In Breton we find "gwenn," meaning "white," and Cornish "guyn" meaning the same. Scottish Gaelic has "fios," meaning "knowledge."

In Celtic mythology, we have two beings that should interest us here- Fintan, the salmon of knowledge, who represents the oldest being in the world- whose memory stretched back to the time before creation. In the aquatic form of Fintan, we have a primordial connection between the "white one of great knowledge" and the source of all Wisdom: Fintan swims in the "world well" or the Well of the Great Mother, itself symbol of her womb or Cauldron of Creation, and thereby has access directly to the roots of creation and wisdom.

The fish is a cold-blooded, water-dwelling creature, the waters themselves referring to the primordial creating power of watery chaos, but they are a link to the pre-mammalian worlds, whence springs the serpent as a symbol of both the Master and the great cthonic Father. the serpent is likewise and a symbol of the knowledge that the Master gifted the mankind with, at the dawn of a truly "human" consciousness.

Through this chain of mystical connections, we come to the mysterious White Stag, which appears in many mythologies, leading those who hunt it or chase it into the Otherworld itself, and to Wisdom.

In Fintan, we can see a connection between the ancient white Horned One and the most primordial sources of knowledge, as well as mystical access to the timeless source of all. When the White Stag appears in our mythologies, there is (as I shall mention later) an immediate "transition" of the people in the tale into an Otherworldly state. The White Stag, like the white salmon of knowledge, is the link to non-ordinary and primordial, non-mammal kingdoms of life, along with the serpent that has a deep relationship with Him.

Vindos, Vindonnus, or Gwyn/Arawn is the White Horned God in the Land, the ruler of the Underworld and He who bears the serpents that symbolize primordial life-force and the sorcery of self-awareness, the true "Lord of the World." He is the giver of familiar spirits or animal powers, as He is the master of the forest and the natural world. The "whiteness" links Him to the Pale People in the Land, the spirits of the dead or the Faery-folk, the people of Annwn, over whom He is said to rule in his underground realm.

He is the master of knowledge, not unlike the chthonic Dagda of the Celts; and as I discussed in the section on "the Master," the "Horned Wolf" now reveals another secret- the wolf and the ravens who surround the God represent His "light and sorcerous shaper" aspect, but the stag or horned beast aspect represents his chthonic and tellurian aspect. They are both met in one powerful being, the Great Godhead of the Pagan world, a power that we are considering from two very important angles.

As we search around ancient Europe, especially in the British Isles, we begin to see this Godly power emerging in powerful ways. In French temples, we find inscriptions to APOLLO VINDONNUS, said to be a God of healing and a sun God. He was associated with the healing of eyesight. It should be pointed out that Apollo, far from being merely a sun God, was the God of light and occult mysteries, and like Woden and Lugh, was totemically associated with ravens, serpents and wolves- and, most tellingly, with "the far north," or Hyperborea- the Isle of Britain.

No Greek God had more rustic shrines raised in His honor than Apollo, who was also a great archer and hunter. Apollo was also the "enlightener" of mankind- the very function of the Master. Anyone familiar with the work of groundbreaking author and philosopher Peter Kingsley will already be aware of Apollo's connections to the Underworld and to serpents.

Few modern Pagans of the British Isles or Northern Tradition care to give a thought to Apollo, for most ignorantly associate Him with white-washed Greek temples and urban life, and snooty intellectualism; but the God Himself was primal and powerful, and from the same rustic, earthy root as the "All Fathers" of the north; I believe that Apollo is nothing less than the "southernmost" drift of the great Master.

In Gaul, we find APOLLO VIROTUTIS, a Celtic God whose name means "benefactor of humanity." Inscriptions to Apollo Vindonnus are known, linking Vindos to the name VINOTONUS – "Vinotonus" being a clear cognate to Vindonus.

Vinotonus is known from inscriptions on altars, all found near the Roman fort of Bowes in North Yorkshire, England, a beautiful and powerful Land that I was privileged to visit during my pilgrimage. Two of the altars identify Him outright with the Roman deity Silvanus as Silvanus Vinotonus, a God of stags, hunters and the forest, of whom I shall speak shortly.

As we approach Northern England, however, a greater picture begins to emerge. At Hadrian's Wall, we find inscriptions to MOGONS, whose name means "the Great One." He is also found mentioned in inscriptions both in Germany and France. There are variants on this God's name, and dedicatory inscriptions to Mogunus, Mogounus and Mountus, all of which are thought to be the same being. The Celtic Goddess Mogontia may have been a consort to this deity. Some scholars have said that this God cannot be linked to any classical deity, but I must disagree on this point.

An inscription discovered in England gave Mogons a longer name- MOGONS VITIRIS - associating Mogons with the northern Celtic God Vitiris.

The deity VITIRIS was also called Hvitiris, Vetus, Vitris, Veteris, Hvitris, Vheteris, and Veteres. Pay attention to these names- many of them, such as HVITRIS, come from HWIT- the root of "white," or the same root as Vindos.

Vitiris was quite a popular deity in the area of Hadrian's Wall, among the ranks of the Roman army in the second and third century. More than fifty inscriptions dedicated to Vitiris are known. Most importantly, some of the altars dedicated to Him are decorated with a serpent and a boar. In light of what we know of the totemic associations of the Horned One and the Master, we have no trouble now seeing what power we are dealing with.

Vindonus

As I mentioned above, Vindonus was linked to the Roman God Silvanus-Vinotonus, the God of the forest.

The Celtic God Callirius was also linked with the Roman God Silvanus. We know this from dedicatory inscriptions found at Colchester, England, and from an inscription that is found on a bronze plaque discovered in an offering pit near a rectangular shrine. In that same pit was found a bronze figure of a stag, which has led most to agree that the God was worshipped as a God who protected stags and the hunters of stags. Callirius was the name of a local woodland God whose name is said by some to mean "king of the woodland" or "hazel wood God" or "God of the hazel wood."

When I did the research that led to my discovery of this, I remembered the hazel staff that I now have in my possession, and smiled.

From the holy root of Vindos, a series of names for the true native God had emerged- Vindonus and Vitiris, the White King in the Land, Callirius the woodland king and lord of the hazel, and Mogons, the Great One. Next to him stood his "Great Queen," Mogontia, who would be the same as Rhiannon (the Underworldly wife of Pwyll, the human king who hunted the White Stag, transitioned into the Underworld to take Arawn/Gwyn's place, and become the king of the Underworld himself) or Rigantona.

Pwyll was no doubt a God of the Underworld whose worship superceded Arawn/Gwyn's, and Rhiannon was probably the original Great Queen of the Land and Underworld, married to Gwyn/Arawn before Pwyll PenAnnwn.

Lord Gwyn, the White Horned king and Arawn the hunter, the White King of Faery- these twin figures emerge in Wales through the powerful symbols of the White Stag, the White Stag-King and Lord of the Land and Underworld, the power that is ancient and forever a part of the body of Nature, and a part of all people- in their very knowing, their very awareness and consciousness, as well as in the life-force of all things.

When the White Stag appears in dreams, in myths, or in real life, a powerful transition is about to occur between this world and the next- it is the symbol of the great Master as the keeper of the Ghost Roads that run between this world and the next, the keeper of the unseen gates and doors inside the Land, through which the shades of the dead and the wandering spirits of mystics pass, to join in the grand Wisdom of the pale world within and below.

Goat Master and Stag-King: Clarifications of the Witch Theology

In the previous sections, I have discussed two powerful spiritual entities that act as the "root powers" of the entire Craft as I know it. These two primary "masculine" spiritual powers are they whom the tradition of Witchcraft (and the folkloric tradition) has manifested a deep relationship with since time immemorial. Through many times and changes, a constant reality has lived behind the images.

These figures- the Master of the Craft and the Horned King, have countless overlaps, and in many places, they run together almost inseparably, particularly in the folkloric hypostasis of the "Devil" figure. I am writing this clarification now to clarify and "sum-up" the relationship between these two overlapping yet distinct figures: The Goat-Spirit or God/Son of Light, who is most specifically and rightly called "Master," and the Stag-God, the White King, or The Hunter.

Throughout my writings, I use the emblem of the goat to "mark" the mercurial Master, and the stag to "mark" the titanic, chthonic and saturnian God of nature. Understanding the relationship between these two is all-important.

Vindonus and Janicot

In some countries, the chthonic Witch God was called the Wild Hunter; in others, the Black Woodsman. He is Scratch, Master Skrat, Old Hobb, Iu-Hu or Hou; and Janicot; He was and is the Two-headed and Crooked-Horned One; He dwells in perpetuity as the Grand Master of the Witches who hold communion with him and with the Old Powers in the secret places of the night-veiled world.

In the Basque countries the God of Witches was called by the name "Basaiaun" or "Basa-Jaun," this meaning "Lord of the Woods," but

Basajaun was also the Azaelian spirit who taught man agriculture and forging- not the same as the dark Saturnian Lord Janicot. Other names have been mentioned to me, wihch seem to be construed or created from the Basque language, including "Akeraiaun" or "Akhera-Jaun," meaning "Goat Lord," and "Beliaun," "Beliajaun" or "Bel-Jaun," meaning the "Black Lord." Any Azaelian hypostasis will be aligned with the symbol and presence of the goat.

"Janicot," according to some, could have meant "Lord who is called" or "Lord God" (Jaun + Cot or "God"). Janicot, when taken as a purely Basque name, is translated as "Blessed" in one old witch chant. Some say that "Janicot" stems from Dianus or Janus, the Latin two-headed God of the oak tree. His name in this case would derive from "Ianua," meaning "Door." This points to the fact that He is the door God, the God of the hidden portals into the netherworld, and the "portal" or gate between one time and the next, of the old year and the new, and of course the threshold between, which is the hidden "third" condition, the transcendent.

This role as great forest or oak-father and God of doorways between this world and the next reveals Janicot's oneness with the figure of Vindonus, which I have already discussed in detail.

As I have mentioned before, a God with two heads, looking into the seen and into the unseen, or into life and death, always implies a "third" invisible head- an invisible "center," a mystical "between-ness" or threshold-reality. This reality transcends the duality of old and new, left or right, inside or out, this world or other, and is symbolized by the Lord of mantic Mystery-Illumination that emerges from the primary fatherly reality of wholeness- this is the goatish Dionysian son of the Great two-faced Oak-Father. The father opens the door for the coming of his son, the shining and mercurial teacher of craft and artifice to mankind, and bestower of illumination and the Mysteries by which humans are saved through realization of the Divine.

In Janicot we see perhaps a more "senior" figure to the goatish lord, a primary spiritual reality that emanates the active transcendental reality represented by the Goat-Master- in Janicot-Vindonus, we can see a darker chthonic and Saturnian reflex of the "Great God" (and Janicot or Janus was associated with the Voor or the Fore-Void, the great Chaos of the Beginning, also called "Misrule," again playing up his Saturnian connections), whereas the Goat Lord, the true "Master" and "Witchfather," was a solar, mercurial, logos-like or "active" manifestation, but still possessed of many dark, chthonic qualities.

It is discerning to realize that the Goat-Angel or the Goat-Master was such a symbol of illumination, the true Witch teacher and Witchfather, while still bearing all the "chthonic" hallmarks and essential nature of His origin- the Goat is often associated with darkness, materiality, carnality, and winter, among other things. This is another hint to the paradoxical nature of the hidden truths encapsulated by these figures; the Goat is the illumination within matter, the Fire in the Land, which is simultaneously free and pure and immortal, bestowed from perceptually "outside" the Land; though in reality, there is no separation- all is one and whole. The darkness in the light, the light in the darkness- these things show full integration and wholeness, defying the dualistic logic that truly limits the higher thinking of mankind.

It could help to use the "son" model- the Goat who is the son of the Oak; the dense overlap between father Gods and their logos-sons, such as God the Father and Jesus from Christianity, and Zeus and Dionysos, is well attested to. Zeus, in common with both his Semitic equivalent El and his son Dionysos, had oaks as sacred to him and wore bull's horns at times. This was the Janicot who bore light to the Witches of northern Spain and France between his horns- that light between the horns representing his logos, his tutelary spirit or son, the "He-Goat Above," whereas the father was the "Horned Beast Below," the Saturnian nature god. The light between the horns represents the fact that the father "bears" the son from within himself, and the son comes forth as the gift of the Great Father, the "transcendent mode" which the light symbolizes.

It is important to see the Grand Master of the Witches in terms of a Saturnian power, over-arching, integral to all of Nature, and darkly, strongly present in all of Nature, in the brooding and "white" omniscient sense, as well as manifest in the goatish and cunning Logos/Light-Bringer and tutelary Master, for these two ancient streams cannot be separated- they overlap in many places, and it can be hard to tell them apart. It may not be necessary to fight over-hard to separate them, for, like many Logos-sons of many Godly fathers, the son completely manifests the essence of the father; the two are as one in this manner.

Basajaun and the Goat-Master

The Golden-Horned Goat, sometimes the Black Goat, is the true Witchfather, and the being that I am usually referring to when I use the term "Master." As has been mentioned before, the Great Vindonus-Janicot is the wild God of nature, the Great White presence, the Lord of the portals between this world and the unseen, the King of the living and the dead, the virile life in nature as well as the ghostly King of the Underworld. This figure of Vindonus is the "strong God" of natural power and force, across the realms of nature, above and below- the Saturnian/Jupiterian "primary" godly power in and of nature. The Dark Stag or White Stag is the emblem of this Godly power.

The transcendent Godly power is the Puck, Buccos or the Master Pouck-the Goat-King. Unlike the dark and chthonic father, the Goat-King is associated with light and the golden spectrum of light and mineral, as well as fire and the stars and the sun. He is rightly called "Master" because He is the primordial teacher of mankind, the awakener to the divine imagination, the transmitter of the primordial fire of the Gods to infant humankind. The "Goat-God" or "Azael" fully embodies this spirit of transcendence and light.

He is the goatish son of the All-Father of nature, but also the Word of the father, who fully embodies the true will of the father in its transcendent activity of awakening and transmutation. As the "Word" of creation, it was the Lord of Light that shaped the worlds into the form they now have, and who sustains them. He is the Light that rose from the Mother-Father darkness of the beginning.

He is the "Lord" who, in his most mercurial roles (representing the spirit of all spirits), guides the released souls to the Underworld after death. As the light of life fades, the dead first see the secret light of the Master, before being led to the timeless white force of the Lord Below, the primal father and first ancestor, the Yama of the Vedas, the Bull-Horned or Stag-Antlered chthonic One as visualized by the Tibetan masters of death.

You will always know the Goat-Master and Lord of Light through his countless folkloric connections to blacksmithing, plowing (the two primary Azaelian "arts" taught to man by the Light-bringer), fires, and the icon of the goat.

Some witches called the Goat Lord Iu, Iasus, Iasu, or Iesu. His wife in Basque countries was Basa-Andre, the "Lady of the Wood" or "Wild Lady," or just Andred, the "Lady"- also called "Benzozia." Her association with forests makes her very much appear in the mold of the Witch-Goddess Diana-Holda or Herodias.

Interestingly enough, the very same relationship that exists between Vindonus and the Goat King exists between Old Fate or Dame Dark, who is the Great Sibylia or Kolyo, our hidden and dark queen of Elfhame- the Goddess whose womb was the source-Chaos of the beginning- and her bright "daughter," the Hyldor or Fire-Queen.

This "Fair" Queen of Elfland, the Hyldor Queen, was a later manifestation of Freya within the folkloric tradition; She was and is the "Feminine Logos" or "Word" of the ineffable, darksome Great Queen of all beginnings; just as the fire of life fades from the dead, they eventually move from the Rose Queen's Bower to the dark/clear void of the ultimate source, the Great White Queen's utter and final embrace as Dame Hel or the Hidden and Veiled Reality, naked of form and adornment.

The "fair queen" or Fire-Goddess was indeed the "Witch Queen," the Goddess of the Witches, as She completely manifests the power of her dark and ineffable Mother, acting as a total mediatrix of that power, in much the same way the masculine word completely manifests and mediates the power of his great father. In much the same manner that the two masculine figures overlap to the point of seeming oneness in places, the same can be said for the dark and bright queens.

All of these powers were worshipped on the "Field of the Goat" or the "Meadow of the Goat"- which in the older language was called the "Akelarre." Of course, it is the opinion of many of those faithful to the Goat-Lord that the true "Field of the Goat" is not a field of earth, but a field of mystically inspired and timeless awareness in which the Old Powers are met and interacted with on an inner level.

An old witch chant to summon the Old One goes:

Har har hou hou!
Eman hetan! Eman hetan!
Har har hou hou!
Janicot! Janicot! Janicot! Janicot!
Har har hou hou!
Yona Gorril, Yona Gorril,
Akhera Goiti, Akhera Beiti.
It is said to mean:

Worm worm hou hou!
Look old! Look old!
Worm worm hou hou!
Blessed! Blessed! Blessed! Blessed!
Lord the Red, Lord the Red,
The Goat in the heights, the Goat below.
The Goat has come.

Notice the association of "worms" with Hou or Hu- "worm" here could also refer to serpents or snakes- all deeply chthonic creatures, and creatures that were associated (like the Bull) with both the chthonic Zeus and his son Dionysos. The song begins by invoking the Lord Hou-Janicot, and ends calling upon the Goat, not unlike Christians invoking God the Father and his Son, who, incidentally, are thought to be "one," the son being a perfect manifestation of the father, the manifestor and mediator to humans and all creation of a greater, more mysterious power. The Goat and the Goat Master is to the Witch what the Christ is to a Christian.

Names and Correspondences

As said before, overlaps between this great source-spirit and His active Logos or manifestation are many, and yet, they are distinct figures. You will notice that some correspondences are held in common:

Vindonus-Janicot is represented by the stag, the white stag or deer, serpents, horses, owls, bulls, hounds, wolves, ravens, and the plant badges of oak, thorn, hazel, and ash. The darker half of the year tended to fall in the "otherworldly" spectrum and was aligned to His great power.

The Goat-Master is represented by the goat, serpents, bulls, ravens (usually ravens with white feathers among the black) and the plant badges of rowan, birch, oak, and holly. The brighter half of the year fell under alignment to His nature as Lightbringer and teacher of the Mysteries of realization.

In the course of my researches, when I have found and used names and titles for these beings, always attempting to discern between the two, the following lists have formed:

VINDONUS-JANICOT: Wild Hunter, Black Woodsman, Old Hobb (the Dark Master can be called Old Hobb in his role as Lord of the Underworld or Hell and king of the dead, although "Hob" is also a nickname for Puck/ Robin Goodfellow, a hypostasis of the Goatish master, and it applies to Him as well), Hu, Hou, Janicot, Arrdhu, Vindonus, Vindos, Vitiris, Gwynn, Arawn, Conal Cernac, Sator, Hob th-rus (Bear in mind again that Hob th-rus can refer to the Goatish master as well.), the Horned One (but the Goatish master can also be called Horned One), the White King, the Great White One, Great Father, Old One (also a title for the Goat king), and Hellekin. Northern heathens can see both Frey and the chthonic aspect of Woden here.

GOATISH LORD: Master, Goat-footed, Goat-eyed, Lord of Light/ Lucifer, Azael, Old One, Ancient Wise One, Firebringer, Witchfather, Goat-buck, Puck, Robin Goodfellow, Robin Artisson, Pouck, Master Puck, Master Pouck, Old Hobb, Hobgoblin, Hob th-rus (for some, Hob th-rus refers to the Old Saturnian King, because "th-rus comes from "thurs" meaning "giant"- however, "Hob, son of th-rus" could be implied as well, making this a name for the Goat-King, and even if it were not implied, the Lord of Light is no less ancient or titanic in His power than the Saturnian being that acts as the primary foundation of His own activity), Sweet Puck, Buccos, Apollo/Apollon, Andras, Lord of the World, the Word, Logos, Teacher, Landwarder (also a name for Vindonus), Reverser (also a name for Vindonus), and Consecrator. The power of Woden as world-shaper and spirit-bestower applies here.

Apollo Vindonus

The inscription from Britain that I discussed earlier yielded the name "APOLLO VINDONUS." I wish to make a note here to avoid any confusion, for the figure of Apollo seems to fit into both the molds of the Stag-Lord and the Goatish Lord, or appears to be simultaneously the chthonic God as well as the God of transcendental light.

We have the great Apollo, Lord of Light, a teacher of occult mysteries, the great "Nourisher of the Kouros," or the youth-figure that represents the realized initiate in Greek Mysteries; Apollo seems to fulfill very well the roles associated with the Master of Light, the bright son or "Logos" of Vindonus. Mythology tells us that Apollo was the son of Zeus, and of course, Zeus represents the great primary "father" power of all the realms of Nature- Zeus was far from only a sky or weather God- his serpentine chthonic hypostasis was universal in the ancient Greek world. The "Great Father" is what is broadly represented by Zeus; and Apollo, in this model, easily represents the messenger or Word of Light that springs forth from Him, to enlighten all.

If you look at the short lists I've made above of correspondences, you will see that Apollo is named as a hypostasis of the Goatish Lord or Lord of Light, the Master; however, the three primary animals associated totemically with Apollo appear in the list for Vindonus- serpents, hounds or wolves, and ravens. Of course, ravens and serpents appear on the Goatish Lord's list as well, and this only serves to illustrate what I am writing here, and what I mention before and later- that the Father and Son are, in mythical and ritual manifestation, almost impossible to separate.

Apollo is the Lord of Light, of occult art and initiation, but He is also the bearer of His father's immense power; He is a perfect mediator of the great dark, deep power of the father-force of nature. Understanding these distinctions is important, so that we can invoke or approach precisely who we need, when we need.

The Light Between the Horns

When the Basque Witches circled around Janicot, they saw the great dark man with spreading horns- and a light between His horns. The dark man is the Saturnian father; the light He bears is the presence of His Word, His son, His gift, His promise, and His fulfillment. In the light that Witches took from His horns came the bright spirit of the Goatish King, the Christos of the Craft, who represents His father's spirit in manifestation and activity. The Dark Father reigns over the dead, and His hunt erupts into the dark fields of the world on the winter-cycles, but He remains an enigma, strangely aloof and dwelling in unimaginable contemplations in the great undivided consciousness of Misrule, only peaking out from the summer foliage as the impetuous and virile spirit of masculine life in nature, the quickened serpent in the Land, ancient and white.

But His son manifests in the very imagination and spirit of all, for His son is the Spirit of the World. The golden and refulgent Goat-Kid cannot be separated from his father, just as light cannot be separated from the flame that throws it, and yet, light is not the same as the flame that creates it. In the Mysteries of the Goat, we pass into a more subtle and transcendental experience of the Great Power that witches and pagans experienced and called by many names. The Stag-Father and the Goat-Master are not the same, and yet, they cannot be separated. When dealing with them on a spiritual level, however, it is important to understand the distinctions- from the Great White and brooding presence deep in all of manifest nature (Vindonus), to the mysterious, luminous, mercurial, and "clear-light" spirit that has such a secret relationship to your own consciousness (the Buccos), one may rise from the other, but they are distinct.

From one, the expectation of the other arises; "now I know that from darkness, comes light" (Nunc Scio Tenebris Lux). But most mysteriously and paradoxically, the great body of Nature was shaped by the Goatish master of light- can the son pre-exist the father? In the timelessness of the great Voor or the Fore-time, there is no "before" or "after." This is the final and greatest lesson of the Spirit of the Goat-King; the Spirit in us is timeless, and "origin stories" and even "mythologies," do not ultimately reflect linear realities. Mythologies take on a new aspect in the light of this perpetual mystery.

Witchmother: The Dark Matriarch of the Craft

The Matriarch, the first of all spirits or beings from craft mythology, is beyond a doubt the most mysterious, powerful, and central to any true "inner" mythology or Wisdom-acquisition. Here we begin to speak of the Queen of Hell or Queen of Elfhame herself.

This is the great feminine spirit of nature, the dark, divine soul within and beyond the body of Nature, within and beyond all worlds.

She is known and experienced by traditional Pagans who merge with the most Saturnian and Tellurian currents as the **Pale Woman lying below the Land**, the **Queen of Faery, Elphame, Queen Hel, the Three Fates, or Old Fate**. The great **Hyldor, Ellorn, or Ellhorn**, was Her own feminine "Logos" or creative spirit made manifest, but She and Her "daughter" were the two faces of a singular mystery- the all-encompassing Great Queen of the Land, of what was seen and unseen. She could appear in triple form, as the Matres, or as the singular Modron, and in Her chthonic role as both life source and initiatrix, She was called in some places the "Harsh Sinister One," **Ondred** or **Andred**, and the Hollan Queen or Hollantide Queen.

Her great being is the dark hollow of the interior places of the Earth, the abyss of the Underworld, the same "timeless dimension" or infinite womb which contains, conceals and sends forth all potentials. This timeless dimension, the Mystery of Her being, dwells at the heart of all things, places and beings. She holds the spindle of Fate, because all things that emerge into manifestation come from this dark Mystery.

Even the Earth itself can be said to be her "gown;" meaning, poetically, that the outward manifestations of Nature's power- the trees, the ground, the waters, and the like- are Her garments. In that capacity, She can be called an "Earth Mother," for as Nature is the cloak of the dark Mystery beyond, the physical Earth or Nature itself is seen as a fertile "manifesting" force, which, when joined with the dark Mystery of origins, becomes the ultimate source of all things, such as animal life and humans, and, on other levels, even spirits, Gods and all beings.

The Queen of Elfhame fulfills the role of the wise darkness, the darkness of Old Night (Dame Dark or Night were are also names for Her.), and in this capacity, She is the figure of Old Fate, the ultimate, supreme, and first being, from whom all things come. She was an Underworld Goddess, the dark and first Queen of the Underworld, because the darkness of the Underworld, which is also the darkness of Fate's womb (and the darkness of Her very being), is the same primal darkness that existed at the "beginning," and from which the divine fire and light, the seed of shaping, flowed. As the darkness within all, the dark of the Underworld, She is the Queen of the Dead, surrounded by the Pale People or the Sidh-folk, called by some the Faeries, the dead who return to the ultimate dark Mystery from which we all come- Elfhame or the unseen. In this manner, she is not just the Queen of the Otherworld, but the Otherworld embodied.

But as She is the origin and source of all, She is the end of all, that to which all returns, before regeneration. The nine worlds of Indo-European mythology were all born from Her womb, and at the world-doom, they were withdrawn back into Her darkness, to await regeneration, and only She remained, as She was in the beginning. She was the spinning Goddess, who spun the threads of Fate, and the stars and moon floated in the darkness of Her immense being, as parts of the weaving.

As the source of life and the place of death, She was depicted as half-fair and half-dark and decaying; the outward life of the Earth can also be seen as Her fair face and the darkness below as Her dark face. In the original darkness that She embodies, which is the darkness of the Mystery of Fate, Her presence acts as a kind of "final and necessary factor" in the regeneration and realization of the cunning witch.

She is of a power and a time older than Gods. She is the First and Timeless being. She is the mirror in which all things are seen; She is the pit of the Underworld in which the living die and the dead live. She is the true source of the craft. She is the true queen of life and of the Land. And the full revelation of Her is secret. But the world remembers Her in the deepest places. She still holds court and greets those who have the desire and the cunning to seek Her by going below and within.

Her living essence also animates the furious activity of life, and in the heat of living beings, in the fecundity of spring and the dangerous, seductive, burning fire of the inspired witch, She appears in the heart of fire, and in the summer-mad fields and forests as a Maid, described by some as a "daughter"- though daughter and mother seem to be two faces of each other- this "daughter" being the beautiful Rose Queen or Dame Venus, the Hyldor Queen of whom we shall speak soon.

The Origins of the Old Veiled Witch Queen, Great Kolyo, or "Old Fate"

While I am a true polytheist, that is, a person who does not believe that all the Gods and Goddesses of ancient times were "aspects" of a greater divine force or God, I must admit, after researching the origins, linguistics, and mythological intricacies of this Goddess, I have become convinced that there is a lot of substance to the theories of the "Great Goddess" that are treasured by so many modern scholars. While I reject the pop-culture, politically slanted feminist interpretations of this concept of the "Great Goddess," I still have no choice but to admit, and to declare my belief, based on what I have seen and experienced, that there was and is a great primordial feminine divine power that stands behind many different European cultural Goddesses. Her original name was KOLYO.

I do not say that KOLYO stands behind all Goddesses- for in my view, the local Land powers, the spiritual double or "Fetch Brides" of living human beings and other living creatures, ancestral clan-spirits that appear in mythology as mothers, and other spirits can be counted as "Goddesses." But I do profess a belief in a supreme being that is female, and who appears in all mythologies, as far back as we can see. She is the power that is "Fate" and "Necessity," and She is also the Queen of the Dead and the Underworld, as well as the Earth Goddess Herself.

This great and trans-functional Goddess, the Great Grandmother of the world-ruling male deities, and all forms of life, the Goddess-source of life and death, the concealed or "covered" one (called the Old Veiled One), the womb-Goddess that birthed all worlds or realms of existence, is called by scholars by the reconstructed name KOLYO.

The three main functions given to Her are the powers of Fate, the produce and life of the Earth, and the Mysteries of the occult, the dead, and the Underworld. To Her is also passed the power of regeneration.
The three functions of Fate, Earth, and Underworld almost always

Hul'da Quene Elphen

overlap in Pagan Europe. Where the more highly developed pantheons had "the Fates" or the Fate Trinity-Goddesses being one thing, the Earth Goddess being one thing, and the God/Goddess of the Underworld being something else, originally, the Goddess of the Earth was also the Goddess of the Dead and the Underworld as well as the weaver of Fate.

Carl Kerenyi, in his work "Eleusis," has shown how Demeter and Kore were not ultimately separate Goddesses. They represented a pair- even called "the Two Goddesses," that were paradoxically seen as two faces of the same Goddess- Demeter being the outward face and Kore the inner, just as the Underworld is the inner dimension of the Earth, and the source of the life that rises up to the surface of the Earth, and becomes embodied in harvests, animals, plants, and humans. Earth and Underworld, body and spirit, the manifest function and the transcendent function, cannot be separated.

Kore or Persephone was seen herself as a Goddess of Fate- judge of the dead, attended in the Underworld by Justice and the Eumenides. The triple Hecate's overlap with the power of the Fates, as well as Kore's mythological overlap with Hecate are also well known, and a good description of this is found in the PGM (Greek Magical Papyri). Demeter Herself (Her name meaning Da-Meter, or "earth mother" or "barley mother") had functions that overlapped with Fate- that of law-giving.

The Underworld, as I said, was thought by Pagans to be the source of all; all animals, humans, plants, all life. As the interior Mystery of the Earth, it was the womb of the Earth, and insofar as the Earth was seen as the "Magna Mater" (Great Mother) and the "Mother of Gods and Men," the Underworld was the source of the Gods as well as their enemies, the Titans or Giants and other threatening monsters that forever struggled against the world order.

Being the source of all, and the place to which the dead return, the Underworld (and its presiding Gods and Goddesses) was also the mysterious territory of Fate, of Necessity, and the deepest Mysteries.

We are dealing with an "older" kind of Paganism when you deal with the chthonic divinities- one that was old before the sky Gods and thunder

Gods took such power in the later centuries. But these two strands of Paganism got mixed together, as native and Indo-European cultures came together, thus forming the pantheons and mythologies that we are all familiar with.

The Germanic Goddess Holda's name is derived from the PIE name KOLYO. The root of that name, the Proto-Indo-European word KOL, is where we get the words, HILL, HALL, HOLE, HOLLOW, HELL, and the name HEL. The Goddess Hel Herself is a later incarnation of Holda, and captured in late mythology as a Goddess of the Dead and the Underworld, and as Dame Hell, the Queen of Elfhame and the Queen of many a coven of Witches.

In modern Germanic folklore, Holda, too, is a Goddess who is found in an underground world by girls who travel down wells, and who is responsible for sending snow and weather up into the world from her home below.

The name KOLYO is from the Proto-Indo-European root word KOL, meaning "covered" and YO, an ending added which means "to gather" or "the thing(s) gathered."

KOLYO is the death/funereal Goddess; "the thing gathered to cover" refers to the grave mound, but also to the earth piled on top of the dead. As we have seen, KOL is where we get the word HEL, which is the name of the Goddess of the dead, as well as the name applied to Her realm- Hell, the Underworld. The name implies that to be in Hell (or with Hel), you were "covered," or buried. It is easy to understand how "hall" and "hill" come from the same root- halls are covered things, and hills cover things, especially grave hills.

The old name for the Elder tree, Hyldor, possibly derives from the same root- KOL or HOL, HUL, and HYL. The Goddess Holda had the Elder tree as sacred to Her, and her hidden people- the dead in the Underworld- were called the "Huldafolk," the Hidden People. However, the name of the Elder tree is said by most to come from Ael, meaning "fire"- and in light of the overlap between the Dark Queen and Her daughter, the spirit of the fire, this is a fine connection.

The name KOLYO, and all its derivatives, implies something that is "concealed," or "masked"- the concealed Goddess, the hider, the veiled one, the concealer, the masker. Not only did She (and the earth) conceal the dead from the living by hiding their bodies under earth, and taking them into the Underworld, but Fate itself, the whole process of universal causality, was a very unknowable, hidden process, seemingly mysterious to humans who had no way of predicting its myriad outcomes, whether they would finally be fortunate or unfortunate ends.

From this ancient word KOL and name KOLYO, we get the names of the Goddesses KALI, KLOTHO, LEDA, LETO, KALYPSO, CAILLEACH, HOLDA/HULDA/HOLLE, and HEL/HELA.

Kalypso means "hider" or "concealer." Cailleach means "old woman," and She was called "the Old Veiled One"- the root of Cailleach, KOLYO, also the origin of KLOTHO the spinning Fate (as we will see below), is truly the name for the "Old Fate" of the Witch-cult. "She is "the coverer;" Kolyo, Kali, Kalypso — as in eclipse and apocalypse. She is "the face covered," "the veiled one," the sun eclipsed by the moon, the sun at once in mourning for, and hidden behind, the ever dying and rejuvenating, ever falling and ever rising.

We should now further discuss the Goddess HEL or HELA and the Goddess HOLDA, whose names are from the same root and are clearly the same Goddess. My point for presenting the information that follows is to prove my contention that the Goddesses or powers of Fate, the Earth Goddess, and the Underworld Goddess, are all faces of the same power, and that cultural manifestations of the Goddess of the Underworld, and Earth, and Fate, are the same being, with a focus on Kore/Persephone of the Greeks and Queen Hel of the Teutons.

The work by the excellent scholar and writer Alby Stone, entitled "The Knots of Death" states:

"(The dead) resided with the dread Goddess Hel in the underground realm variously known as Niflhel, Niflheim or simply as Hel located in the far north. This Goddess of the dead was said to be Loki's offspring, conceived and born while he was in the form of a mare following a dangerously mischievous escapade.

Actually she can be traced back to Proto-Indo-European times and her original name has been reconstructed as Kolyo, "the coverer." As Bruce Lincoln puts it in his book, "Death, War and Sacrifice" (1991), 'Her domain is underground and she physically conveys her victims thence by fixing a snare or noose on their bodies and dragging them down. Her bonds regularly fall upon the foot or neck of the victim, the same places where domestic animals are fettered. The deceased are thus led away like animals by Death, in whose bonds they may struggle, but which they cannot escape, caught in her snares and dragged under.'

Lincoln presents an impressive body of evidence to support this summary, from Ancient Greece, Rome, Scandinavia, India and Iran. The theme has altered from place to place and from one age to another but the essence has remained. He also notes that the Middle High German term for a noose was "helsing," which he translates as "Hel's Sling." He argues that German sacrifice by hanging, generally related to Odin or Woden, was actually a ritual enactment of the seizing of the victim by the Goddess of death. Given the mutual concerns of Odin, Hel and the Nornir, it seems to make little difference either way.

In Old English texts the term "Wyrd" is, despite its other connotations, frequently used to denote death rather than a structured and unfolding future that is suggested by the functions of the Nornir and their Greek and Roman counterparts. There is of course an intimate relationship between the two concepts and death is after all the Fate of every being. Scandinavian myth makes it clear that there are only two things which the Gods cannot avert; Fate and death. In Norse myth the name of the senior Norn is Urdr, a word in Old IceLandic that can also denote a burial mound or cairn. "Beowulf" and other texts characterise Wyrd as a weaving of webs but the word usually means nothing less than the moment of death, or at least the events leading up to death.

The "Beowulf" motif is revealing, however; it has already been noted that the Fates tend to be spinners or weavers and in this instance there is also the idea of a snare, which can refer back to the Indo-European Goddess of death as described by Lincoln. Like Hel, the Nornir reside in the far north, at or near the celestial axis and like her they reside "below ground," where the World Tree has its roots. The Nornir determine life, span and the time of death, while Hel takes the dead to her cold bosom. All these characteristics are shared to some extent with Odin, as is their femininity, apparently adopted by Odin in order to engage in seidr - the natural magic of womankind.

At the very least, Hel and the Nornir are closely related, perhaps even deriving from the same Proto Indo-European Goddess..."

The Fates of Greece and the Wyrds/Norns of Northern Europe have a great overlap to Earth and the Great Earth/Nature Goddess figure- the Norns are Urd, Verthandi, and Skuld- and the name of the first Norn, Urd, means "Earth."

The names of the Fates are "Klotho, Lachesis, and Atropos"- and Klotho is the Fate that spins the thread- and Her name comes from KOLYO, the same place as Holda's name, Hel's name, the Celtic Great Mother "Cailleach," and the Greek Calypso.

Though the Fates are often pictured as three sisters, it is thought that originally they were pictured as one being, "Old Fate" Herself, before evolving into three "sisters." In the North, that would have been Urd, or Earth, or Kolto/Kolyo/Holda- the earth/funeral Goddess of the burial mound that covered the dead. Again, overlaps all around with Fate and Earth.

In some southern regions, I am convinced it would have been Klotho, the spinning Goddess who appears in so many mythologies from southern and eastern Europe, just as a spinning or spindle/distaff Goddess or Faery Lady appears in so many northern folktales.
Alby Stone writes:

"While the Nornir each have individual names in England, they go by the name allocated to the eldest in Norse Tradition. The eldest of the three is called Urdr by the Norse, which is cognate with the Old English 'Wyrd,' hence the three 'weird sisters' of Shakespeare. Thus they are a three-in-one being in the same way as the Irish war Goddesses known as the Morrigu. Like the other, inevitably triadic, Indo-European Fates, the Nornir spin and weave destinies. One of them is also named as a valkyrie."

Kolyo is of course connected with the bonfire, just as a connection has been made with Her name and coal, and burning embers below. Her connection to fire and thus fire Goddesses (Hestia was regarded as a "Great Mother" type Goddess, source of life to all the Gods, and now this is easy to see why) is important- but in fire, we find Kolyo's connection to Venus. Freya, the fire Goddess of the North, has always been seen as the northern equivalent to Venus/Aphrodite, and this is not by accident. Kerenyi has shown how Persephone was a fire Goddess, also.

The love that brings to life, and the life that leads to death, are two sides of the same coin. Freya was also a Goddess who collected dead to Herself and had an Underworldly realm for the dead- Folkvang. Dr. Peter Kingsley has mentioned the connection between Aphrodite and Persephone, life and death, in his own works. Brigid, another "triple" or Great Mother Goddess, who as we will see was called "Great Queen," is similarly a fire Goddess, a Goddess of the dead, a Goddess of cows- the cow being the mother animal whose milk sustained the cosmos in northern myth- and a manifestation of Kolyo.

By the way, the word bonfire means "bone fire." The Welsh word for the same is "coelcerth," a cognate to Kolyo. The Kol- prefix is root to the English "coal," from the Old Norse "kol," which means "burning ember."

Hel and Persephone are the same Goddess. This is without a doubt; both are queens of the Underworld, and queens over the dead in the Underworld. Persephone's name consists of the parts "phero" and "phonos," with the meaning "she who brings destruction." The Romans called Her Proserpina, which is said to mean "fearful one," but that name seems to be related to the Etruscan "phersu" and to the Greek "prosopon," both meaning "mask." She is the great Kolyo. The people of Athens also gave to Persephone the title Persephatta, which our Greek teachers tell us comes from "ptersis" and "ephapto," with the meaning "she who mends destruction."

Persephone is the Goddess to whom the Greek Iatromantis-mystic Parmenides journeyed, to learn the secrets of Reality itself- interestingly, when he visited Her, She performed a rite in which She "destroyed death"- literally caused death to cease to be. As the supreme being, and Goddess of Fate and life and death, She could do this, and it is more interesting that Her title Persphatta should mean "She who mends destruction"- She is not only the Goddess of death, but life and regeneration. Parmenides' schema of the universe has this "Goddess," the Queen of the Underworld, at the center; She sends forth life and receives at death; She occupies the central place of power. It is easy to see why, in light of what we have been discussing.

Brigid was worshipped as Brigantia by the British Celts, and the name Brigantia is the same as "Rigantona"- B(rigantia). It means "Great Queen"- which is also what Morrigan means: Mor-Riga "Great Queen" or "Great Chieftainess."

The Welsh form of Rigantona is Rhiannon- and here is where we can connect the figure of the "Great Queen" to the Queen of the Underworld; Rhiannon was the ghostly bride from the Underworld- from the world of Annwn, who married Pwyll PenAnnwn, Pwyll the Chieftain of the Underworld. Pwyll and Rhiannon are themselves dim memories from Welsh mythology of the primal king and queen of the Underworld, Kolyo and her husband/consort. Rhiannon was a horse-Goddess, just as Morrigan was. She was first seen near a burial mound, riding on a mare.

The Goddess Hel had been reduced to only the Queen of the Dead, in late Norse mythology, due to the great distance between the primal beginnings of the Indo-European mythology, and the patriarchal nature of the later Norse Paganism, which is what most modern Asatruar and Germanic reconstructionists base their religious beliefs on. Originally, Hel/Kolyo was the Great One, the true All-Mother.

Holda's appearance in Germanic myths show the same pattern- Holda was Herself a "Great Mother" that preceeded the Gods of Asgard, and whose many powers and magical items were passed on to later Goddesses. The path of the Milky Way was associated with her as a road that souls walked after death, only to be given over to Woden/Odin. Freya's necklace, which represented the cycle of the seasons and natural power, was derived from Holda, as well as the spindle that spun Fate, given to Frigga. Holda's (mostly female) followers are always pictures as witches and as members of a previous, probably native European order, hostile to Asgard, in which we can see conflict between Old Europe and incoming Indo-European invaders.

Of course, the names Cailleach, Holda, Hulda, and what have you, are of Indo-European origin, but they were used by the invaders to refer to the cults of equivalent Goddesses that they found in Old Europe. Cailleach, particularly, has always been thought to be the native Goddess of Britain and Ireland, a true native titan and Earth/Underworld Goddess. What her native, non-Indo-European name(s) were, we cannot really know, but the being is the same being.

In KOLYO, we have the great All-Mother who stands behind the drama of the Gods themselves, as their mother and consort. The "White Goddess," the "White Lady" who appears inside and from within the Land, has a secret and all-encompassing identity, here revealed. She is the Mystery of Indo-European Paganism, the omnipresent and ubiquitous. She is the immortal and eternal that gives rise to all, and regenerates all, the true supreme being of the Pagans. Her Mystery is such, though, that She is subtle and hard to grasp without the "children" and realities that she births and upholds- the focus has always been outwardly on supreme male beings, but the Mother-Source of even the greatest of Indo-European Gods, DEIWAS, from whom we get Zeus/Jupiter and many other great sky fathers (but who is also a more abstract and transcendent "masculine ordering principle") was Kolyo- She was the power behind them, from which they arose, the Old Night that even Zeus gave fearful respect and worship to.

She appeared to every living being as the Queen of the Underworld, to whom all had to go at death, so while KOLYO was the most distant and over-arching of all cosmic powers and Mysteries, She was at once also the most personal and, while fearsome, was pictured as compassionate and friendly by turns- this fitting into her light and dark natures, Her face half horrible and half beautiful. She embodied the totality. It was to Her that all human beings and all mystics and poets had to go for the inspiration and guidance needed to achieve Wisdom and art.

She alone is Truth and the guide to Truth- Truth is hidden, concealed, hard to see, and to find Truth is to find Her- the Greek word for Truth, "Aleithea," means "to uncover, to reveal." "Aleithea" was also a name for Nature, as a Goddess.

She was the establisher of the great Mysteries, and the Otherworldy woman/lover that brought about the internal great marriage that led to the union of soul and spirit, the destruction of ego, and immortality- or perhaps madness and death. Her will was final, and Her appetites and Mysteries implacable. She alone survived the world-destruction, and gathered all back into Her womb, and regenerated the cosmos at the end, for the beginning of a new era or aeon. As Kingsley pointed out in his work "Reality," anything you do will be for nothing, unless it leads you to the Goddess of the Underworld- for in Her, we find the Mystery of the timeless and everlasting.

The Daughter of the Great Queen, the Feminine Spirit of the Fire

Kolyo, Old Dame Fate, or the Mother, has a daughter. Of course, when we speak of Her "daughter," we are talking about a particular manifestation of this supreme source and being- we are talking about the fire. The flame, the fire, the Goddess or feminine spirit of the fire- this is the "Fair Queen of Elfland," in contradistinction to the darker face of the Funeral Queen- this is Dame Venus, the "Secret Presence." This is the Rose Queen, the Maiden, the feminine spirit of life.

The Elder tree, sacred to the dark Queen of the Underworld, is said by some to gain its name from "Ael," meaning fire- because the pithy center of elder twigs can be removed, and used as a blowing tube for fire. This is an interesting connection between chthonic mother of dark and death and bright or heat-filled daughter of life. The "daughter," who is associated with both fire and cats, is the **Dame Hyldor, or Aelda**- the Fire Mother, but also the Mother deep below, among the dead and near the wooden cat in the tree amid the Elder Grove. As an initiatrix, She can be very terrible.

Even though her "Mother" Hulda or Hel/Kolyo, the Old Fate and Veiled One has the Elder or Hyldor tree sacred to Her, the name "Hyldor," or fire, refers to the manifestation of this great dark Mother in the form of this daughter-being. In this way, the name "Hyldor Queen" can refer to both, but in the knowledge of the fire-hollow, it usually refers to the daughter. Both are hypostasis of the same being-reality.

This feminine spirit of the living fire is the manifestation of all the Mothers. Her secret name was the secret name of Fate, the "name" of the unfolding of Fate, of manifestation, of the secret nature of things.

Istara Hyldor

This is because the feminine spirit of the fire rises up from darkness and from the earth, the "active" mother, the maiden of fiery life and lust, the soul of the earth and nature, burning and living within all natural forms.

The Name of Fate cannot be said, because it is not possible to name such a force, the force of All, within all, and beyond all. Besides, an old story tells us of a man who knew the secret name of God- a highly secret name, which to his culture would be the Pagan equivalent of the Name of Fate- and he was killed because he refused to tell it.

Friends of his had him exhumed, and magically revived him, just so they could get this powerful and needful name from him- for without it, they couldn't bless their sacraments and temples. But the revived dead man didn't give them the name- he gave them a "substitute" name instead.

Many have wondered why, but the answer's simple. Because when you are speaking of such names, such concepts, it is not the "name" that is important- it's the ongoing search for understanding the power or concept that the "name" refers to that is important. Wisdom is not a destination, not a name- it is a road, a search, a way of engaging life.

To give someone the name of the "supreme being" would be not only impossible (our minds simply couldn't contain it), but foolish. It would do something to the "supreme being" that cannot and should not be done- lock it down to a simple word, leaving the person who "knows" the word to think that their search is over. But coming to know the Name of Fate is a process, the process of existing, of becoming truly human. Her name is everything that you have ever experienced, and will ever experience, plus many, many things beyond which you can imagine.

This feminine spirit of fire was called Frea or Freyja by the Norse and Germanics; Brigid/Brigantia by the Celts and Britons. She is the **Dame Venus**, the **Rose Queen**, the Kore or the **Maiden**, the Young and Fair Queen of the Craft, who is the Witch-initiatrix.

She is the "bright" face of the pair Brigid/Cailleach, the young daughter and dark, cronish or harsh mother- Fate's daughter and Old Fate herself, representing summer and winter. They are the same, yet different.

The young one, the fire-spirit, Her name is very secret; as you well know by now, Frey and Freya were not names, but titles- meaning "Lord and Lady." It is believed that Frey's *actual* name was Ingvi- but no one ever knew what the secret name of Freya was. Those who did know, weren't talking.

To those of the Witch-cult, this spirit will reveal Her secret names when the person is ready.

The Pale People, the Good Folk, and the Master Men

"The Pale People" refers to the dead. These are the "Feeorin" of Lancashire, those who have died and merged with the Land, and entered into the Elfhame or Underworldly state, where they undergo a metamorphosis, becoming the Pale Folk- the Fae, the Sith or the Sidhe, or the Alfar- the Elves. By merging with the Land, they become almost indistinguishable from the powers of the Land itself. Indeed, there may be no difference between the two, as the rebirth-cycle of the dead can bring them into being as spirits attached to certain phenomenon of nature.

The condition of "being pale" or "mound dead" refers to the post-mortem state of existence of humans and beasts, although when used by myself or others, it almost always refers to the post-mortem human soul. Red is the sacred color of life, and the paleness of the dead refers not just to paleness of their corpses, but to the fact that they are cold- for the redness or fire of life and passion has left them. The whiteness also refers to the color of bone. The death-experience reduces the dead to "bone" on both inner and outer levels, for the flesh does decay off, and internally, the person is returned to the ancient and timeless white Mystery that underlies their mortal being.

To coat the bones of dead animals with red ochre or paint is an ancient method of sympathetically magically returning them to life- and the same process could be applied to the remains of human beings.

The Pale People dwell in Elfhame, and emerge at certain times of the year, in an event sometimes led by the Queen of Elfhame or the King of Elfhame, or by both of the great rulers below- this event is called by many folktales a "Faery Rade." They occur chiefly around the four hallows, or other powerful "red and black" nights of the year. They lead a mysterious and subtle existence in the meadows of Elfhame, and certain among them can be dangerous at times, for not all of the dead rest easily or lightly.

The only other time one of the Pale Company in the deep earth can emerge is when the rulers of the Underworld have given permission for them to do so, or when their Fate moves them onward to a new condition or home in the cycle of their destiny- and of course, those two conditions are not necessarily different things. Mortals who use necromantic workings to summon the dead would represent another point in the Fate of the dead, where that Fate connects with the mortal world through the mind and body of a living user of magic or necromancy.

The Land spirits proper, the spirits of trees, stones, and the rivers and the like, are themselves (as said before) sometimes indistinguishable from the spirits of the dead, for good reason- the dead are in a condition- the Elfhame state- that is literally and symbolically at the "heart" of all things.

The Underworld is not just under the ground; it is under/within the surface of every leaf, under the surface of every human thought, under the surface of every pool or water, and deep in the infinite heart of even a tiny pebble. Within each rock or river or leaf, the dead in Elfhame can be reached, but also the power and spirit of that natural phenomenon, who often appear as distinct entities apart from the host of the dead. Sometimes, as said, it is a spirit of the dead that takes "rebirth" as the spirit of a rock, or a river, or a place, usually for some special reason- something binds them to the place, or to the phenomenon. Either way, many Witches see the two types of spirits as distinct, and many others simply join them together in their understanding. The respect due to them both is the same.

Lewis Spence mentions, in his book "British Fairy Origins," that the "Bansidhe"- literally, the Ban-Sidhe, or the "Woman of the Hill" (referring to the burial mound) was not only an appearance of the ancestral power of a person's family- literally the appearance of an ancestress, or the collective totality of the family's spiritual force and root- but also of the Goddess of the Land herself, the Dark Mother, the "Fate" of the family. He writes:

"In Aberdeenshire, two hills were pointed out where wont to propitiate the Banshee with cakes of barley-meal, and if such an offering were neglected, death or misfortune was sure to ensue."

This connection of the Bansidhe with the "breasts" or the "two hills," shows a connection with the ancient earth and barley-mother cultus, of whom the "Woman of the Hill" is an appearance, and a further overlap of the "Woman of the Hill" with the ancestral female spirits of each family and a sacred locus that was a gateway to the Underworld. The great Veiled One, the Kolyo, was the "Bansidhe," but "Bansidhe" also referred to the ancestral mothers of each family line. Kolyo is the first ancestress of all lines, and thus the overlap is immense.

Sometimes, the inhabitants of the Innerworld or the Underworld are classed in two categories, dark and light- the dark represent the oldest ancestral spirits in the deepest parts of the earth, as well as the "common" Pale Folk, and the light ones, who are also called the Master Men, the Grand Array, the Holy Ones, or the Hidden Company, who represent the presence of fully realized and advanced beings who have undergone a mysterious metamorphosis into a state of "wholeness"- which is what the word "holy" refers to- and no longer return to earthly life compelled by hard and unconscious Fate. They have metamorphed into a fullness of "Faery Nature" as it is told.

These "whole" beings cannot be commanded or compelled by morals, and the best we can hope for is that they shall visit us, guide us, and teach us their Wisdom, that we can be like them one day. The "master" or "mistress" witch is indeed thought to be someone who has become whole in this life, before the shedding of the flesh, a "justified" person who is at once alive and in the Company of the Hidden, and who will fully join them in the unseen at death, and to what ends they will then journey or work, none but they can know. No doubt they return only to do their part in fulfilling Fate's great and unfathomable will, and to guide and test spiritual seekers who are close to the final wholeness.

The "Grey Women" were like a feminine equivalent to the Master Men, being women who, according to folklore, were given a "Faery Nature" through enchantments from the Otherworld.

Collectively, all of the inhabitants of the unseen world are ruled over by the Queen of Elfhame herself, who represents the force that is dominant in the Innerworld. Even though I have mentioned it above, I cannot stress enough that you must remember that the term "Hidden Folk" or "Pale People" can refer not just to the dead, but to the spirits of the Land itself, that is, the spirits of places, trees, forests, valleys, etc. The overlap between the human and animal dead who go into the spiritual dimension of the earth and the natural spirits of the earth is great. Oftentimes, the distinction is blurred. They may be one and the same power.

The Strangers

Land spirits, whether seen as spiritual powers in nature, inhabiting some specific place, or as the powers of the dead, emerging through the Land at that place, were always venerated in Pagan religions across the world- and for good reason. Aside from the sheer politeness and Wisdom of befriending and honoring the local powers in the Land, the Land-spirits had power over the harvest and over human well-being, insofar as humans depended on the Land.

The Dead or the Pale People are powers of the Underworld, and the Land spirits are powers of the various aspects of the Land in expression- but both come from the unseen reality at the heart of the Land- and that unseen world, or Underworld, has always been thought of as the source of wealth and fertility. Crops grew up from the depths of the Underworld, just as the under-earth contained mineral wealth. Thus, the veneration of the inner Land dwelling spirits of the dead and the veneration of the spirits of nature have a similar goal, beyond politeness- to secure food and plenty.

A powerful example of the survival of genuine Land-based Paganism into Christian times, complete with a veneration and propitiation of Land spirits, was recorded and retold by Katharine Briggs, in her essential book "The Encyclopedia of Fairies."

A woman named "Mrs. Balfour" collected a good deal of folklore from an area of Northern Lincolnshire, where the fens had been drained. This area was called "the cars," and she preserved the notes she took down as the stories were being told to her. Some people didn't believe her, on account of the macabre nature of what she found and published, but time has proven that she was correct- information found in other works on the folklore of the Fens has corroborated what she wrote.

The people in the Fens called the Land spirits "the Strangers," but also the "Greencoaties," the "Yarthkins" and the "Tiddy people," this final name being on account of their diminutive size. In many folklores around the world, the spirits of the dead are presented as being small- a reference to the "reduction" of the dead into the inner dimension of the world, the "going down" into the Underworld.

Her account contained actual folk rituals done with the ancient megalithic stones found around England, and so it interests all traditional Pagans of this tradition. Let me begin by quoting one of her contacts directly- a Fen-man who was recorded in the late 1800's, in a very dense local dialect; what you read here is my transliteration of what he said, but you can see the original on page 383 of "The Encyclopedia of Fairies":

Mrs. Balfour's contact told her:

"But about the Strangers…you know what they be- aye- you're gettin' ready with the word, but it's chancy to call them such! No, and if you'd seen them as much as I have, you'd twist your tongue into another shape, you would. Folk in these parts, they call them mostly the Strangers, or the tiddy people, or the Greencoaties from their green jackets; or maybe the Yarthkin, since they dwelled in the mools. But mostly the Strangers, as I said before, for strange they be- in looks and in ways…

On summer nights they danced in the moonshine on the great flat stones you see about, I don't know where they come from, but my grandmother said how her grandmother's grandmother told them that long ago the folk set fire on those stones and smeared them with blood and thought a deal more on them than the passion bodies at the church…

And on winter evenings the Strangers danced at nights on the fireplace when the folk went to bed; and the crickets played for them with right good will…

Folk thought the Strangers helped the corn to ripen, and all the green things to grow and that they painted the pretty colors on the flowers and the reds and browns on the fruit and the yallerin leaves. And that's how, if they were fratched (offended) things would dwindle and wither and the harvest would fail and the folk would go hungry. So, they did all they could think to please the tiddy people and keep friends with them. In the gardens, the first flowers, the first fruit, and the first cabbage or whatnot, they'd be taken to the nearest flat stone and laid there for the Strangers; in the fields, the first yearn of corn or the first potatoes were given to them and at home, before you began to eat your vittles, a bit of bread and drop of milk or beer, was spilled on the fireplace to keep the Greencoaties from hunger and thirst."

Katherine Briggs continues the story in her own words- words chilling and powerful:

"According to the Story, all went well with the people and the Land as long as they kept up these habits. But as time went on, the people became careless. No libations were poured out, the great flat stones were left empty, and even sometimes broken up and carried away. There was more church-going, and in time a generation sprang up that had almost forgotten about the Strangers. Only the wise women remembered.

At first nothing happened; the Strangers were reluctant to believe that their old worshippers had deserted them. At last they became angry, and struck. Harvest after harvest failed, there was no growth of corn or hay, the beasts sickened on the farms, the children pined away and there was no food to give them. Then the men spent the little they could get on drink, and the women on opium. They were bewildered, and could think of nothing to do; all except the wise women.

They got together and made a solemn ceremony of divination, with fire and blood (presumably on the stones) and when they learnt what was making the mischief, they went all among the people, and summoned them to gather at the cross-roads in the deep twilight, and there they told them the cause of the trouble, and explained the usages of the older people. And the women, remembering all the little graves in the churchyard and the pining babies in their arms, said that the old ways must be taken up again, and the men agreed with them.

So they went home, and spilled their libations, and laid out the firstings of the little that they had, and taught their children to respect the Strangers. Then, little by little, things began to mend; the children lifted their heads, the crops grew and the cattle throve. Still, there were never such merry times as there once had been, and the fever still hovered over the Land. It is a bad thing to forsake the old ways, and what is once lost can never quite be recovered." (Briggs, 384-385).

Mistress Briggs is quite right- it is bad to forsake the Old Ways, and it is true that the full power of a former era or age can never be recovered, for the world's procession of "ages" is moving along, until the end, and you can't go back. But you can spiritually revitalize yourself and your world, in accordance with what is possible for your own age, and the Strangers occupy an inner world of timeless power, which is still available to all that have the courage and love to make the fires on the stones and spill some blood for them.

Stories like this, from the 1800's, should make the hair turn white on the nay sayers who claim that Pagan customs never survived into the modern day. This second-hand account from Mrs. Balfour clearly identifies the various features of traditional Paganism in the British Isles- a reciprocal exchange with Land powers or Innerworldly powers, libations, "wise women" who understood the origin of these rites and methods of divination, meetings at the "crossroads in deep twilight," ancient stones and hearths as interaction points with the unseen world, and the dangers of losing the Old Ways.

The Twilight Art:
The Secret Doors of Trance and Fetch-Flight

Awakening Awareness: The White Tree, the Ghost Tree, or the God Stone

This section of our book of craft details techniques that can be practiced and learned, to bring about powerful altered states, and which can lead to "inner contact" with the Land itself and the powers that dwell in it.

I will reveal to you now what these techniques are intended to do. When you have mastered them, you will fully realize and fully experience the most important fact about your very being- that your awareness, the silent, passive "experience point" within you and around you (for truly, your awareness is not limited to your body or head) *is* the center of all things, and is intimately involved with all things, people, plants, Landscape features, spirits, or worlds.

This is the key and the secret to both the trance, to clairvoyance or "Witch-sight," and to the ability to "send forth the Fetch" and experience what seem like "journeys" in the unseen world.

Awareness is the entire key and point. Awareness has been described as the "listener" in you that "hears" your thoughts, the quality of your being that makes you "know" what your senses experience. That quality is not dependent on the senses for knowledge, however, because it can "know" things that are internal to you, such as thoughts and dreams, and it can "know" the unseen world, and "know" things in a very mysterious manner- a manner that is sometimes called "intuition" or that "strong feeling of knowing."

The awareness in you is the center of all things. When I say "center of all," I mean exactly that- awareness *is* the "world tree" or the "White Tree;" it is the ghost-haunted "totality" of all, the ghosts here referring to the forms that all things seem to assume when they appear to your senses, consciousness, and awareness.

There is a totality, a unity that is Nature and Reality. That totality is boundlessly aware- all things, beings, object, phenomena have a share in the Mystery of awareness. While you experience life as a seemingly differentiated being, you still partake of that awareness- you just mistakenly think of that awareness as "yours" or "isolated to you"-

and many people mistakenly associate their "knowing" with the brain. Awareness is not dependent on the brain. The brain and the primordial or root awareness merely work together cooperatively to engage the human experience that we are all having. Part of that human experience- a defining part- is the naturally formed yet illusory feeling that "you" are "aware" and isolated in a "body," "cut away" and separate from everything and everyone else.

That awareness that you experience as though it were "in you," that "listener" that silently and passively adds the element of "knowing" to what you think, see, hear, touch, taste, feel, or dream, or to what you experience when you have an intuition or vision, is the timeless, deathless Mystery. It is also the great center of all things.

Without awareness, the most essential and eternal quality in us and in all things, you could not be aware of what you become conscious of. There are thoughts in your head, but if you watch your thoughts carefully, you will see that some silent part of you is also aware of what you are thinking. It is fine and well to understand this, but you must eventually go further, and come to understand that what is aware and the things that "it" is aware of, are not two different "sides" of a duality; they are not two different "substances"- they are the differentiated, but not separate; they are one.

The seeming difference between the things experienced and the experiencer is a part of the "seeming of duality" or differentiation that we all have to deal with as human beings- but do not ever let yourself be fooled into thinking that there is an absolute separation between things, just because things naturally seem differentiated to your mind as a human. That seeming is part of the human experience- and it is just a seeming, albeit an important one for our ability to communicate, think rationally, and to maintain our sanity.

However, as mystics from all times and places have discovered and reported, you are not separate from things, despite the seeming. The mystic or witch can and should gradually realize that they are simultaneously one with all *and* experiencing differentiation. These two things run together, and are always twin conditions with each other. We do not seek to obliterate one in exchange for the other, only to realize the absolute Truth of oneness, and allow it to transform how we experience the necessity of differentiation. We allow the Truth of oneness to destroy the "cut away" and "isolated" feeling that so many people suffer under all their lives.

No one is isolated or alone, and when the Truth of your condition is made clear to you, you will have access to the boundless forms and unities of Nature or Reality itself. This is not only the path to being able to extend your consciousness into the secret, hidden places that most humans cannot see or touch, but also to peace.

When you break out of the prison of seeming isolation, your awareness suddenly is seen for what it is- a timeless and eternal reality that is one with all things, the center; awareness is an immense and perfect circle the size of the cosmos itself, the size of Reality, which passively takes in all things, and is involved with all things. When your mind loses its false "body and sense only" focus, you discover the bridge, the connecting factor, between your consciousness and the ancient spirits in the Land; you discover "where" the Underworld is. All of reality is arrayed within the great field of awareness, and is in fact *an appearance* of that great timeless field of awareness.

The spiritual forces above and below can "hear" you and experience you, because they have gone beyond egocentric limitation; they engage the "center" or awareness in a whole manner. "Be whole" is the greatest blessing you can offer to another, and it comes from the same root word as "holy"- to be holy is to partake of wholeness.

This is how the spiritual powers that exist in the Underworld or the Otherworld are ever more aware of us than most people could ever be of them; we live lives cut off from the boundless and living reality that our very awareness- the simplest and most intimate aspect of our being- is both a gate to, and the presence of. This silent gate to eternity is easy to miss, unless it is pointed out to you, and awakened with various spiritual exercises.

To begin the path of the traditional Witch or Pagan, you must internalize the worldview of the Old Ways, the Land-centered worldview. The first part of this book was specifically devoted to that.

To continue the path, you must now master awareness. You must be able to utilize the trance-art, know the secret of the trance, which I have talked at length about here.

The following four techniques are the most treasured techniques that I have discovered over time, from various contacts. When used as I suggest, they will begin to awaken the fire of awareness in you, extending it out into unfathomable regions of whiteness and infinity, merging what you once called "you" with the massive and timeless event that is the true "you." A great "White Tree" or a great spreading reality will extend out from you, and become involved in all times and places; the universal center will become your awareness, which is everywhere, just as the center is everywhere.

Using this "center," this axis and many-branched reality, you will be able to access any spiritual entity, to come to know them and their minds, and to communicate with them- including the dead. You will communicate in the silent places of the awareness that has become whole, a dream-like marsh of primordial images and great, unspeakable "knowings." You will be able to be wherever and whatever you like, because you already are everywhere and everything, at the deepest level. What you must do now is learn how to become truly conscious of that.

This Art is not without danger. The mind cannot always handle such experiences, and thus, you must be prepared to leave behind your old sense of self-definition. Holding on to your former methods of defining yourself will hold you back from going as far as you need to go- but not everyone can do this. Death will do it for you one day, and the wise choose to do it before death forces their hand. If you are brave, and ready to go beyond the Fate of mortal men and women, you should proceed, with audacity and caution.

The Witch is that person who has made the journey into the place where only the dead go. These techniques and the experiences they lead to can bring about an initiatory "death" of the ego, and that is as it should be. You exchange limited self-definition for Wisdom. The risk of madness is the gamble the Witch takes, just as warriors gamble against death to gain the glory and excitement they seek. When using these techniques, along with the "invocation" techniques discussed in a coming portion of this book, wherein the mindstream can be placed into direct contact with the immense powers of the Master Spirits that rule over the Old Ways, there is more risk- these powers are ancient and vast, timeless and potent- this is something you have to prepare for, accept- because you will fail at the Art if you are only prepared to invoke powers that fit tidy, preconceived notions of "what spirits are"- you have to open yourself to their immensity and power, which can be raw and disturbing and even overwhelming at times. This is how you know their power and the authenticity of your contact.

The four techniques in this section are the *Witch-sight* or clarity technique, the *Hissing of the Serpent* or the internal transformation technique, the *Serpent in the Land* technique, and the *Left-Way Road* or the *Widdershins Walk* technique.

The first two are meant to be used in conjunction, even though you must learn them one at a time, and practice them separately until you have mastered them.

The third technique, the Serpent in the Land, is meant to be used after you have mastered and engaged the first two- it is a technique for bonding with the power of whatever Land you happen to be on, and the reason why you need the first two techniques before you use it is because the first two help you to "feel" or experience it fully. Done by itself, it will probably fail. The first two techniques (which are quite simple techniques, by the way) put you into a mental condition of full openness, which allows you to sense the subtle power of the Serpent in the Land.

The last technique is the most complex and powerful- it does nothing less than open doors in the Land, and allow you to pass through them, in a manner that becomes a full "out of body" experience. This is the doorway technique that gets the Fetch and consciousness of the Witch to the Sabbat itself, to deepest communion with the Witchmother and White King of the Underworld, and to the ancestral dead. They are the true initiators.

This is how you should begin with the techniques I am about to describe:

Begin by reading and absorbing the Witch-sight essay, and put it to practice, as much as you can- as you will see, it is a technique that can be done any time of day or night, and can be done regardless of where you happen to be, or what you happen to be doing. Spend time with this technique, and really internalize it- after weeks of practice at it, you will begin seeing the world quite differently, with the "new" kind of clarity that it discusses.

Once you have entered into that technique well enough, read the Hissing of the Serpent technique, and try it. From this point, when you practice, start with the Witch-sight technique, and follow it immediately with the Hissing technique. Then, when you have finished the Hissing session, end with another Witch-sight. The pattern is Clarity- Hissing- Clarity.

You should do these two in tandem for a long time. Eventually, you will be able to engage the Serpent in the Land technique- and when you make the decision to do so, always do the Clarity-Hissing-Clarity practice *before* you engage the Serpent in the Land.

The Clarity-Hissing-Clarity practice should be done before any serious work, because it opens you and puts you in a position to sense the powers you are engaging afterwards.

After you have truly mastered the Witch-sight technique, the Hissing technique, and the Serpent in the Land, you will have made miles of progress into the powerful and genuine experience of the power in the Land and in yourself. You will, in fact, have gone further than 99% of people who claim to be involved in "trance work" or "magic" or "Paganism."

When you are doing the Clarity-Hissing-Clarity sessions, after the final Clarity, let yourself move into the "awareness" that will have woken up in you, and realize- truly realize- that the powers you wish to contact and work with are *with* you, within you and without you- and fully aware of you and your thoughts, words, and deeds. Realize that you are in a perfect, intimate oneness with them, and being open, feel and sense what they are doing in conjunction with you. That is the key.

After you have become so awakened, and had these depth experiences, you will be prepared for the Left-Way Road, and you will be able to use it to great effect.

I. Attaining the Witch-sight: Second Sight and the Great Quest of Humankind

"The great spiritual powers desire that we be like them- fully, consciously aware of the circle of All. The witch seeks for the Grand Seal, the supreme Wisdom, just as the Druid of old sought inspiration or illumination. To be as the Gods is to experience the world as the Gods do- this experience is found in the mind of light, the mind in the grip of inspiration."

What astounds me is the great simplicity of the mystical path.

We came into the life condition we currently experience from a timeless chain of previous experiences. When we leave this life experience, we will flow into others. Life or existence, from the human perspective, is a neverending flow of experiences. Your thoughts flow from thought to thought, your emotions from emotional climate to emotional climate; your opinions flow and change- everything about you. A million deaths, a million rebirths, occur in each person's lifetime.

The circle of the soul is the size of all reality, and it flows through all things. Reality is itself a great circle, a perfect circle. Moving, yet still; changing, yet unchanging. All things, all events describe a great circle, from the life cycle of a man, to the circle of the seasons, and the sun and the moon. Human perceptions are also a great circle.

Life is a quest. We are perceptually moving from experience to experience, searching. All beings want the same thing- lasting peace and satisfaction. The problem begins when people get false ideas in their heads about *what precisely* will bring them lasting peace and happiness.

Materialists believe that a lot of money and possessions will make them truly happy- but when that mistaken belief warps their senses, and makes them destroy the world and hurt others in greed, they discover that all the money and possessions in the world only make them happy for a while. Then they feel hollow again, and try to fill it with even more material things- a neverending paper-chase, a neverending fight for what they can never attain enough of.

On the same token, there are other things that people mistakenly decide will satisfy them- religious beliefs, pet theories, some supreme scientific or philosophical explanation for life, sexual satisfaction, titles, positions, and so forth- and people spend lives chasing these things, chasing them until they die.

The Quest for the Young Puck

Life is a quest. Deep down, we all have the impulse to find what will give us the lasting peace we incline towards. What *will* give us this lasting peace is nothing short of the Truth: the Truth about life, the Truth about what we are, and what the world is. "What is my life?" is the supreme question you have to ask upon self-examination. What is the Truth of things?

Mystics from all times and places have experienced reality in such a manner that the Truth was made known to them- or they followed a mystical path that led them towards some lesser or greater realization. The role of the mystic is precisely that: to mentally, spiritually, and emotionally go where the vast majority of mankind does not- into mysterious reaches of experience, where Truth is encountered in a more direct, naked way.

From the primal shaman, whose task it was to leave the tribe and enter the Otherworld, and then, to return and mediate the power, Wisdom, and healing of the Otherworld to his people, the mystic of the modern day has no less of an important task- to go into the direct experience of Reality that most people will never have in this life. In the modern world, such an experience is couched in terms comfortable to monotheists- they say the mystic "directly experiences or has knowledge of God."

As a modern Pagan, and someone who thinks more in line with Meister Eckhart, I see this language for what it is- an attempt to describe something rather indescribable, nothing more; "God" in this context means "source of All," and "Truth" and can rightly be seen as the great fertile Mother-Reality that gives birth and sustenance to all- the "Godhead" of Eckhart, and the "Great Mother of Gods and Men" of the Pagans.

In some way, we have no choice but to all become mystics, at some time or another. If not now, in this life, then in some other time or condition or place. The human being has a quest to fulfill, and that quest can only be completed by a mystic.

This quest was summed up very shortly by me in an earlier writing, where I stated:

"...When the immense life and awareness of All-Mother Nature (the divine source of All) finally dwells consciously in man, through true consciousness on the part of man (a experience we call inspiration), the Mabon, or the Divine Youth is born through the body, soul, and mind of man- the "Child of the Mother" comes, in immortal youth and freedom. But he must be stolen away by shadowy forces first; threatened by the forces of chaos, and hidden, and only found through quest- through our personal, individual efforts towards true clarity of consciousness and awareness- before the travails of the stolen and lost Divine Youth come to an end, and he is freed. This is a metaphor for the human condition; each of us has the potential for the coming of the Mabon, the Divine Youth."

It is important to point out that an initiate into the Mysteries of ancient Greece was called a "Kouros," meaning "youth," and referring to the undying, eternally youthful or immortal portion of all of us. Not surprisingly, the feminine version of the word is "Kore"- a maiden- and the oldest and supreme Mysteries of Greece were held at Eleusis, where the drama of Kore/Persephone, the daughter of Demeter, were held, and where the initiates reported achieving a lasting happiness, a joy in this life, and a "great and secret hope" for life beyond.

The Divine Youth or Kouros/Mabon is the spirit that can be born within and through each soul- the supreme mystical experience, which represents the Illumination of the human being- the Druidic Imbas or Awen. Those who are so illuminated have lasting peace and continual awareness of the Truth- a wordless, "deep" awareness of what is real. Few illuminated mystics from history who have tried to express this condition in words have been able to do so, for this condition is necessarily impossible to communicate directly.

Words are finite and of limited use when it comes to describing what can only be experienced. Words can, however, help point the way. Also, in the Bardic traditions of Britain and Ireland, the Bard- the fully illuminated master of verse, memory, song, and poetry- had the power of "naming"- of speaking the Truth about whatever thing they spoke of. Here, "Truth" or "Naming" refers to creating words that have a mystical value, in the sense that they bring the person who hears the words into a sort of "state" where the inner nature of the thing referred to is experienced, normally in a wordless, direct manner- a feeling, or a sentiment, or sometimes a strange insight.

The human quest is just another expression of the quest that all life follows- a quest for lasting peace and satisfaction. Animals seek for lasting satisfaction, but lack a deeper capacity to be aware of it, in such a manner suited to finish the quest- but they fight for satisfaction, daily. When hungry, they seek out food; when in danger, they run or fight the danger off. For beasts, the closest approximation to lasting satisfaction is stability- a food supply that keeps away hunger, a safe haven that protects from predators or a safe place full of prey, and without competing predators; a place where the climate is agreeable, and where they can find mates.

They do not and cannot think far beyond these immediate needs, except in mystical moments of a strange, primal clarity that may sneak into their dreams, but which is lost by the brutality, short-sightedness, and basics of their animalistic condition. Animals experience an intensity of emotion unique to them, and emotional reactions unique to their condition- and when in domesticated contact with humans, they can display great affection. But overall, they lack the higher abstract and spiritual capacity to complete the quest.

I believe, however, that their quest extends from the beast-experience, into greater and more aware states, beyond this life. On this point, however, we stray into the Fate of other creatures that have their own path to follow- and I am talking about the particularly human path in this short essay.

You came into this life, this experience, this world, according to the strands of Fate that wove you here, into this time and place. You came seeking lasting peace, illumination, Truth. No matter what sort of person you are, spiritual or unspiritual, eternalist or nihilist, religious or atheist, you seek the same thing- Truth; lasting happiness and satisfaction. Everyone gets a different idea inside them about what will bring them to this point, and chases after it.

If you find it, you have found the Mabon, the Puck-child of the craft. You find divinity, this ancient being who is as much a potential within all things, as he is a God- you find an experience of Reality which frees you from illusion. You find the Truth. Then, the quest is over; the experiences and conditions that now await you are not for those who have not completed the quest to know.

If you don't find it, you continue looking- even after death, you continue looking, driven on to stranger and newer life-experiences, in an infinite number of other forms- perhaps as a tree, a wind, an animal, another human, or any number of unseen beings. When you die in those forms, on you will go searching. You will search all of the perfect circle of Reality for the Truth.

Many times, under the influence of falsehood, you will think you have found it, but lack of true peace and the revelations of death will tell you otherwise.

All of nature, all of its parts, plus Nature as a whole, is flowing, seeking, and gradually, as beings find the Truth, all of Nature is rising into the light of Truth; Nature is slowly being filled with the light of true illumination, as though a great spiritual dawn is arising. The Mother is constantly giving birth to the Youth, the Child of Light. In all of Nature's movement and flowing, still the reality of things- awareness- stays utterly still, with a seeming of motion but never moving, quiescently eternal. You search in a long quest but ultimately, the quest is stillness.

All of our lives we've desired Truth, wondered, searched- "died" a million times to certain ways of being and thinking, and got "born" into new ones- the entire space of our internal and external lives is a model in miniature of a greater, universal drama. Do not doubt that death is only another passage into a new birth, wherein the quest continues.

The Key to the Quest

There is only one key to the path- clarity. Life, as we experience it, is like a dream. We live our lives in a state that is near total unconsciousness, no matter how "conscious" we think we are. If one day you ever stop, sit down, and let yourself feel *all* of your bodily sensations, really feel everything- then, move on to what you are hearing without letting go of what you are feeling, and then, add what you are seeing- and go into a state of total "all-around" consciousness, a total conscious awareness of every input coming from every sense, simultaneously, you will see precisely what I am saying.

Don't think. Just feel, hear, look, taste; do not ignore any sense in exchange for the sensory input of another sense. Let yourself go passive and take in your entire sensory experience, with a mind silent of thoughts. When you do this, make certain that you *know* that you are seeing, feeling, hearing- you have to "arouse the mind" to the task of this pure and sharp consciousness- arouse the mind, but don't rest it on one thing in particular, but on the totality of your experience.

Normally, people let a stray sight or *tons* of stray thoughts and daydreams lead them off to lost places within or without themselves. When you start ruminating on a thought, or staring at a television, or anything like that, even though sounds are reaching your ears, you are not hearing them. Even though something might be touching your skin, you don't feel it. This is the condition of almost unconsciousness that people live their entire lives in- stuck, dazed and drunk on fantasies, thoughts, feelings, objects, whatever they favor over other things.

Never do people become *truly* awake and consciously aware- purely aware, purely conscious. To do so is to achieve the Witch-sight, the second sight that cuts through the darkness of human sleep and ignorance.

Here's a short formula for it:

1. Sit or stand comfortably.

2. Let yourself "feel" all of what you are feeling. Are you hot? Cold? Feel the pressure between your bottom and the chair or ground? Do you itch somewhere? Feel your clothes brushing against you or weighing on your skin? Feel everything; do not judge the feelings, just be aware of them.

3. Now, without taking your mind off that, allow yourself to also be aware of all sounds that you hear- background noise, noises near you, all the noise reaching your ear.

4. Without taking your mind off your experience of feeling all/hearing all, become aware of whatever you happen to be seeing, whatever is right in front of your eyes. Just let yourself see, hear, and feel everything that is occurring to you. Don't think about it- just let your mind go silent. You must have every intention- you must know what you are doing- you are seeing, hearing, feeling, tasting- in other words, you are *being consciously aware of the totality* of your experience.

You are not only seeing, but you know that you are seeing. You are not only hearing, but you are *wordlessly aware* of the fact that you are hearing, and so forth. But you are doing it all at once, in a wordless, clear way. I know it sounds hard, but try, work it out. It is not as difficult as you think. The hardest part is really not thinking "word-thoughts" in your head.

5. If you find that you have trouble getting rid of mental chatter, there is a secret to making it easy- pretend that you have just awakened from a coma, and have severe amnesia, amnesia that has made you forget your own language. You can't speak *or* think in English, or whatever language you speak. Imagine what that would be like, then let yourself play the game, slip into the role. What would that be like? You couldn't think with words, because you've forgotten all words. You could just see, hear, feel, and be aware. Play the role. It is far easier than you think.

6. If you manage to capture even three seconds of total, still clarity, a total "full sensory" conscious awareness of your sensory inputs, you will become aware of something: you will see how dim and unconscious "ordinary" everyday conscious experience is, by way of comparison to the state of true clarity, or the state of true and full consciousness, full conscious sensory perception.

But then, within seconds of capturing this perfect clearness, or this non-selective "full" conscious experience, you will begin to think about it. Thoughts will arise, and you will discover that you wandered off following some thoughts, and went back to looking, but not seeing; or, you went back to hearing, but not listening; or you will realize that you weren't feeling your bodily impressions anymore.

7. As soon as thought has invaded, the clarity ends. As soon as you start automatically showing preference for one sense input over another, the clarity ends, and you go numb in some way; some sense starts to dim and dull out; it is still operating, but you are not consciously experiencing its operation. You are falling back into unconsciousness, even though you *think* that you are fully conscious. What we call "full consciousness" is actually a dim shadow of true consciousness, true clarity.

Once you can do this technique, you will have everything you need to complete the quest. As you walk through your days, or run, or drive, or eat, or lie down to sleep, or pray, or play games, or make love, or any other activity- you will remember the state of clarity, and at any time, you can do it- you can become fully consciously aware.

If you are eating dinner, become aware of all you are tasting, feeling, hearing, seeing, at *that* moment, the moment you think about it. See if you can have a good, pure few seconds of open conscious awareness of your experience. You can do it anytime. Do it as much as you think about it; I am doing it as I write this.

Great changes will begin occurring in you. If you introduce this practice- the practice of Witch-sight (though when I say "sight," I am referring, obviously, to more than just eyes) you will begin to get better at it, and have longer and longer experiences of it- soon, you may be able to "have" clarity for minutes at a time- and the longer you maintain this condition, the more insights you will begin having about your presence or existence "in" Nature, or "in" Reality.

You will gradually become untangled from illusions you might have held about reality; but you will not "escape" the world- such a thing is impossible. There is no other "Reality" or world to escape to; the world is one, whole, undivided- as is awareness. There are only fantasies and delusions about Reality that you can escape, through clarity, and there is a dim state of unconsciousness that you can turn into true openness and perfect, mystical wakefulness.

As you practice this technique, which you should often, even if it is for a few moments, you will become aware of something "greater"- a quality about the world of your experience, which you share and which all things "have"- something timeless. You will begin to "see" with clearness, have awakenings of intuition and idea. You will begin to develop the Witch-sight; the "Two Sights" as they called it in Scotland, because the more you do this practice, the more you start to realize the Truth: That what you call "different" occurrences, different feelings and experiences, are all really *one* great experience; the world is one great occurrence, and you are experiencing its many shades.

But what appear to us to be the "many" parts of the world all come together in clarity, as inseparable from the whole, and the whole is one great, grand divine occurrence- the timeless expression of Fate *as* the world of our experience. What we call "past" and "future" even come together, in the uroboric circle of Reality, which you begin to experience on a deep, deep level. Your eyes lose their false focus; as your sessions of clarity increase in time and in number, you will begin to awaken. You will be victimized less and less by the long bouts of unconsciousness and dazed half-consciousness that most people lead their lives in.

You will start to really *see*- not just what appears to your eyes, but things beyond sensory perception; they, too, will begin to "occur" to you, in ways that cannot be described, but chiefly in strong "knowings" or "feelings." You will start to see- and become aware of- things that other people do not; you will have a better memory, a better sharpness of mind, a better reaction time, and a better alertness, over time. But more than that, you will gain subtle awareness of things that were always there, just unnoticed by you, or by the vast majority of mankind.

You will start to sense a crystalline "eternal still wholeness" that all disparate shapes and forms and people and beasts seem to be parts of. It's a "new thing" for most people to sense, but it is very real; it is Reality. It is hard to focus on, because you can't focus mind or selective senses on it; it "emerges" or rises in conscious awareness when your perceptions are "whole" in sensory attention, and yet, seems to draw your perceptions beyond what they are experiencing. It vanishes with broken attention- an odd effect, one that makes people call it "difficult" to find, when in reality nothing could be easier or harder. It just takes "letting go" and paying full attention to all things.

Dreams, Death and Destiny

Stay alert. Do not let "other realities" appearing tempt you away from clarity- even if you were to see another world, *remember* that your task is to stay totally consciously aware of whatever presents itself. If you wander off into fairy-land, you will be just as lost and asleep as you are if you wander off in this world.

When you sleep at night, you may dream. If, during your waking hours, you practice true clarity every time you think about it, then eventually, when you are dreaming one night, you will find yourself "thinking about it" in the dream- and if you have built an almost automatic habit of doing a clarity session in your daily life each time you think about it, then in the dream, you will probably do the same thing- and then, you will discover precisely how "lucid dreams" can be created. If, in your dream, you "become fully conscious," you should suddenly realize that you are dreaming- or, even if you don't, you will suddenly be aware of many new things; dreams will become more clear, powerful, and in your control.

Either way, one day, you *will* have this clarity in your dreams, and then you have made great progress. When you die, and death's experiences come onto you, this same impulse to stay in "clarity" can transform your entire experience of death- an experience that drives most people into darkness and unconsciousness, and unconsciously propels them onward to new states of being, some comfortable, and some frightening or painful- but with clarity and full awareness, even that Fate can be transformed. The Vajrayana Buddhist "Tibetan Book of the Dead" deals with this theme a good deal- the Theme of "lucid dying."

But this essay is not about dreams and death, primarily. It is about daily and nightly clarity; it is about the key to the quest for the Horn Child, the Puck-Child, the Mabon, or the Child, which means the quest for illumination. This one simple technique of clarity is all that you need; it is armor, shield, and sword against delusion and the dim states of unconsciousness that Hard Fate traps us all in as mortal beings. These dim states of sleepwalking are actually what define us as mortals, compared to the Gods, who have great and permanent clarity; the Gods are totally consciously aware of all; their minds trace the perfect circle of Reality, taking in all.

To the Gods, mortals are like stumbling, dazed creatures, yawning and sleeping as they walk and sit down and go about life; we stumble by the Gods without ever seeing them, or the many worlds beyond. We hurt and kill each other, and hurt and kill ourselves, without ever seeing or suspecting the greater implications of our real condition, nor being aware of how large a role our own unconsciousness played in our own tragedies.

Reality- the Great Mother- is a great divine whole; and the Source of All is within us and it surrounds us. Reality is one, whole, and undivided. Our minds break it up for us into pieces, treating the pieces as though they were separate from each other, but all things are from the whole source, and sustained by it, every moment of timeless time. Nothing is apart from anything else; we differentiate ourselves and all things from other things, but differentiation is not the same as separation.

Every strand in the tapestry of reality is part of the whole; without one strand, the rest of reality would "come apart" and cease to be.

When you stop thinking in terms of separation, Reality begins to dawn on you- you begin to see the whole "coming together" again, as it always was.

The perfect and tightly bound circle of Reality becomes complete, through your conscious awareness. You become complete, because you, too, are part of it all; what you call "the world" and "yourself" are just two labels you use to situate what you think is "your" experience. But there is no "you" or "self" apart from the world, and no world apart from "you." "Your" experience is the world "happening," and the world's events are your events. As the great philosopher Dr. Peter Kingsley has pointed out, you reach a point where you realize that "instead of being born into the world, you see that the world was born in you."

All things depend on all other things, just as all points in a circle depend on every other point to be there, or the circle would cease to be a circle.

Be clear and open; practice clarity. Don't think or analyze; just see, feel, hear, taste... sit in pure and unselective experience. All is perfect, and as it should be- truly see, and you will begin to change, to experience something deeper- but even in that, stay clear and stay conscious of what is occurring, of what you are experiencing.

The great Mother Reality will finally fully "spill into you"- your full experiences and practices at "taking it in" with full clarity will eventually cause the birth of the Divine Child; you will "find" what you always had; what was potentially waiting to happen through you will occur, you will recognize reality, and undergo a transformation that cannot be described. You will, however, have lasting peace, and all humans will see that on your face, and you won't adequately be able to tell them how it came about. You will simply try to tell them "just look; hear, feel, be here and now, and don't over-think it. Just see."

In seeing clearly and truly, you begin to experience the "roots" of what presents itself to you as sensory inputs- the roots of the Reality, the Underworld, which is also the root of you. Then, you come face to face with the Truth. The Divine Child is found, and "comes" to be realized, actualized through you, as you. Death, obscurity, despair, and fear are defeated; Wisdom is born, and clarity and peace.

That is the Way, the quest. The great Mother Reality acts in conjunction with the soul, mind, and body that is fully conscious of Reality, and She brings about the natural and spontaneous realization of Truth, which is the birth of the Child.

It is our task, our Fated goal, to be seekers and the vessel of this experience. The horse that we ride to this goal is our body; the weapon and armor that protects us is our clarity of consciousness and our efforts towards the same.

Are you looking for the Divine Child, or are you the Divine Child that was lost and hidden? In the circle of Reality, both are true, at the same time. Fail or lack in your effort, and the forces of illusion, glamour, chaos, and darkness will drag you off to sleep again, and eventually, overwhelm you in death.

Should this happen, you will move off to a new "country," a new test, a new time and place, a new branch of the quest, where hopefully the Gods will see fit to help you further; I know that they answer all prayers for aid in this human experience and quest. They answer these prayers, for they, too, once quested.

II. The Hissing of the Serpent, or the Voice of the Master which Transforms

"Trance" is the experience of extra-sensory reality.

We can be certain that the range of our standard human senses do not expose us to reality in full, but to reality as we humans need to see it, in such a manner that we react properly for our own survival. This is sensory reality. Our senses tell us of potentially dangerous situations, predators, sounds that are important, tastes and textures that can reveal danger or comfort. Our senses reveal to us what we need to know to interact with the world in such a manner that our comfort and survival is provided for.

This "primacy of sensory reality" which absorbs our minds most of our lives is our heritage from the animal kingdom. The gift of the All Father or Cunning Father to mankind was the Spirit of "Wod" or inspiration; this gift was the awarenss of the immortal spirit that interacts without and within us, and awareness of the sorcerous fire; the fire of the Gods.

This strange and weird power, which is the seat of our own divine imaginations, our imaginal ability, exists for one purpose only: it is a doorway into an experience of Reality which is fully divine, or should I say, an experience that is whole or full. The Witch Fire, the divine element of consciousness in mankind which is a gateway to consciousness of the infinite, is there that we, too, may be like the true beings, the spirits, or undying ones.

The true beings, spirits that have been called "Gods," are Gods because they have a wholeness of awareness and a wholeness of consciousness. There is nothing that they do not see or experience. The same cannot be said of humans most of the time, if ever. But when the trance comes, and opens into a strong experience of extra-sensory reality, you find yourself on the threshold of your own mortality; this is why Trance and death are similar. The true and full trance is The immortal hour, the hour of the Gods. It is the doorway to a world that is entirely not ours, and yet, a world that cannot be said to be "apart" from ours- for Reality is *one*, *whole*, and *undivided*. What is different is perception- and even perception is part of the whole.

In this manner, we can say that the divine world of the undying ones is not the same as the human world, and yet, it is not different; we can say that our worlds are not one, and yet, they are not two. This is a subtle point that must be understood.

The trance does not begin strong, but it grows strong as your divine, imaginal capacity or invisible Fire is fanned higher and higher, inside your essential being. This is why effort or practise is necessary. A day will come when the trance will destroy you, as a fire destroys anything. But the destruction will be only of the "you" that was based on your memories and experience of mortal, sensory reality, and it will be the birth of a new "you" that freely partakes in the wholeness of things; a "you" that will now be able to experience Reality with the "strong" senses or the eyes of cunning, the eyes of a Witch.

You will "look" upon the faces of the unseen ones, and know them as your true companions. Indeed, even now, they are far more involved in us than we mortals could ever be in them, by virtue of their great mastery of what we call "the trance."

The trance does not exist apart from sensory reality or the body, and yet, what makes it possible is not limited to sensory reality or the body. We are dealing with a Mystery of the spirit, of a dark and wondrous immortal fire that was bestowed on mankind by beings that are beyond our mortal understanding, in "ancient times," or within the mythical dimension of our existence.

After the bestowing of the fire, we were no longer merely mortal things, but immortals in fugue, seeds of the Gods waiting to break forth.

The metaphysical pain of our human existence is only the deepest, most buried divine reality in us which knows full well that it is no slave to death or limitation, and yet, it is forced to deal with fear and limitation- again, a side-effect of our animal heritage, and the Hard Fate of our mortality- the blessing and curse of beings that are no longer merely mortal and yet not fully immortal, straddling the strange space between these things.

What strange times these are, and strange beings we are. the trance introduces us to "the secret history" of what we really are, what has been forgotten, and what awaits us. We are Capax Dei, "capable of Gods"-capable of being far more than we ever dreamed, for even most of our dreams are mere mortal fantasies.

The flame itself has some mysterious relationship to the area behind your navel. If you want to fan it brighter, it is to the Mystery of the inconstant air that you must go, just like wind fans flames the higher, or the bellows makes the fire in the furnace higher. Your body is the furnace in which an infinitely wise spiritual being is forged, a spiritual birth- never mistake this or forget it.

When the Mystery Night comes, a divine being will be born- but who will it be? This is the beatific vision, the culmination of Fate. The identity of the Horn Child or the Divine Child is the central Mystery of the awakening, and the name of this being the name of destiny. But that is for another time to puzzle out. I will return now to the basics of this technique.

The area behind your navel is a secret key. Something begins to happen when you affect it with your breath. This simple technique begins all growth towards changing the subtle body into a vehicle of trance.

Ten is the number- you take ten easy but deep breaths, and as you do so, you imagine in your head that balloon is filling behind your navel. It gets pretty big, so you should effortlessly allow your stomach to expand out, and then, when you let your breath come rushing out, let it out slowly but generously, and allow the wind escaping to make a hissing noise through your teeth. This is an important detail.

This is the Hissing of the Cunning Serpent, the Old Cunning One. This high-pitched hiss affects deep layers of the brain and mind, and yes, I am asking you to take my word for this. Give it a chance; if you do as I ask, you will start to change. This is the sound of the hiss, the sound of the piper, the sound of silence, the supreme password of the Mysteries. The stars themselves make this sound as they cut through the void of space.

As the breath comes out into the hiss, you must think of nothing else but the out breath. All of the world should vanish, leaving only your breath.

Sit with your back straight and your neck straight to do this. Ten breaths, doing as I said each time. In, inflate the balloon, out with the long steady hiss, and all you should fix your mind on is the out-breath and the sound of the hiss. Don't force your mind to do this; gently direct your mind to the out-breath feeling and sound. If stray thoughts arise, you gently come back silently to your breath. As the breath completes its exit, you think "one." Then you start the next breath, and at the completion of the "in-inflate balloon-out-hiss" process, you think "two." You do this until you reach ten.

Only the sensations of breathing, the feeling of breath, the sound of the hiss, and the number should exist for you. Close your eyes if you need to. If any other single mental image or thing intrudes, you just come back to your breath.

This is not hard to do; just remember to go gently- don't force. Don't be fast or hard. Be steady, not too lazy and not too hard, just somewhere in the middle, with a steady temperament to you.

This is the basic "meditation" in which the power-center of the body is enlivened, and the cunning serpent's hiss rises in your consciousness. There is no trance work (or really, any other work) that does not begin with this seemingly simple exercise. The point of this exercise is to relax and center you, but also to rouse the serpent, awaken the deep mind, and empower you. You should do this exercise daily, and usually more than once a day; after all, any few minutes in your life can be set aside for ten slow, steady breaths and a little of the serpent's tongue.

What you must remember is that each time you complete a set of ten of these, you have become a different being; you have changed a bit, transformed on a deep level, become more capable of moving closer to that arousal of power and awareness that will eventually break through the misty wall that separates the slumbering world of mortals from the eldritch world of the deathless. Neither the inconstant air nor the hiss of the deathless serpent can leave even a single thing totally as it was before.

Do not be fooled by the simple appearance of this technique; it is a foundational technique. I suggest that you always do it before you go to sleep, perhaps when you lie down at night.

As an aside, if before you go to sleep, and after you reach breath ten, you allow yourself to "let go" of and relax into bodily and mental stillness- as though you were a corpse- you will start to notice a change in your dreams. This is an "entry point" into the advanced technique of "incubation" or dream divination.

Now, before we can continue, I have to discuss how important the element of "understanding" is. It is fine to begin the ascent into internal transformation, using the "foundational technique" above and others I will discuss; but without understanding, none of this is useful. All of the trance techniques in the world, and all the capabilities in the world will mean nothing without understanding what they are. To have these techniques and the experiences they bring without understanding is the same as having a heap of very expensive building materials. A heap of building materials is not a house, and without understanding how they work together, they never will be.

You have to understand that Reality is one, whole, and undivided. Human minds chop it into a billion pieces, abstract parts of it away from the wholeness of Nature, and label those various "parts" as different "things"- but it is still one. Your mind takes an oak tree and *thinks* of the oak as a thing different from Nature, but the tree, like your own body or mind, or any other thing you label as "something," is still inseparable from the wholeness.

Please do not ever forget this; You are not "in" the world; you *are* a world. You are only different from the body of Nature insofar as you perceive yourself as such. It just so happens, however, that as an individual being, you will always perceive yourself in that manner, in any world or condition you may come to inhabit. It is precisely that mode of perception- that you are "apart" from all things that you perceive- that defines you as a mortal being, or as a spirit, or what have you.

Many people think that the point of "spirituality" is to lose the self in absorption with the Great Allness of Reality; to become absorbed into the "one with all" state. But such a thing is absurd. You do not ever cease to exist as a being with perception- what ceases is your absolute sense of separation from Nature. You can be both aware of yourself as a "thing" apart from Nature, while simultaneously being totally aware and conscious of your oneness with all.

That is the secret. A being that has *both* of these modes of awareness at the same time is no longer really a mortal. A mortal is precisely the sort of being that has pretty much 100% of their everyday awareness cast only in terms of separation and differentiation from the world "around them." They have no ability to also realize their great oneness, their intimate and natural connection with Nature. Of course, that oneness always exists; it is the true condition of all things, no matter how unconscious of it we may be.

But to have both modes of perception makes a person both a mortal *and* an immortal; because the immortals have a wholeness of awareness that takes in All That Is. They are aware of All. They are totally aware of the mortal and the immortal, the limited and the unlimited, the finite and the infinite, simultaneously. By "existing" in both modes, a being actually (paradoxically) becomes both *and* neither! This is the symbolism of the Veiled One's face- half light and half dark, half living and half dead; She unites both "halves" of reality in one great being. The symbolism of the Dark Master and the Lord of Light, being two faces or aspects of one being, is the same.

They become a "third new thing" which is beyond all and nothing, beyond absorption and individuality, and yet, still capable of enjoying both of these perspectives. This is the deathless state, the condition of the Hidden Company, or the Grand Array. These are the "Master Men" or the "True Beings" of Lore.

The path to this awareness begins with the technique I discussed above. Humble beginnings, a simple soil for a seed of reality- a simple soil like so many soils that produce crops in abundance all over the earth. Never scoff at simplicity or simple beginnings.

III. The Serpent in the Land: The Power Below and Within

The Serpent in the Land technique is familiar to most modern day Pagans. Similar techniques abound in many fine books on the subject of earth-Mysteries and related subjects. The idea of "drawing up power" from the ground below is a nearly ubiquitous idea in modern Pagan metaphysical systems. There is a reason for this; it is one of the most profound and simple methods of forging a real connection with the force or power of the Land in a certain place.

"Drawing up power" is the union of the circulating currents of power in the body with the circulating currents of power in the Land beneath you, and the creation of a state of awareness and experience in which the body's flowing powers and the Land's flowing powers seem to become as one.

The following technique is a simpler technique that should be done after Witch-sight or clarity practice, after you have come to a clear and perfect "openness" to yourself and your surroundings, and after you have hissed like the old serpent, and awakened the subtle forces in yourself. This technique can be done repeatedly, as you move about the landscape, to "tune" yourself to whatever place you happen to be in.

I find that it is most useful for "getting to know" a place, by first opening yourself, and then walking about and pausing to perform this technique at key spots. If this is kept up for several days, and if during that time, you perform the Housle or Red Meal (which we will discuss in a coming chapter) to the spiritual forces in and below that Land or place, and if you go even further and endeavor to sleep outside or as close to the ground of that place as you can, the inner levels of the Land will tend to reveal themselves to you in strange and powerful ways.

The revelations will normally begin in sleep, when dreams become affected by the subtle forces in the Land, and can evolve to become full blown mystical encounters, as your mind-body complex becomes suffused with the power of that place.

To do the "Drawing up," stand straight up, with your feet touching the Land itself- barefoot, if possible. Ironically, this same technique will work if you are elevated above the Land, such as on a building or in a tree, for instance. You simply have to be aware of how you contact the Land.

You begin by opening yourself to the Land all around and below you, and quieting your mind into a great quiet receptivity, until you sense a great power below you. It is impossible *not* to sense this, if you are on the earth anywhere, and if you can quiet your mind to any extent and let yourself really feel. When I say "feel," I don't mean "feel" as in emotion- I mean feel as in sensation. It is occurring every day of your life, all day- forces of your environment are having an impact on you, from the most subtle to the most apparent, and you have simply grown numb to the constant barrage, and learned to ignore them.

When you go quiet, and become receptive, concentrate on the way the air feels around your skin, and around the area of your body. Concentrate on the "whole feeling" of the place you are in. Forests, for instance, "feel" different from an open field. The trick is to realize that you are probably already feeling what I describe- the spiritual "atmosphere" of a place- but you probably have it in your mind that this "feeling" is just your normal "feeling" or "nothing at all." But it is something.

If you journey from place to place, you can see how different places feel differently. Some creepy, some calm, some turbulent, some deep and vast. Sometimes the feeling of a place is covered up by the feeling of breezes on you, or with the feel of the rain, but you must be careful- sometimes, what you think is a wind or a simple shiver in your spine *is* the feeling of the place.

Pay careful attention, in a silent, internal way, and with an expansive, open mind, to your total body and mind experience, and you will realize that there is "something" coming from "around" you, and it even extends to "inside" you, in most cases.

Once you realize that you are "feeling" the power of the place, let your awareness go downward into the ground, and "feel" there. You must use the center to do this- the whiteness of awareness that touches all places and is all places.

Feel deep down. Then, allow your mind to "picture" the feeling of the deep power in the ground as a ball of softly luminous light. Concentrate on it, and breathe in and out lightly, fixing your whole mind on it. Then, when you feel its reality as strongly as you may, take a long, slow, and deep inhale, and raise your hands from your sides, slowly, very slowly, as if you intend to bring your hands together above your head.

As you breathe in and raise your hands, will the light to rise into your feet and legs, and move up into the area behind your navel. See and feel it move into your chest and your heart, and come to rest there. Your hands should be straight out from you, but not higher than your shoulders, by the time the light arrives in your chest. Here, breathe out, and as you breathe out, see and feel the sphere of light expand suddenly, to encompass your entire body, and suffuse it with the power of the ground below.

Breathe in, and feel more power rising from below and filling your chest, and then, when you breathe out, feel it expand and fill your whole body, radiating out from your chest.

In your inner sight, you should see your body as though it were a brilliant, clear body of light, and the navel-center and your heart should seem like contrasting dark spots, whirling with motion. There should be a motion in your head, as well.

Finally, allow yourself to receive the subtle impressions that it will get from the powers of the Land swirling in your system.

At the point before you return the power to the Land and end this technique, you should also endeavor to stop thinking of your body as different from the ground that you are standing on, or thinking that your inner self is different from it. You should see yourself and the Land around you as one thing.

You should breathe out several times and lower your hands slowly back to your sides to allow the power that you raised to flow back down into the ground, but it never totally leaves you- it remains behind in traces, just as part of you goes back down into the ground with it. You have just forged a lasting connection with that place.

Never do this technique with anything other than respect and a sense of awe in your heart- because more than just power rises from the ground. The subtle force of the ground carries with it echoes of all powers, above and Underworldly, including the sleeping forms of archaic Gods, living spirits, the ancestors, and the dwellers in the inner reality of the Land. Tread softly on the Land you walk upon, because you tread upon the Gods! When you draw up the power into you, and become part of it, you draw the divine potentials locked within the Land below you into your consciousness and deeper awareness.

The traditional Pagan "spiritual current" is very earthy and simple. It is strongly focused around the reality which is at the heart of all things, metaphorically pictured as "below" everything; the eternally renewing and expressive "power" of the Underworld.

The great dark and hidden Mother of the craft, the feminine power that dwells below and in the Land (aside from Her existence as a divine being), represents the exchange that occurs between what we call "this side of life" and the source of life, the mysterious "other reality" that is such an essential part of this one; indeed, it is the sustenance and eternity of what we perceive as "this reality."

As I have said before, the Fate of all beings who live perceptually "on the Land" or "above ground," is one of merging. The living who have gone before, the ancestors- they have entered into full perceptual oneness with the eternal reality at the heart of all things. They have merged with the ground, the trees, and all that you see; the body of Nature is the body of both the living and the dead. Burial in the ground is only a profound symbol of a deeper reality.

These beings, these merged beings, become the souls of the ancestral dead, as well as the spiritual forces of Nature. Some are cyclically reborn into our perceptual state; others remain within all things, moving towards some other mysterious Fate.

The Great Ancestral Mother who stands behind and within the entire process of Fate and emergence and re-integration, is the great being who is the mother of all peoples and the key to the craft. The life that is exchanged is Her life; her gift is truth, though Her soul is change and transformation.

This is the heart and core of the Land-based mystical Art, and the Land-centered worldview. To learn to integrate ourselves into this transformative process or "merging" in new ways, and to gain Wisdom and insight, is the point of the Art and path of realization. This is a very earthy and simple way of approaching the Mysteries of life; there are no complex and foreign Gods and philosophies, no over-ceremonialism; just clean, organic approaches to the realities within, which have the "feel" of the quiet, dark ground and creaking trees, and silent stones.

The Old People have been laid beneath the earth, with stones raised above them, with staves and beakers at their heads and feet, and they act as merged guardians of more Wisdom in the Land than anyone could ever imagine. It is the Witch or mystic that must act as mediator for that Wisdom, which sleeps and lives within the sacred Land. Tread softly on the Land, for every stone, hill and tree is a doorway to the Gods and to living essences.

IV. The Widdershins Walk: The Left-Way Road or the Crooked Path, and the Doors in the Land

The "Left-Way Road" or the "Widdershins Walk" is the name given to a technique for gaining entry into the Otherworld. This technique is a means of inducing a "waking dream," or a lucid state of neither wakefulness nor total sleep; a "between state" in which outer and inner realities lose their perceptual boundaries, and in which the spiritual forces and living potencies of the Otherworlds can interact (and be interacted with) by the mindstream of the one who engages in the rite. This is a "journeying" or a "shimmering" technique which is very powerful.

The person who shared this technique with me only said that it was "very old;" I believe him, because its sheer simplicity and yet power is the same feeling that I have come to expect from the workings of the true "Old Persuasion."

Many have used this technique to gain entry into the Underworld, to interact with the powers there. Many have used this technique and the Underworldly contact it allowed them to have with the Horned Master to gain identification with their Puckril, or the Fetch-beast, the animal form borne by the spirit when it makes the first "ground level" contact with the mortal human.

True "instruction" in the craft comes from the potencies of the Underworld, and the unseen world. To identify with the Fetch-beast or Puckril is a vital and important step for all of the cunning because the Puckril, or the Familiar spirit, then acts as a guide and protector in the unseen realms of the mind and of the world, and can help guide the witch into further and deeper contacts, eventually leading up to the culminating marriage with the Fetch-mate, whom the Fetch-beast is the animal face of. Such an internal marriage is a transformation into a greater wholeness, and an initiation into new reaches of experience. It is, in fact, the culmination of the entire path of the Witch.

The basics of gaining the Puckril are simple; one must know how to use the Widdershins Walk to find access (through the Land) into the Underworld; they must meet the Horned One or the White King of the Under-wood; they must have made devotions and offerings to this goal for usually a long while beforehand; they must then make the descent and approach the Old One and ask to have their Familiar bestowed upon them. This "Left-Way Walk" technique is *the* passport or key into the realms of initiation, the means by which all five pattern-points of the "Witching Way" are actualized.

This requires the asker to have embraced, in their heart, a true Pagan worldview, and to have total devotion to the Horned Master and to the spirit of the Old Ways. There has to be a certain amount of willingness to accept this power, this new inner knowledge, and to accept a certain amount of danger and responsibility that will come with it- Fate can demand a nasty cost, even from those who seek deeper Wisdom or power. One must also be willing to continually contact and Housle with the Familiar, to keep its relationship strong, to keep this Otherworldly contact wedded strongly with "this" world.

Once a person knows the basic techniques of entering into the spectral reality at will, and can build positive, strong relationships with the Master, the Witchmother or Dark Matriarch, and the Fetches and shades of ancestors, and when they can gain identification with a Puckril, there is no end to what lore or power can be gained or found, and no limit to the Wisdom and transformation that can be won.

The true "initiation" into being a fully fledged Witch-man or woman is quite simply the realization and demonstration of the ability to interact, reasonably at will, with Otherworldly contacts, in such a way that personal transformations (or other transformations) can be produced. Further mastery of the craft leads to higher reaches, but it is not from human hands that such further grades come, but from the subtle reaches within, from the hands of the Hidden Ones, and the Grand Array, and the Old Ones themselves.

All that fellow men and women can do is teach the basics, orient one to the path and show them the door; the rest is up to the Witch and Fate.

"Initiation" will be a time when the experiences that the witch has had lead to a profound series of inner transformations that ripple out into all aspects of life. This series of experiences will have no true "ending."

The Widdershins Walk is an important technique, because it is a very central technique to those who wish to traffic with the netherworld, or to have contact with the endless reaches within themselves, and within the Land itself- both of which happen to be the *same place*. I consider the Widdershins Walk to be the heart of the craft, and of any mystical relationship with the Land, because it makes the inner reality of any Land accessible.

The Walk also makes the inner reality of any symbolic or oneiric Landscapes accessible; how the Widdershins Walk can be used to reach these things is simple, once a person understand the Walk itself.

Basically put, the Walk is a two-layered journey that can give access to even deeper perceptual layers of reality. It begins with you physically traveling to a place, a place of some traditional power or of some suspected overlap with the unseen world; great trees, stones, hills, mounds, churchyards, gravesites, mountains, forests, springs, vast fields, traditionally "haunted" plains or moors, ruins, marshes, hedges, wells, rivers, or what have you.

The site that you choose should have the depth and uncanny feel of an "overlap" point with the unseen world. Failing that, it should have a great and powerful wildness about it, or a great age. The ghost roads in the Land often connect these kinds of places, places as were all mentioned above. Trance work, working with local Land powers, and investigation all can lead to understanding how the inner Landscape overlaps with the outer.

When you have discovered a focus point, you have done the first part of this technique. The rest is easier.

Going a short distance from the focus point, you select a starting point. From the starting point, you make a walk- a circular or semi-circular walk, from your starting point, to the focus point, and back to the starting point, all in a big circular or semi-circular path. (To use the clock example, the starting point would be the 6, the focus point would be the 12, and you would keep going "around" to get back to the 6- a big counterclockwise circle walk.)

The walk shouldn't be over a mile at most, and not less than 50 or so feet. The focus point should be visible from the starting point.

When you make your first counterclockwise walk, you must select two features of the terrain or two features along the path to the focus point, which are called "markers," and commit every detail of them to memory. Then, you must study every detail of the focus point itself, and commit it to memory.

Finally, on your return path, you must select two more markers or interesting sights and commit them to memory as well. When you arrive back at the starting point, after this counterclockwise hike, you are ready to begin at any time. It is best to wait for twilight to perform this technique, after you have done this initial walk, but that is only a suggestion. This can be done at any time, day or night, though the wise know how some times can be easier to work upon and within, and should time matters accordingly.

When twilight comes (in this sample instance), you go to your starting point and achieve a good trance, light a Watchfire, perform a Housle or Red Meal to the Master himself or whatever Otherworldly power or contact you wish to act as your guide down the Widdershins Walk and into the unseen world or into the Land, and then you "Tread the Mill" counterclockwise around the fire. We will cover the Red Meal and the Watchfire in the "Ritual Book" section of this work- for now, it is enough to read on here.

"Treading the Mill" is a simple trance-strengthening technique where you walk counterclockwise around a fire or some other "point" that you fix your mind and eyes on- you have to walk with your shoulders facing straight ahead, and only your head turned to the left to gaze at the center of your "mill" or circular walk that is around the fire (or stone, or whatever you have chosen to be your treading attention point.)

If you have a stang and would rather use it to be your focus for treading, that is more than fine. Once you have trod counterclockwise enough and built up enough power and presence of your contact, and begin to feel the otherness coming, the feeling of being in "many places at once," or a strong sense of separation, you take to the ground, lie down, but (and this is difficult to describe), you "continue" to move, in a more subtle way- you simply allow the momentum of the mill treading to "carry you" onwards, in your inner eye, away from your prone body, and straight into the counterclockwise walk you took earlier, before you trod.

In your new state, you "recreate" the walk you took, in your mind. To help do this, all you have to do is "see" yourself doing the walk, and "see" the first marker you selected to remember, and come to it. Examine it again, in full detail, just like the first time you saw it, and then "walk" on to the next marker. These markers help your mind to put you "further away" along this Widdershins Walk you are making, this time on a deeper level within.

Once you have passed the second marker, you should be "approaching" the focus point- the focus point, of course, being the place that you wish to attempt to gain access "through" to the unseen worlds beyond. "See" and experience the focus point again, in all detail that you can recall, but this time, you are looking for something that wasn't there before- you are looking for a light.

Somewhere, either near the focus point, or distant from it, but still visible to you, you should see a ghostly light, which is the Otherworldly reflection of the worldly Watchfire that you created back at your starting point. As I said, it may be a distance away, or it may be very close.

The spiritual forces you invoked to guide you are the ones who place it where it needs to be; go towards it when you find it, even if it means going into an unclear, murky or dark region. If you can't seem to find it, it is a sign that your contacts have refused, or that this place cannot be used to "pass through" into the inner reality, perhaps because the guardians of the place won't allow it, or because the place naturally has no "door." Fate may simply be against you; try again later or in another place.

Let me again reiterate how important positive relationships with the guardians of various locations are, especially if you wish to undertake this kind of work. If the powers of the place don't want you working there, you will find it very difficult to lie comfortably, leaving your body exposed as you detach subtle layers of yourself to "leave" and deal with inner realities; you will probably feel menaced or unsafe as you try, or simply find that you can't finish the walk. Many other things can go wrong.

You should always do this technique in a place where you are on very good terms with the guardians, and use some protection for yourself at your starting point- a good compass round is always useful if you feel you need it, but the best protection is always the presence of your Puckril (if you have identified with it yet), a burning Watchfire, and your Otherworldly contacts.

At any rate, this example assumes that you do actually find the "other light" of your Watchfire; and that you go towards it. It can take many forms, but it is there to guide you. When you reach it, you must focus your other eyes on it, and spin, move, or tread around it counterclockwise, very quickly. Spin around it quickly, staying focused on it, until you find yourself hurled away from it, and let yourself just fly as a blur over the ground, until you naturally stop. When you get your bearings again, look about for the focus point, and go back towards it.

When you arrive "back" at the focus point (and you might never had to go far from it to find the other light in the first place), look around. You should see a door, a gate, a hole, or an opening, something that wasn't there before. That is your opening. That is what will give you access to the inner regions within and beyond. This technique reveals it. All that is left is to go through it.

What lies on the other side, far below or beyond, only you can know or experience- but please, never forget this- should you find a tunnel or a shaft downward, or some passage that seems to go on a long way, do *not* hurry to get to the end or the bottom. Patiently allow yourself to walk or sink down to the end, and do not start "imagining" that you have found the bottom or the end, or the "other side." You must calmly let the transition from the surface state you were at, to the deeper state symbolized by the passage or tunnel or shaft, happen at its own pace.

You will *know* when you are "doing it right"- because if you can control your impatience, you will literally *feel* a great, strong "otherness" or "deeper world" coming near you, or you will feel that you are getting "near" it. The Underworld sometimes feels like a great "deeper layer" far below this world, and when I say "far below," I mean very far. It may seem maddening, like you will never get there, or that it keeps getting further from you as you "deepen" towards it. But that will pass, and you will enter into the depth, if you are patient and persistent. Just go with the sinking flow.

Your mindstream is entering into the depths of reality, the place where all things come together, where all things exist at once; the indescribable fullness of the source-world. To the dead who have not Wisdom, the utter fullness of it seems like a void of emptiness, of suffocating extinction. To the wise, to the living voyager into the deep, the deep void is known as it is- a great fullness of All things. You will merge with it, for you *are* it- and you will share in the deep Wisdom of the land of the dead *as* a living being- two worlds come together. You are going to the hidden source of Wisdom, the place where Wisdom is found.

Thomas the Rhymer rode with the Queen of Elfhame for what seemed like 40 days and nights to him- and the transition to Otherworldly states of experience can seem like a gruelingly long process. Do *not* hurry it, or you will only delude yourself. The longer it seems to take, ironically, the better. It means that you are making a deep transition to the roots behind and beyond reality. Do not try to imagine what the Otherworlds or Underworld will look like; let what appears, appear. It can be anything, from any time or place, any terrain, or totally amazing things that you cannot describe or conceive of. It can be abstract, to formless, to dark, to anything. Most locations will be tied to the inner history of the Land, and its former inhabitants, but there is still more at work here. The guardians can be encountered at the doors, or in the passages, or anywhere in your inner sight once you have started this technique. Just let what is, be.

If you have identified with your Puckril, it can be called or encountered anywhere once you have gone through the "door" your technique revealed, or sometimes even before, once you have begun the walk on the inner level. Once you have passed through and entered into an experience of another realm, remember your manners, and your politeness with beings you meet- and remember to be truthful and honest at all times. One of the main reasons to have a Puckril with you is to protect you from hostile beings; if all else fails, leave. Unless you have come specifically to banish or destroy a hostile being, do not remain in a place or around a being that makes you feel threatened.

When you have found the thing or being you came to find or meet, when you have been guided to where you wanted to go, or when you are otherwise done, return the way you came, emerge from where you entered, and finish your walk- go to your third and fourth markers, in order, and get "back" to your starting point, where your body awaits, and when you see your Watchfire, or your prone form, merge again back into your head-body awareness knot and open your eyes.

At various times during this whole experience, depending on how good you are at this, and on the depth of your trance, you can feel as though you never left your starting point- that is, you can "see" the whole experience taking place, on one level, while still being aware of lying on the ground at your starting point on another level. That is fine; sometimes, the shimmering trance allows for a sensation of being in two places at once, or even many places at once. It is all very subtle, and it becomes stronger the more you work with it.

Lastly, I would like to mention that the Sabbats, or the hidden festivals of the year, are all traditional times to use the Widdershins Walk; there are even traditional places to do it, based on the Sabbat; hills for Candlemas and Roodmas, mounds and graves for All Hallows, and so forth. Bodies of water are also traditional places. Long-standing groups of practitioners have their own traditional locations that they have used for sometimes very long times, wherein they have permission and lasting relationships with the Land guardians, to operate and practice their craft. This technique is the "passageway" to the Sabbat- the true Sabbat, which is a spiritual experience, a gathering of many fetches into a timeless and spaceless location, marked by a certain "outward" time and location- the "sacred times" are when the "ways" open for the approach to the true Sabbat.

The current of witchery is based on the "transition" into the unseen, especially around the Sabbats, and the merging of the fetch with that Otherworldly celebration, which is an initiation in and of itself, each time. It is the direct time of experiencing the Veiled Queen and the Lord of the Craft, as well as the ancestral forces and the powers of others wise in the craft, who can extend their "truth bodies" into the timeless.

Symbolic Landscapes, or Landscapes and terrain that are described in folktales or faery tales, or even created in the imagination of the cunning

Witch can be "entered" using this technique as well- because all places and objects of imagination are part of awareness. A totally symbolic landscape can still give entry into the center of All.

If a person wished to use the Widdershins Walk technique to "enter" into a symbolic or oneiric Landscape, they would use this technique as explained above, except instead of choosing a focus point, they would simply make a counterclockwise walk in some lonely area, a relatively lengthy walk, and choose to remember in detail four markers spread out equidistantly along the path (skipping the "focus point" because this version of the technique does not use a physical world focus point, only a physical world starting point and four markers), and then, having committed this walk to memory, they would return home.

That evening, they would lie down in their home, in a comfortable dark place, close their eyes, and take the walk again, slowly and focused in their heads, going along this counterclockwise walk, arriving at each of the four markers in turn, and going back towards the starting point, but, instead of arriving back at the starting point, they would find themselves instead arriving at one of the places described in the tale or in the description of the terrain. The rest of the Landscape and the locations and beings and the like should be totally memorized from careful study of the story, and now can be interacted with, as a symbolic inner oneiric landscape, in this new relaxed, inner experience.

The point of this oneiric landscape is to *use its symbols to help access inner realities*. It is especially useful if one finds himself or herself forced to live in an urban area where rural and powerful natural locations are hard to come by or visit. On the oneiric level, one can always have haunted forests or ancient mounds nearby, to use as passage points.

A "hill" in the inner landscape, or a mound, or a well, which you can "approach" and "enter into" or "go down into," can serve as a strong symbol for the mind to attempt to "shimmer" or alter itself into a state where the deeper layers of reality can be reached. Of course, once you have "walked" through the landscape of a folktale and came to a "well" (or some other traditional interaction point) and gone "down" it (and please remember what I said above about not hurrying transitions), you are no longer operating on the oneiric landscape, you are making a transition into the deeper realities, into the "genuine experience" which only you can see or have, and there is no way to go on describing what you will see, for only you will see it.

This is how the Widdershins Walk technique is used in conjunction with any oneiric landscape that the cunning mind takes the time to create. It is beneficial for a working group to share a commonly created and decided upon inner landscape, for this strengthens the current that informs the oneiric landscape, and makes it a valuable tool for gaining Otherworldly passage.

The other use of the Widdershins Walk is the more common and traditional of the two- that of using it to gain access through actual places and through landscape features, into the Otherworlds. The "conjunction" technique where it is used to give access to inner, imaginal Landscapes, is useful, but not the full use or traditional use of the technique.

The Secret Tradition:
The Hidden Wisdom of the Old Ways

The Secret Tradition: The Hidden Wisdom of the Old Ways

As I mentioned in the introduction to this book, the Old Ways did not vanish; they turned inward and went to live inside the Land, and in the hearts and souls of men and women. When they re-emerged, they emerged in the folk-ballads and folklore of many parts of the world. By looking to the symbolism of these timeless expressions of folk-memory, we can discover much Wisdom. In this part of our book we will examine the symbolism of a few of the many ballads that help to point us on the way to Wisdom.

Understanding the symbolism and the Wisdom contained in these ballads and stories is crucial, because it gives us a grounding in authentic tradition, and a basis from which to articulate themes as important as morality, the sacredness of life, the importance of honesty, and Land-centered veneration. Without these things, the Old Ways would have no substance, nor we as people who claim to follow them. What so many "new age" religions are lacking is precisely that substance, grounded in the folk-soul of the ancestors.

The Cruel Mother
A Traditional Ballad

There was a lady lived near York
All alone and quite lonely
Courted was she by her father's clerk,
By the bonnie Greenwood side.

She leaned against the tall thorn tree
All alone and quite lonely
And two pretty babes were born to she,
By the bonnie Greenwood side.

She took a thin knife long and sharp
All alone and quite lonely
And pierced those babes through their hearts,
By the bonnie Greenwood side.

She dug a shallow grave by the Moon
All alone and quite lonely
And covered them over with earth and stones,
By the bonnie Greenwood side.

One day she was making for church
All alone and quite lonely
When she spied two pretty babes on a porch,
By the bonnie Greenwood side.

"Lovely babes, O babes if you were but mine
All alone and quite lonely
I'd drape you both in satin fine"
By the bonnie Greenwood side.

"O Mother, Mother when we were thine
All alone and quite lonely
You didn't treat us half so kind"
By the bonnie Greenwood side.

"Babes, O my babes, can you foresee
All alone and quite lonely
What my future will hold for me?"
By the bonnie Greenwood side.

"You shall be for seven years a fish in the flood
All alone and quite lonely
And for seven years fly as a bird in the wood,
By the bonnie Greenwood side.

"You shall be for seven years the tongue of a bell
All alone and quite lonely
And seven years more a porter in Hell"
By the bonnie Greenwood side.

"O, I welcome the Fate of a bird in the wood
All alone and quite lonely
And welcome that I be a fish in the flood,
By the bonnie Greenwood side.

"And I welcome the Fate of a tongue of a bell
All alone and quite lonely
But the good Christ deliver me from Hell"
By the bonnie Greenwood side.

The "Ballad of the Cruel Mother" presents modern Pagans with a powerful treasure-horde of Wisdom. The Wisdom hidden here is the key to the central moral theme of human life: the sacredness of life and the dark Fate that awaits those who destroy it for wrong reasons. All life, all things, are connected, so what happens anywhere in the web of reality affects everything else.

In this ancient tale, we are presented with a mother who murders her children, after giving birth to them leaning against a thorn tree. We are not told why she felt the need to commit this act, but we are left to assume that her father wouldn't have been too happy to find out she had been engaging in illicit intimacy with one of his employees.

The thorn tree, in folklore, was a traditional "gateway" tree to the Underworld. It was a symbol not only of sacrifice, but of a gate or a liminal place, whereby the power of the Underworld emerges into this one, and the power of this world returns.

For a place of birthing, it takes on a sinister tone. A woman's womb and the process of birth itself creates a certain "liminality" as well, because the power of the womb, and the process of birth, just like death, is an interaction point and an interaction event, a flow between two worlds, the seen and the unseen, and the inner and outer.

The presence of the thorn tree, however indicates (normally) that the power or the person in this world is going into the Underworld or into the unseen- it is a tree of entrance to the land of the dead, and initiatory death. The thorn has dark connotations for this very reason. In Thomas the Rhymer's ballad, he begins under the Eildon Thorn, a traditional "gateway place" where he meets the Queen of Elfhame.

Giving birth leaning against the thorn is a grim sign, and rightly so, because the children are murdered and buried near it, before they can take very many mortal breaths.

What the mother has done is disrupt the flow of life from one world to another. When a human being engages in this sort of disruption, they do not emerge from it untouched; they make themselves forever a part of the disruption, and become bound to the consequences that must follow it.

In the mother's case, she has disrupted life flowing between this world and the other, and now, her own Fate is entangled with the disrupted flow; her own Fate-threads are entangled with those of the children she killed. She buries the bodies of the children; they return to merge with the ground and the Underworld, and the mother leaves, thinking the deed is finished and done, and not imagining that it will come back to haunt her, quite literally.

Life is precious, and the web of power- all interconnected and flowing from one world to the next one transformation to the next- is vast and mysterious. Through her actions, the mother has made herself a part of a chain of cause and effect that will be the worse for her, as she discovers on her way to church one morning.

She sees two lovely children watching her, and does not recognize them as her children- until she speaks to them, and they reveal that they are her children; they tell her that they were once hers, and naturally, they know of her cruel treatment to them. So does the mother; it is impossible to truly lie to oneself for very long. Her heart recognizes these phantoms, and she fearfully asks them what will become of her- she seems to know that her children have the power to reveal her Fate to her. There is a good reason why she should think so.

Her children are no longer her children. They have become "elfin grey" or Pale People- they have become Feeorin; they have passed through death and merged with the Land itself, and they have gone beyond their human limitations and become an aspect of the Other reality.

When her children reappear to her, they are no longer merely ghosts of children, though they may also be seen as that- they are "faces of Fate," for they have merged with the dark and fatal power of the adamantine and unforgiving Underworld- they embody what is and what must be, outside of human illusions and sentimentality.

The justice of the Underworld or the Otherworld cares nothing at all for human complaints of "unfairness" or other notions based on a limited view of Truth and Wisdom. This is why Fate and Justice, as Underworldly powers, have been surrounded by an aura of fear among humans since time immemorial.

Some ancient peoples in Northern Europe believed that the dead became very wise, and this is because the dead have to enter into the Truth. The pale children are now omnisciently knowledgeable about the chain of Fate- further proving that they are no longer human as we know "human"- and they are able to tell their mother what awaits her, beyond this life.

Some people say that the cruel mother was trying to spare her children from a life where they would be unwanted or unloved- but this is a very flawed perception, and it is part of an apologetic line of modern thinking that is used to justify the killing or abandonment of many children today. All people deserve a chance to mature and find love and acceptance, even if that love and acceptance will be rare in their formative years.

Luckily for many of us, love and acceptance can be found after we grow up and take control of our own lives, and for many, sad though it is to say, the only true love and acceptance they ever find is after they have become adults. It is not for humans to decide that other humans shouldn't have a chance at the fullness of a life, just because the beginning of their lives, or the first 16-18 years, will be hard.

The children in this tale know the whole situation from the perspective of Truth; they know exactly why their mother did what she did, and the people who think that the cruel mother was doing her children a favor might take notice that they aren't appearing to thank her. They- and Fate- are quite stern and brutally honest with the mother. The phantom children are acting as agents of Fate's message, faces of Fate; and She/they say, "A dark Fate awaits you for your cruel and unjustified disruption of life."

It's not the Great Dark Mother (who is sometimes called Old Fate) as a personal being that will punish the mother who murdered; the Old Ways do not teach that the Gods function in such a manner. It is Fate in Her most impersonal form, an impersonal and unavoidable series of subtle and universal reactions to her actions, which will guide and force the mother to her transformations. It is universal consequence. There are spirits that "lay the fetters" of Fate upon the mortal world and its beings, and spirits who "name" Fate, or who embody it, and some spirits who embody the torment of conscience- but the pure consequences of her actions (like ours) are hers and hers alone.

The mother will have to undergo transformations after she dies- four different transformations, each for a period of seven years- a highly symbolic number, which doesn't necessarily mean a literal seven years; as we will see when we discuss the "Ballad of Tam Lin," "seven years" can refer to an entire age of the world- or, in the perceptual difference between the seen and the unseen world, it can represent seven literal years to human beings, but ages in the Otherworld.

The mother will have to undergo a series of shape-changes or transformations, which are all metaphors for the post-mortem Fate of her soul. Shape-changing and transformation are both metaphors for death, whether the controlled death of the mystic or the Witch in ritual circumstance, or the final death of a person, where the soul has to follow its "rebirth cycle," through many worlds and forms, as it seeks for Wisdom, peace, and wholeness. The driving force of the cycle is Fate, and the great dark blanket of ignorance is threaded throughout, there for the overcoming as the soul moves through pain and mistake, love and insight.

The mother will have to enter, after death and the loss of her mortal identity, into many conditions bonded to each of the three realms of nature- a bird in the sky, a fish in a river, and even an earth or mineral transformation, as the metal tongue of a bell- which would then be followed by the penultimate transformation- and the only transformation that the presumably Christian mother fears- "a porter in hell."

A porter is a gatekeeper or a doorkeeper, and the idea that she should have to be a gatekeeper in Hell, or the Underworld, is very significant. She has a consequential responsibility to the life-forces she has diverted, and thus, she has to become a factor that is directly involved in "righting" that flow, or restoring it. No one is in a better position to alter and control the flows of life-force into and out of the Underworld, than the person who controls the portal, or the porter.

So, at some point, she will have to be consigned to the Underworld and be directly responsible for opening the door by which life emerges from the unseen, and presumably, being a part of the chain of Fate that leads to the correcting of what she wronged.

Interestingly, to use a modern example, 19 very ignorant and wicked men flew airplanes into the World Trade Center on September 11, 2001, and killed thousands of people. Their deeds must cause them to become involved in a practically neverending chain of Fate, a chain that includes not only the oblivion of their own personalities and memories, but a nonstop and unconsciously oppressive cycle of rebirths in many different forms- many no doubt painful or hopelessly sunk in ignorance- all culminating at some point in these men's strands of Fate assuming whatever forms and becoming involved in whatever powers are necessary to pay their great debt.

The mother's debt was said to require four periods of transformations at seven years each- which, as I mentioned before, can be four ages of time. Her crime was to murder two infants- how much more complicated the twisted strands of Fate for the men that murder thousands and thousands? Transformations in the Otherworld and between the Otherworld and this world deal with a timeless Mystery, so time is really irrelevant; however, the symbolic naming of time is still important.

It is a good time to consider the notion of preserving life and taking it, and what it can mean to each of us. Life is the highest cause, the most precious force and substance, and we know, instinctively, that we should not take it without good reasons. But what would qualify as a "good reason," and why should that "good reason" exempt us from having to become involved in the disruption of the power of life, and the consequences of it, as the cruel mother had to be involved?

The question becomes whether or not the act of taking life- of disrupting the natural transfer of life between this world and the next- is either consequence free, or free of negative consequences.

The answer is this: disrupting the flow of life, the transfer of power between this world and the next, is never without consequence. It is always an action that carries weight, and it leads to further involvement with the life force that was diverted, and the chain of Fate.

However, negative consequences can be avoided, depending on the nature of the act, and in some cases, the act of diverting life can be a part of the chain that leads to illumination. This is certainly not the case in the cruel mother, for a very simple reason- she does not kill to preserve life; she kills for selfish reasons.

It is as though Fate has made killing for the preservation of life an act that does not bear a penalty, because the life that is diverted is compensated by the life preserved. If you were to kill a deer to feed yourself and your family, the deer's life actually lives on inside you, and gives you the power to live by its sacrifice. There is no debt to life, for life continues on in you, if you realize this and honor the sacrifice with conscious awareness.

If you disrupt life to save the life of another, then in the life that is saved, the diverted life is compensated. Again, the element of preservation of life acts as a balance to the debt of diverting life.

Gold has to answer gold, and silver, silver. If a life is disrupted with no life to compensate- such as in the case of killing for the sake of greed, selfishness or convenience- then it is wrong.

When the mother killed her children, no life was preserved or saved; their life-power was disrupted and all that was there to compensate it was the selfishness of the mother; an empty, egocentric desire to not be inconvenienced or embarrassed by her children outside of wedlock. This is not enough to pay the debt of life. Thus, the mother's action was imbalanced and truly "wrong," and the price she is Fated to pay is just. It is not only just, but needful to maintain the integrity of the system of force and Fate.

This same understanding can be extended to the taking of your own life- the question becomes a matter of what compensates for the disrupting of your own life.

The mother hopes, in her typical Christian way, that "Christ" will save her from Hell- but Fate is more powerful than any God, and Fate doesn't let people off with mere apologies. People can be sorry, but the scales also have to be balanced, debts to life and Fate have to be paid. When we are dealing with Fate in this manner, we are dealing with it in a very mechanical and impersonal manner, not unlike gravity. If you jump off of a building, and fall fifty feet, no matter how much you regret jumping as you fall, you still have to hit the ground and probably get hurt.

Christ cannot deliver the mother from the consequences of her actions, though perhaps Wisdom can help deliver the mother from having to suffer as she completes the circle of her soul and Fate. In fact, Wisdom is the only thing that can help her, as she stares into a future that practically all humans stare into- a future of death and cyclic rebirth, dominated by the unconscious processes and irresistible commands or fetters of Hard Fate. Those who seek clarity and insight, those who seek Wisdom, will be the only ones who manage to transform Hard Fate, and gain a "second destiny" based on clarity and Truth.

This ballad begs us all to consider the cost of disrupting life, and not to do it, except in circumstances where the debt can be paid to balanced ends. It reminds us of the interconnected nature of all things, and forms the basis for the true "natural morality" which is the heart of the morality of the Old Ways.

Eyes of Wood, Heart of Stone: The Hidden Metaphysics in the Ballad of Tam Lin

Tam Lin
A Traditional Ballad

"O I forbid you, maidens all,"
That wear gold in your hair,
To come or go by Carterhaugh
For young Tam Lin dwells there."

"There's none that goes by Carterhaugh
But they leave him a wad,
Either their rings or green mantles,
Or else their maidenhead."

Janet has kilted her green mantle
Up above her knee,
And she has braided her yellow hair
A little above her brow,
And she's away to Carterhaugh
As fast as she can go.

When she came to haunted Carterhaugh
Tam Lin was at the well,
And there was found his white steed standing,
But away and unseen was he.

She had no sooner pulled a double rose,
A rose but only two,
Up then started young Tam Lin,
Saying, "Lady, pull you no more!"

"Why pull you the rose, Janet,
And why breaks you the wand?
And why do you come to Carterhaugh
Without my command?"

"Carterhaugh, it is my own,
My father gave it me;
I'll come and go by Carterhaugh,
And ask no leave of thee."

***** *****

Janet has kilted her green mantle,
A little above her knee,
And she has braided her yellow hair
A little above her brow,
And she's away to Carterhaugh
As fast as she can go.

Four and twenty ladies fair
Were playing at the chess,
And out then came the fair Janet,
As pale as any glass.

Out then spoke her father dear,
And he spoke meek and mild;
"Alas, my sweet Janet," says he,
I think you go with child."

"If I go with child, dear father,
Myself must bear the blame;
There's not a lord about your hall
Shall give my child his name."

"For my love is no earthly knight,
Aye, he's an elfin grey,
I would not give my one true-love
For any lord here today."

"The steed that my true-love rides on
Is lighter than the wind;
With silver he is shod before,
With burning gold behind."

Janet has kilted her green mantle,
A little above her knee,
And she has braided her yellow hair
A little above her brow,
And she's away to Carterhaugh
As fast as she can go.

***** *****

When she came to haunted Carterhaugh,
Tam Lin was at the well,
And there she found his lone pale steed,
But away and unseen was he.

She had not pulled a double rose,
A rose but only two,
Till up then started young Tam Lin,
Saying, "Lady, pull you no more!"

"Why pulls you the rose, Janet,
Among the groves so dark and green
And all to kill the bonnie babe,
That we got us between?"

"Oh tell me, tell me, Tam Lin" she says,
Oh you must tell to me,
If ever you were a mortal knight,
Or mortal hall did see."

"Oh I was once a mortal knight
Till, hunting, from my horse I fell,
The Queen of Faerie she caught me here,
In yon green hill I came to dwell."

"And pleasant is the faerie Land,
But, an eerie tale to tell,
Aye, at the end of every seven years
They pay a tithe to hell;
And I am so fair and full of flesh,
I fear it may be myself."
"But this night is Hallowe'en, my Lady,

The morn is Hallowday;
Then win me, win me, if you will,
For well I want that you may."

"Just at the mirk and midnight hour,
The faerie folk will ride,
And they that would their true-love win,
At Miles Cross must they hide."

"But how shall I know you, Tam Lin,
Or how my true-love know,
Among so many Faery knights
The like which I never saw?"

"Oh first let pass the black, lady,
And then let pass the brown,
But run you up to the milk-white steed,
And pull the rider down."

"For I'll ride on the milk-white steed,
A gold star in my crown;
For I was a brave earthly knight
So they give me that renown."

"They'll turn me in your arms, lady,
Into a snake or sharp adder,
But hold me fast and fear me not,
For I am your child's father."

"They'll turn me to a bear so grim,
And then a lion bold,
But hold me fast and fear me not,
As ye shall love your child."

"Again they'll turn me in your arms
Into red hot melting iron,
But hold me and cast me in yon well,
I'll do to you no harm."
"And then I'll be your one true-love
I'll turn into a naked knight;

Then cover me with your warm green mantle,
And cover me out of sight."

***** *****

Gloomy, gloomy was the night,
And eerie was the road,
As Janet in her dark green mantle
To Miles Cross she did go.

About the middle of the night
She heard the bridles ring;
This lady was as glad for that
As for any earthly thing.

First she let the black horse pass,
And then she let the brown,
But she ran up to the milk-white steed
And pulled the rider down.

She pulled him free from his white steed,
And seized the bridle fair,
And up there rose an eldritch cry,
"True Tam Lin, he's away!"

They turned him, he changed in her arms
Like to a hissing snake;
She held him fast, feared him not
That he would be her mate.

They turned him to a sooty bear
Then a snapping lion wild;
She held him fast, feared him not
For he was father to her child.

And then they turned him in her arms,
Into iron hot with red fire;
She held him fast, feared him not
This was her heart's desire.

At last they changed him in her arms
Into molten lead;
She thrust him into deep well water
She cast him in with speed.

So well she minded what he did say,
That young Tam Lin she won;
And covered him with her warm green mantle,
Warm as the coming spring sun.

Out then spoke the Faerie Queen,
And an angry wight was she;
"Shame betide her ill-shaped face,
And an ill death may Janet die,
For she's taken away the bonniest knight

In all my company."
"But had I seen, Tam Lin," she said,
What now this night I see,
I would have taken out your two grey eyes,
And put in two made from a tree."

"And had this I known, Tam Lin," she said,
Before we came from elfin home,
I would have plucked out thy heart of flesh
And given you a heart of stone."

The traditional "Ballad of Tam Lin" is one of the most important and symbolically deep ballads of the entire folk tradition. In it, we are treated to the remnants of authentic British Isles Pagan afterlife beliefs as well as native notions of rebirth into a new human life from the Underworld, through the agency of a mother's womb.

The ballad also details the Faery rade, that is, the supernatural intrusion of the inhabitants of Faery Land or the unseen world as they "rade" or ride through the world of humans on Hallows Eve- a potent symbol of the immediate interactions between this world and the other.

In this ballad, which is a inexhaustible well of mystical insights and symbolism, Tam Lin, a former human inhabitant of our world, was killed long ago in what seems at first to be a horse riding accident, but where he fell was "sacred ground" to the Faeries or the old Powers of the Land, and their Queen, the Queen of Elfhame or Elfland.

Tam Lin's death on this hallowed stretch of ground results in him being taken by the Queen Herself into a "green hill," a traditional gate into the Underworld, and Tam Lin becomes Her lover. He also becomes a sort of prisoner in the unseen world, for the "Elfland" he inhabits is not the usual land of the dead, but a special realm, kept and overseen by the Queen Herself, where the inhabitants live in a "halfway state" somewhere between this world and the deep Underworld.

To maintain their seemingly immortal half-state, every seven years, they must "pay a tithe to hell," or a "fine" to hell, which means they must give up one of their number to the deeper Underworld, where that person is given forever into the dark Mystery beyond, given up to the powers of dissolution and rebirth.

Some versions of this ballad mention the fact that Tam Lin did not fall from his horse onto just any ground, but onto 'holy ground." This fall from a horse, in what we are led to believe was an accident, may in fact be a memory of a sacrificial ritual in which he, representing the sacred king, was killed on a holy site- the horse was an ancient symbol of both kingship, as well as the Land-Goddess Herself, whom the king was wed to in a sacred union, and to whom he had to return in a periodic sacrifice- in some places it is said every seven years! Thus, the "tithe to hell" of those in Tam Lin's Faery realm is significant.

Also, Tam Lin's appearance as a guardian of a plot of land in the Ballad suggests that he was sacrificed to become a fixed land guardian of a sacred place- or that he simply was killed in an accident and became a land guardian through the mysterious whims of Fate. He appears to Janet when she disrupts the flow and exchange of power in Carterhaugh, by "pulling and breaking" roses that grow there, forcing Tam Lin to manifest.

The fact that only his horse appears at the locus of his "merging," to represent his unseen presence, is telling- the horse is not only the symbol of the hippomorphic Land-Goddess, but also of Tam Lin and his sacrifice. It calls to mind the horse mated with by the Irish kings in Pagan times at the bestowal of their sovereignty, and the horse ridden by the man undergoing sacrificial death by stabbing, hanging, and drowning. What is also significant, as Katherine Briggs has pointed out, is the hint of ritual cannibalism found in Tam Lin, perhaps practiced by the natives of the British Isles, that is mentioned in the ballad. When Tam Lin tells his fears about the "seven year tithe to hell" to his lover, he mentions that he is afraid that he will be the next sacrifice to hell- for he, according to his own description, is "So fair and full of flesh."

The cults of the Sacred Kings in Ireland and doubtless other parts of the British Isles practiced a form of ritual cannibalism, in which the parts of the king's body were consumed by the tribe or gathering (certainly in Scotland, where quaint folk festival customs up to the last century still contain blatant symbolic references to the "game of chance" random human sacrifice of one unlucky attendee). Tam Lin fears that he is being maintained in his strange post-mortem state, because he is intended to be the next sacrifice to the powers of the Underworld, so that the Faery realm he is trapped in can be maintained free of dissolution.

Tam Lin desires to escape and to live again as a human- and through the agency of his human lover, Janet, who symbolizes not only the transformative power of love, as well as the necessary feminine other half of his whole being, a harmony and union with whom is required to do true "magic." He manages to do this.

As a mortal woman, Janet is one half of the magical relationship, with Tam Lin representing the "Otherworldly" half, as well as the masculine- a symbolic marriage of the Fetch-husband with human wife, through which a child is conceived- a "virgin birth," truly- a child of an Otherworldly father, who in fact will be Tam Lin reborn.

But it is Love which is the secret key force here, allowing for the necessary bravery to win this soul-prize from the Otherworld, as well as the devotion to overcome the fear and power of the illusions of the Faery folk, who fiercely attempt to stop Tam Lin's escape.

But when he escapes into a human rebirth, at the end of the ballad, the enraged Queen of Elfhame shows Her darker face; She savagely curses

Janet and makes dire threats to Tam Lin. The Queen, angered at the loss of Her lover, angry also at the possible loss of a seven year sacrifice, but mostly angry at the fact that Tam Lin circumvented Her authority as the ultimate arbiter of death and rebirth, tells Tam Lin (who is, for a time, safely out of her reach) that:

> "But had I seen, Tam Lin," she said,
> What now this night I see,
> I would have taken out your two grey eyes,
> And put in two made from a tree.

> "And had this I known, Tam Lin," she said,
> Before we came from elfin home,
> I would have plucked out thy heart of flesh
> And given you a heart of stone."

Eyes of Wood

We will discuss the heart of stone soon; first, we have to concentrate on the concept of "eyes from a tree" or the "eyes of wood."

RJ Stewart makes mention in his excellent book "The Underworld Initiation" that the eyes of wood reference refers to a mode of perception that Tam Lin has, which the Faery Queen wishes She could deny him. Now that Tam Lin has been saved directly from the Underworld, to return to this world with his memories and experiences of that place intact (unlike most rebirths from the Underworld, where memories of that place, and the things discovered there, are all lost to time and forgetfulness), he will have the power of the "staring eyes" or "second sight"- he will be able to see both this world and the Otherworld.

Stewart believes that the Queen would not desire this for Tam Lin, and even though Stewart does not go into detail explaining why, I believe there is a very good reason. Beings from the Otherworld are not allowed to return to this one once they have experienced the sights, sounds, and life of the Otherworld- this is why eating food or drinking the wines of the Otherworld traps a person there forever.

Reference this to the story of Persephone in Greek mythology who was permanently bound to the Underworld because she ate the food of the Underworld- and recall Thomas the Rhymer, who was prohibited from ever speaking or asking a question of any being in the Underworld, lest he be forced to stay forever.

The Underworld contains some secrets and powers that are not meant for the living. In mythology, all of the great shamanic heroes who journey to the Underworld or the realms of the Gods, and bring back important items or information for mankind, always do it against the will of the Gods- and often in mortal danger! Taliesin gained the supreme poetic insight from the Underworld, only to have the Queen of the Underworld, Cerridwen, try to kill him before he could escape with it. Prometheus was likewise tortured and penalized terribly for stealing the fire of the Gods for the use of humans- who were never intended to have it.

The gifts and powers of the Otherworld are things that belong to the Gods, to the unseen powers, and not to man. They are dangerous in the hands of man- even the biblical story presents Adam and Eve as stealing forbidden knowledge through sin, and being penalized terribly for it. God never intended for them to have the particular and deep knowledge reserved for the divine- and even God (or the Elohim), in anger after Adam eats the forbidden fruit which endows him with the forbidden knowledge, exclaims, "Now man has become like us; now he knows good and evil."

Adam, who represents mankind, steals a dangerous and unintended gift that day- the gift of the knowledge of Good and Evil, and the world plunges into suffering, because when humans get their hands on Godly power, suffering is an inevitability, because man's nature is no longer naturally held in balance, and man lacks the Wisdom, as a whole, to wield the powers of the Gods. Good humans will use these powers for good, but greed and anger and pride will cause other humans to despoil the world and hurt others, and so does it stand. Some Godly gifts are withheld by the Gods for a reason.

Tam Lin has knowledge that no mortal is intended to have- when he was dead, and in Elfland, he was "safe" to have and experience his condition. But he was never intended to go back to a human condition with this knowledge intact- the living are not meant to know what Tam Lin knows, and he is not meant to be among the living with the knowledge and perception of one dead!

Like many other mystics from mythology, Tam Lin will live as a wise person, a seer, with forbidden power stolen and tricked out of the Underworld or the land of the gods. The motif of humans tricking Gods or stealing power is actually not an uncommon one in mythology, and makes quite an interesting statement about what the ancients thought about the true abilities of man!

The Queen is telling Tam Lin that She would have stripped his eyes away, which is actually another way of saying that She would have killed him Herself if She had known of his escape plan- because the eyes of wood are another way of referring to the eyes of a dead person; fixed, lifeless eyes that have no animation.

Of course, traditionally, the concept of "fixed staring eyes" is *also* a symbol of second sight- eyes that see past this world into another.

The key to understanding the paradox is to realize that Tam Lin, before his escape back into the human realm, is a part of the spirit world- and to have wooden eyes as a spirit means the opposite of what it means here. For a human, to lose eyes and gain new "hollow" or "staring" ones is a way of saying that the human gained second sight, or even a spiritual form of awakening.

For a spirit who already *has* second sight (which all spirits do; they have a totally different mode of perception from us) to have his eyes plucked out is another way of saying that he loses this special sight.

But there is one more point that has to be made- an old saying goes that "the eyes are the windows of the spirit"- and this is important. (Recall that people who think of soul and spirit as the same thing sometimes say "the eyes are the windows of the soul," but in more traditional and other occult understandings, spirit and soul are not the same, and in the case of this saying, spirit is the appropriate use.) The spirit is the basis for the "awareness" in each being, the "basic experience point" of a being, so the eyes, as the chief awareness organ in the human, are symbols of the deeper reality that allows a human to have a basis of perception- the primordial mind/perception, or the spirit. By plucking out Tam Lin's eyes, She would have been carrying out that sacrifice to hell that Tam

Lin feared; She would have been giving up his being to the powers of dissolution and rebirth.

Sacrificing one's eyes to gain a new perception, a spiritual perception, is an old motif which has a precedent in Germanic Paganism- Woden tears out one of His eyes so that He can gain second sight. That same legend, which is no doubt based on shamanic ritual realities among the early Germanic peoples, implies something that modern Pagans often forget-you don't gain anything without danger, pain, and sacrifice.

The Queen of Elfhame, the Queen of Faery or the Underworld, is shown in the ballad to be pretty far from the "loving warm and fuzzy mother Goddess" of modern day neo-Paganism. She is not only unwilling to allow one of Her lovers to have second sight, but She is more than willing to curse his true love and destroy him before he escapes with it. New-agers and other neo-Pagan Goddess worshippers should carefully consider this.

The implications of the ballad are simple- it is easier for a living person, through sacrifice, to gain things from the Otherworld, than it is for those who are absorbed into the Otherworld to escape with what they have. Either way, the Otherworld resists people who attempt to take its powers for their own; one has to prove themselves worthy of it, often through bravery and cunning.

The Otherworld, far from being a "Pagan heaven" of pink cotton-candy peace full of tinsel-winged fairies, is a place of restriction and Fate- and while Tam Lin's world is also described as a beautiful, magical realm of wonder, where he is even a lover to the Queen of Faery Herself, remember- every seven years, someone was being sacrificed to the darkness below to keep it that way- and Tam Lin was probably going to be next.

In other words, even the happy afterlives of the traditional Pagan religions probably weren't thought to last forever; the greater cycle of life, death, and rebirth continued on for everyone, eventually, even if they found a place of rest and happiness for a while.

Only those rare beings who had attained the supreme Truth or Wisdom seem to have escaped the necessity that bound beings to these hard realities. This is not to make the Otherworld seem only a dark or bad place for the dead; far from it- it is full of many wonders and joys; but we must never forget about the "other" realities of this place.

A Heart of Stone

As we discussed in great detail above, Tam Lin escaped from his imprisonment in Elfland or the Land of Faery chiefly through the power of Love- the love that was shared between him and his human lover Janet.

Tam Lin's escape, his transition between worlds, happened through Janet- through her mind and body, and it is through her body and womb that Tam Lin returns, naked to this world, symbolically as a man pulled up from a well by Janet and wrapped in a green cloth, but literally as a newborn babe, pulled out of the well of a woman's womb and birth canal, and wrapped in swaddling cloth. This babe will have all of Tam Lin's memories, as well as second sight, for he escaped the Underworld with these things before they could be stripped from him by the natural powers of dissolution in the deepest Underworld.

The Queen of the Dead or the Queen of Elfland is furious that Tam Lin has escaped, and as a two-part curse, She tells him that if She had known of his escape intentions, She would have plucked out his heart and replaced it with a heart of stone- which is clear in one meaning, but not so clear in another.

On the most direct level, it's quite simple- without his heart, the traditional seat of love and emotions, he never could have had the shared love with Janet that saved him. His magical, transformative escape never would have worked, for it was fueled by the sheer power of Love- and that same love is what allowed Janet to resist the powerful illusions and painful spells cast at Tam Lin, which were affecting her as well, through him, but which she needed to resist to save him.

Janet herself cannot be harmed or even seen by the Faeries, because she is protected by her love for Tam Lin- and not even the power of the Underworld seems able to overcome a Love this true- a unique lesson for modern Pagans and people who doubt the existence of love, or the power of the same.

But aside from robbing him of his ability to love, "plucking out the heart" also refers to something else- just as plucking out the eyes was a metaphor for destroying the Soul, or giving it up to dissolution and rebirth in the Underworld, the heart, as the warm, vital pump of the body's fiery living essence in the blood, and the seat of emotions, is a symbol of the vital soul- and when a being is going to be reborn, they must first face the powers of dissolution in the Underworld, wherein the soul is dissolved and re-shaped anew, minus the memories of the previous life, and what remains within the dead person of the immortal spirit (much, but not all of which flees at death) is finally fully liberated to move on to new forms.

It is again, another way of the Queen of Elfland to tell Tam Lin that had She known of his plot, She would have destroyed him, rather than let him escape. Some may wonder at how the Queen of the Underworld, who represents the force of Fate itself, could not know about Tam Lin's plot- and the answer is not easy; RJ Stewart has mentioned one explanation, that She appears in two forms in many ballads- as a Goddess-type individual being, and as the representation of the impersonal force of Fate.

In the Ballad of Tam Lin, She can be seen as a personal being, a spirit who simply doesn't have to have access to the full workings of Fate, or She can be seen as representing the impersonal force of life, death, and rebirth- and if this is the case, her anger is just a poetic way of Nature itself rebelling against the aberration of Tam Lin's magical rite whereby he violates nature's flow- but there are two other explanations that are more enlightening for us.

One is that the Queen allowed him to escape because She herself is fulfilling a Fate She created; She decided beforehand that She would not know, and then be angry about his escape, and the need for his escape was for the good of mankind- death and the Mysteries of death are hard things for most poor humans to deal with, and every now and then, at least one person has to go against the flow, to give hope to mankind that death is not greater than life.

But there is another explanation- that Love is just that powerful- that True Love (itself born of Fate) can even *seemingly* contradict Fate. Such a thing would be a statement that mystics or magically active people should pay close attention to! If the "Ballad of Tam Lin" tells us anything, it's never to stop loving our dead friends and relatives- but more than that- Love can and will save you from the darkest of Fates. A heart of stone is not a good thing, for anyone.

The Seven Year Tithe to Hell

The concept of seven and a waiting period of "seven years" is relatively common in traditional lore- as common as the "year and a day" waiting period or testing period for admission into occult Mysteries.

Most often, we hear of sacred kings who must be subjected to sacrifice every seven years, for the fertility of the Land or the good of his people- though as it happens, sometimes proxy kings or substitutes can die in his place, winning him seven more years. In the "Ballad of Tam Lin," we see that seven years is the fixed period that the inhabitants of Elfland have to wait between making a "fine" or a "tithe" to hell, or sacrificing a member of their world to the deeper forces of reality, to continue their idyllic existence.

There seems to be a deeper metaphysic operating here- the number seven is not arbitrary; it seems to be a reflection of a deeper principle tied into death and regeneration. In ancient Greece, it was a number sacred to Apollo- an important God of occult Mysteries with deep ties to the British Isles. Apollo was the God who gave purification from the taint of miasma or ritual impurity, and washing or repeating actions seven times seems to have invoked His purifying power. Insofar as purification is a symbolic "death" from one state to another, a regeneration, there is an overlap to be seen there. Pythagoras believed that the number seven had great esoteric power and meaning, as well- not surprising, as he was a devotee to Apollo.

But in the British Isles native tradition, seven years seems to be the number of years that people who are staying in Faery Land or in the Underworld have to stay, before they leave to return to this world, with the knowledge won from that place. When they re-emerge, they are "coated in green" or dressed in green (Tam Lin is likewise wrapped in a green mantle at his escape.)- showing that they have merged with the Mystery of the Land itself, and now speak on its behalf.

In many ballads, seven years is mentioned as the time that a person will have to stay in the Underworld or the Otherworld, or in some condition before they can change to another- in the "Ballad of the Cruel Mother," for instance, she will have to undergo shape changes for seven years each, before she does her final seven years in Hell itself.

Seven years seems to be an Otherworld "standard measure" of time, which represents an entire lifetime. To us, in serial time, it seems to be seven years as we know them, but to the inhabitants of the Otherworld, who do not experience "time" as we do, it is perhaps a lifetime, or the time it takes for a "complete Otherworldly cycle" to pass, which to the inhabitants of the Otherworld, may be an "eternity" or an entire age or era. The paradox is that it's still seven years to us, and perhaps to them, simultaneously alongside its seeming eternity.

There are seven planets, representing the seven archetypal powers of the chief Gods of the Pagan world; seven stars in the heavenly Wain, seven days in a week, seven "chakras" or power centers in the body according to Indian lore, "seven deadly sins," "seven cardinal virtues," "seven sisters" appear in many ballads, "Seven Whistlers," and the concept of seven makes many other appearances in human mythical lore.

In the pre-Christian Isles, and perhaps other parts of Europe, oaths and trial marriages seem to often have been arranged for seven years- and all of this suggests that there was an Otherworldly reality to the concept of seven that made it important. The fact that human sacred kings were sacrificed in some places every seven years shows that humanity sensed the need to be "in time" with the Otherworld as well, or to honor the concept of a series of seven measures of time as being in harmony with an Otherworldly cycle of total regeneration, which the death of the king was tied to.

In some traditional witches' covens, the Magister or male leader has to step down every seven years, and pay some sort of penalty before re-assuming his office. In older days, he may have had to die or step down permanently.

This is in keeping with the same logic of the sacred king's sacrifice; every seven years, or every seven measures of time is symbolic of a total era; time itself is "regenerated" at the end of a cycle of seven-for those who do not believe in linear time (which most pre-Christian societies didn't, and animistic societies even today don't) every day, every season, every year is the same as the one that has gone before it, just regenerated; the years are not seen as unique, but regenerations of the old one, regenerated to begin again after it ended. Every seven years, the king must change; must die; be regenerated into a new form suitable to the new spiritual era, for he is a king in the Otherworld as much as this one, as befitting his title of sacred king.

Be aware of the concept of seven- when you make vows or oaths, work in this concept- if you vow a change in your life to "pay" for Otherworldly favors, make that change for seven days, seven months, or seven years, depending on the magnitude of the favor- or if you wish to make a life change, doing it for seven units of measurement will make it more powerful, because in the Otherworldly sense, if you have done it for seven days, months, or years, you have done it for an entire era.

In much the same way the concept of three is tied to Fate and to the structure of Reality (and thus, making oaths three times, or making magical commands three times is a way of giving them much power), making oaths or magical pronouncements seven times is a way of endowing them with great force in the Otherworld. If you live in your own home, every seven years, you should have a very large purification of your home and property, and have a "fresh start" living there; act as though you just moved in again on the night of the renewal, and repeat any rites you did to open or consecrate your home at your arrival.

Riddle solving forms the basis and soul of this ancient ballad. The child who, with honesty and wit, answers the False Knight's challenges on the road is actually saving his soul from the devil in disguise. One wrong answer, however, and you're caught away to hell. For cunning people who follow the Hidden Tradition and the Elder Rite, however, these Christian glosses can be seen through. The False Knight/Devil is nothing other than the guardian of the paths to the unseen world, where Wisdom waits, and the road is the straight track leading below. The initiate/dead person who is facing him is being tested against the measures of both fear and honesty- the heart that will not yield and the tongue that will not lie.

* * *

The False Knight on the Road
A Traditional Ballad

O where are you going?
Said the False Knight upon the road
I'm going to school
Said the young boy and still he stood.

What is that upon your back?
Said the False Knight upon the road
It is but my peat and books
Said the young boy and still he stood.

I came by your door
Said the False Knight upon the road
A hedge lay in your way
Said the young boy and still he stood.

I tossed your dog a stone
Said the False Knight upon the road
I wish it was a bone
Said the young boy and still he stood.
Whose sheep are they?

Said the False Knight upon the road
They are mine and my mother's
Said the young boy and still he stood.

How many are mine?
Said the False Knight upon the road
All of them that have tails of blue
Said the young boy and still he stood.

O I wish you were in yonder tree
Said the False Knight upon the road
With a good ladder under me
Said the young boy and still he stood.

I wish that ladder to break
Said the False Knight upon the road
And for you to fall down
Said the young boy and still he stood.

I wish you were in yonder sea
Said the False Knight upon the road
With a good ship under me
Said the young boy and still he stood.

And the bottom of that boat to break
Said the False Knight upon the road
And for you to be drowned
Said the young boy and still he stood.

I hear the sound of a distant bell
Said the False Knight upon the road
It's ringing you to hell
Said the young boy and still he stood.

The Truth as it is Born

When a person "knows" the Truth, spiritually speaking, he or she knows things As They Are. When you know things as they are, speaking that fact carries a magical force. To speak or act from Truth carries with it the authority of Truth, which is the same as saying the authority of things as they are- which is yet another way of saying "Nature," the Mother of All, who is the source of All, and the manifest force of Fate. "How things are" at this moment is the unavoidable and unchangeable configuration of the forces of Fate- the Truth of what things are at this very moment is unalterable. To see "the way things are" and speak it, is Truth-speaking.

Nature, both the manifest body of Nature and the dark mysterious interior of Nature, or the void of the Underworld, is constantly bringing forth What Is- and What Is, is the Truth. The Truth is things as they are, aside from how we want them to be. Ultimately, as I have said, Nature and Truth are one. Truth is another name for Nature, and was so in ancient Greece.

Of course, it is very hard for mortals to gauge the complete picture of how things are- many of Fate's forces are hidden, or concealed, but no less important and crucial when one wishes to discover the reason behind any moment's Truth.

The kind of Truth that we are discussing here- full truth- is usually the kind that is only known from mystical insight or inspiration, or from powerful clarity. The Witch, the mystic, the initiate and the dead have, at times, access to a deeper "sight" that shows them the all- and they are beholden to the Truth, to Fate, to state what they see, if they wish to pass the test of the guardians.

When a person's words and thoughts spring from a mystical communion with the ultimate essence of the reality of any situation, or just the ultimate mysterious essence of Reality itself, they speak the Truth. What is said may seem mysterious to people who hear it, but these words always carry with them transformative power, and are usually later seen to contain more than their share of relative Truth.

When a person speaks in accordance with Truth, they are aligning themselves with the power of Fate, and can cause changes to occur by adding an element of awareness, on their part, and on the part of their listeners, to Fate or Nature as it exists about them and within them at that moment. This has a mysterious magical and transformative power- but then, honoring the Truth with expression and respect always does.

The Test of the Guardian

In many folktales and ballads from the British Isles, Innerworldly guardians or beings "test" people who are trying to pass them on the road or get by them somehow. Sometimes, they ask "simple" questions, deceptively simple ones- like "where are you going" or "What are you doing here?" Sometimes, they ask very dense, strange, or hard-to-answer questions- and the answer to any of their questions, without fail, is *never* something that you need to spend time thinking about to figure out. In the Innerworld, the way to answer to the questions of guardians is simple: you must speak the Truth.

When I say that, I mean that the guardians don't want to hear how clever you are- human cleverness seldom means anything to the Otherworld. They don't want to hear your well-planned-out and well-thought-out answer. The guardians want to hear that you honor and uphold Truth, no matter what, and that if the Truth is clear to you, that you will state it as clear as you see it. That is all. They want to see if you will clearly and without distortion express what you are feeling, seeing, and experiencing at that moment.

It sounds like an easy test, but it is not truly, for most people. Most people, all their lives, prefer untruth to the Truth, mostly on an unconscious level.

People live their whole lives believing things simply because they want to believe them, or because these beliefs are comfortable for them, *not* because these things accord with Truth, or the Way Things Are Truly.

This is a common thing among human beings- and when the guardian asks his challenge question, which is one that seldom seems to make sense (much like a zen koan), what he is seeking is for the person to express, completely and clearly, the Truth as they are currently experiencing it. The challenge of the guardian is not a "riddle" that points to the riddle's answer, but a challenge that points at you, and into you, the person hearing it. The answer *is* you; the answer lies in the totality of your experience at *the moment* you hear the riddle, or perceive it.

The guardian is waiting to see how well you can spontaneously and honestly simply state what you are feeling, thinking, seeing, and experiencing at that moment.

It doesn't have to "sound" good or make any "sense" in relation to the question asked- it is simply a statement of the Truth as you see it, in accordance with your full clarity and Wisdom, at the time of the challenge. There is no "wrong" answer, just as there is no "right" one- the only wrong answer is the one that you over-think or say because you think it's what the guardian would want to hear; the only right answer is the one that simply and spontaneously states what you are seeing, feeling and thinking Right Then.

The Hard Road of Spontaneity

If you think that sounds easy, try it. Speak out loud, right now, what you are feeling or thinking- and don't dress it up to sound good. You will find yourself hesitating and trying to "phrase things right"- but why? Because you have a desire to make things sound the way you think they should sound- not the way they are.

Try expressing this to another person- when you are around a friend, play this game, and ask, at random times, for the other to "express their Truth to you." It is funny how people have such a hard time doing it- but what could be easier than honestly and openly just saying what they are thinking, feeling, or seeing fully and without "changing" it to suit your tastes?

The key here is to understand that in Truth, is safety. What the guardian wants to do is test your essential character- he is testing the extent to which you will express the Truth when it is shown to you- and no matter how you choose to understand it, this much is plain: Fate is not an accidental combination of powers and events. Your every waking moment of life, and your every experience after death, is Truth being made plain to you, if you would just see it.

It is Fate that you encounter every thing that you do. Your only task, your hardest test, in return, is to be truly and fully aware of what you experience, and when the time comes, state or express aloud, with all clarity and honesty, what you have seen and felt. You are naming Nature when you do- saying What Is. You have a single choice to make in your human life- to truly be aware of What Is, or to turn away, into a fantasy life, dressing up Truth in mortal guises and preferential falsehoods.

In Truth, is safety- no being in the cosmos can fault you for taking shelter in the Truth as it revealed itself to you, as you felt it.

Even if the Truth is embarrassing to you, or humiliating, or terrible, it is still True- and the Truth is the only safe place to be, because the Truth cannot be resisted by untruth or by beings that delight in falsehood and ego.

Think of the Truth as the ground, the Land, the stable floor, upon which you stand. Now think of human contrivances, lies, and rationales as piles of books that get higher and higher off the floor- the higher they get, the more unstable and unsafe they are- but to a person standing on the floor, stability is assured.

In Truth is stability and safety- because after all, you can't fall off the floor. No magical spell can penetrate the Truth; and a person that passes the test of Truth can pass any guardian. That is the magical power of speaking the Truth. It is the key to any door.

After death, it is believed that guardians can be met on the pathway to the Otherness, towards the supreme revelation. This can happen in a trance, or even after death. They will challenge you. Do not hesitate, nor try to over-think them, or out-think them, because it is simply not possible. The guardians are masters of clarity; they see and perceive all; they are beings who know Truth. They know you, inside and out; because they see Fate clearly, they see all. You cannot deceive these beings anymore than you can deceive your true self. Their questions are not "to" you, their questions are about you, and part of you, part of Fate.

What is Right and What is Easy

What the guardian will ask you to do is both the easiest and the hardest thing in the world.Nothing could be easier than simply spontaneously expressing whatever you happen to be seeing, hearing, thinking, and feeling at any moment. Nothing could be easier than letting go and just letting it all flow out of you, not caring for a moment what it sounds like; there is so much pressure and tension built up inside us, pressure and tension to control our thoughts, our words, to say "the right thing," not to say offensive things, so many judgmental "I shouldn't be thinking or saying" this or that- so many walls and inhibitions which are all built around our need to analyze and re-shape What Is Pure, Clear, and True.

Nothing could be easier than just letting that tension go and speaking and thinking and expressing everything with clarity.

And nothing could be harder, because we have spent our lives, and built up our personalities around that very tension- people will tell you "I am a thoughtful person- I think things through before I say them"- or they will say "I am pretty quick on the uptake, I can say what I mean in some sharp ways"- people have lots of disguises, lots of programs, ways, and methods they "dress up" what they are experiencing, normally so that they can express it in such a manner that it supports a self-fiction, or so that it doesn't offend the self-fictions of others.

That is very mortal, very common. Sadly, the guardians are eaters of mortals, destroyers of the common. They stalk the pathways between worlds, and guard the doors to greater Mysteries, allowing only those who have put the Truth before their own mortality and preferences to carry on.

When you are sitting in clarity, seeing with Witch-sight or the Two Sights- seeing that which is real and that which appears- when the two become one, that is, when what is real *is* what appears (and you will know, in the most silent and mystical moments within, what I mean), be prepared to be totally comfortable with Whatever Is- no matter how your emotions or mortal tugging may rise to act upon it.

Just realize the safety in the Truth, the power in it; it is a power that can be relied on for all time, and in any situation. Cleanse your mind of the need to change what you perceive and feel, and become what you perceive and feel. This is the key to any door.

A Final Mystery

The guardian has appeared as a False Knight for this poor little boy- but the little boy has a kind of clear honesty to what he happens to be feeling or seeing at any moment- the moment the False Knight states a challenge/wish that the little boy should be stuck in the high branches of a "yonder tree," the little boy states simply what most of us would be thinking of- his own safety. He simply responds that if he were to be in the tree, he'd like a ladder under him.

For the young boy being subjected to this test, that is the right answer. If you happened to have been in the little boy's place, you might have preferred to have a trampoline under you; if you had said so, that would have been the correct answer, then and there, for you. As long as it is *truly* what you felt, and *truly* what you *first* thought of, at the moment of the challenge, it would have been "right," because it would have been the Truth.

But the False Knight goes on- he tries to shake the little boy by taking away his security ladder- and he states that it will break. The boy responds with a strange answer- he tells the False Knight "and you will surely fall."

Why? The False Knight, in this scenario, isn't the one that would be in the tree- the little boy would be in the tree. And yet, the little boy turns the danger that would be on him, into danger on the False Knight. How? Why?

Simple. Because the False Knight is not separate or different from the young boy. The False Knight is a "self-display" of the little boy; the tester, the challenger, is an inner portion of this boy's own self, perhaps the Fetch-teacher come forth to harrow the boy, either in a vision, or after the little boy's death.

The fact that danger to the little boy would also be danger to the guardian, the False Knight, reveals a unique bond between them, and it reveals that the little boy already knows what is truly going on, in this challenge- he knows that this False Knight is an aspect of himself, and that this is a self-challenge, a series of self-doubts and self-attacks, that everyone has to face throughout life... and after death.
If you allow confusion to take you or falsehood to comfort you in the face of these tests, whether dead or alive, you will fall into a dark Fate, whether in this world or the next- you will move on to some pretty bad places, places of deceit, forgetfulness, and inevitable sorrow.

In this life, as well as on the Ghost Roads after death, when the challenges come (whether from your inner voice, or from visionary beings that appear in ghastly forms to frighten you or test you), you must remember not to be afraid and to take shelter in the Truth- be calm, spontaneous, and truthful to what you feel, see, and think at any moment.

"I am frightened" may sound like a bad answer to a challenge given to you by a guardian that seems intent on stopping you- but if it is totally true- if fear is the thing that grips you totally at that moment, it is the Truth, and has total power. But you must overcome fear, or it will not allow you to continue on with the contest- realize that every guardian, every tester, every test, is *your* test, or is not apart from you, but pointing *to* you, within you. Do not fear, and say without hesitation what you feel at any moment, and what you know to be True.

The Tale of the White Serpent: A Hidden Wisdom Tradition

The Tale of the White Serpent
A Traditional Story

1. A long time ago there lived a king who was famed for his Wisdom through all the Land. Nothing was hidden from him, and it seemed as if news of the most secret things was brought to him through the air. But he had a strange custom; every day after dinner, when the table was cleared, and no one else was present, a trusty servant had to bring him one more dish. It was covered, however, and even the servant did not know what was in it, neither did anyone know, for the King never took off the cover to eat of it until he was quite alone.

This had gone on for a long time, when one day the servant, who took away the dish, was overcome with such curiosity that he could not help carrying the dish into his room. When he had carefully locked the door, he lifted up the cover, and saw a white snake lying on the dish. But when he saw it he could not deny himself the pleasure of tasting it, so he cut off a little bit and put it into his mouth. No sooner had it touched his tongue than he heard a strange whispering of little voices outside his window. He went and listened, and then noticed that it was the sparrows who were chattering together, and telling one another of all kinds of things which they had seen in the fields and woods. Eating the snake had given him power of understanding the language of animals.

2. Now it so happened that on this very day the queen lost her most beautiful ring, and suspicion of having stolen it fell upon this trusty servant, who was allowed to go everywhere. The king ordered the man to be brought before him, and threatened with angry words that unless he could before the morrow point out the thief, he himself should be looked upon as guilty and executed. In vain he declared his innocence; he was dismissed with no better answer.

In his trouble and fear he went down into the courtyard and took thought how to help himself out of his trouble. Now some ducks were sitting together quietly by a brook and taking their rest; and, whilst they were making their feathers smooth with their bills, they were having a confidential conversation together. The servant stood by and listened. They were telling one another of all the places where they had been waddling about all the morning, and what good food they had found, and one said in a pitiful tone, "Something lies heavy on my stomach; as I was eating in haste I swallowed a ring which lay under the queen's window." The servant at once seized her by the neck, carried her to the kitchen, and said to the cook, "Here is a fine duck; pray, kill her." "Yes," said the cook, and weighed her in his hand. "She has spared no trouble to fatten herself, and has been waiting to be roasted long enough." So he cut off her head, and as she was being dressed for the spit, the queen's ring was found inside her.

3. The servant could now easily prove his innocence; and the king, to make amends for the wrong, allowed him to ask a favor, and promised him the best place in the court that he could wish for. The servant refused everything, and only asked for a horse and some money for traveling, as he had a mind to see the world and go about a little.

4. When his request was granted he set out on his way, and one day came to a pond, where he saw three fishes caught in the reeds and gasping for water. Now, though it is said that fishes are dumb, he heard them lamenting that they must perish so miserably, and, as he had a kind heart, he got off his horse and put the three prisoners back into the water. They quivered with delight, put out their heads, and cried to him, "We will remember you and repay you for saving us!"

5. He rode on, and after a while it seemed to him that he heard a voice in the sand at his feet. He listened, and heard an ant-king complain, "Why cannot folks, with their clumsy beasts, keep off our bodies? That stupid horse, with his heavy hoofs, has been treading down my people without mercy!" So he turned on to a side path and the ant-king cried out to him, "We will remember you- one good turn deserves another!"

6. The path led him into a wood, and here he saw two old ravens standing by their nest, and throwing out their young ones. "Out with you, you idle, good-for-nothing creatures!" cried they. "We cannot find food for you any longer; you are big enough, and can provide for yourselves." But the poor young ravens lay upon the ground, flapping their wings, and crying, "Oh, what helpless chicks we are! We must shift for ourselves,

and yet we cannot fly! What can we do, but lie here and starve?" So the good young fellow alighted and killed his horse with his sword, and gave it to them for food. Then they came hopping up to it, satisfied their hunger, and cried, "We will remember you -- one good turn deserves another!"

7. And now he had to use his own legs, and when he had walked a long way, he came to a large city. There was a great noise and crowd in the streets, and a man rode up on horseback, crying aloud, "The king's daughter wants a husband; but whoever sues for her hand must perform a hard task, and if he does not succeed he will forfeit his life." Many had already made the attempt, but in vain; nevertheless when the youth saw the king's daughter he was so overcome by her great beauty that he forgot all danger, went before the king, and declared himself a suitor.

8. So he was led out to the sea, and a gold ring was thrown into it, in his sight; then the king ordered him to fetch this ring up from the bottom of the sea, and added, "If you come up again without it you will be thrown in again and again until you perish amid the waves." All the people grieved for the handsome youth; then they went away, leaving him alone by the sea.

9. He stood on the shore and considered what he should do, when suddenly he saw three fishes come swimming towards him, and they were the very fishes whose lives he had saved. The one in the middle held a mussel in its mouth, which it laid on the shore at the youth's feet, and when he had taken it up and opened it, there lay the gold ring in the shell. Full of joy he took it to the king, and expected that he would grant him the promised reward.

10. But when the proud princess perceived that he was not her equal in birth, she scorned him, and required him first to perform another task. She went down into the garden and strewed with her own hands ten sacks-full of millet-seed on the grass; then she said, "To-morrow morning before sunrise these must be picked up, and not a single grain be wanting."

11. The youth sat down in the garden and considered how it might be possible to perform this task, but he could think of nothing, and there he sat sorrowfully awaiting the break of day, when he should be led to

death. But as soon as the first rays of the sun shone into the garden he saw all the ten sacks standing side by side, quite full, and not a single grain was missing. The ant-king had come in the night with thousands and thousands of ants, and the grateful creatures had by great industry picked up all the millet-seed and gathered them into the sacks.

12. Presently the king's daughter herself came down into the garden, and was amazed to see that the young man had done the task she had given him. But she could not yet conquer her proud heart, and said, "Although he has performed both the tasks, he shall not be my husband until he has brought me an apple from the Tree of Life."

13. The youth did not know where the Tree of Life stood, but he set out, and would have gone on forever, as long as his legs would carry him, though he had no hope of finding it. After he had wandered through three kingdoms, he came one evening to a wood, and lay down under a tree to sleep. But he heard a rustling in the branches, and a golden apple fell into his hand. At the same time three ravens flew down to him, perched themselves upon his knee, and said, "We are the three young ravens whom you saved from starving; when we had grown big, and heard that you were seeking the Golden Apple, we flew over the sea to the end of the world, where the Tree of Life stands, and have brought you the apple." The youth, full of joy, set out homewards, and took the Golden Apple to the king's beautiful daughter, who had no more excuses left to make. They cut the Apple of Life in two and ate it together; and then her heart became full of love for him, and they lived in undisturbed happiness to a great age.

* * *

Here is a commentary on this tale, revealing the esoteric meanings within, written with numbers to refer to the numbered sections above.

1. This tale begins by telling us of a king and his servant- and the king is renowned and feared for his great and mysterious Wisdom. The servant, through curiosity and cunning, manages to secretly seize a portion of the miraculous source of the king's power, thus making himself an equal to his master.

This first portion of the tale can be compared to the myth of Eden- where Adam and Eve (or mankind) are living in Eden, while the creator God dwells in a position of authority to them; but by Eve's curiosity, and the cunning of nothing less than a serpent, this situation is changed, and mankind is given access to a special gift- a knowledge and ability to be like God, the Gift of Knowledge. To the ancient Gnostics, Ophion, the Serpent of Eden, was a savior to ignorant humanity, by bringing them primal Wisdom or Gnosis- knowledge, thus making them equal to and superior to the God that had trapped them in ignorant servitude in Eden.

In this tale, it is again a serpent that is the source of the secret Wisdom and knowledge, and the servant is a symbol of the Initiate- a symbol of a human being who is a slave to his "king," or material ego. This king is renowned for his power and Wisdom, and so the servant would never think to challenge him, or to be anything other than a servant, until he, too, is given the special gift that makes him *aware* of reality in a new way- he is able to "hear" what animals are saying. The sheer amount of animistic force in this tradition marks this fairy tale as ultimately deriving (as most fairy tales) from an ancient root.

The ability to "hear" or understand the language of the animals is both descriptive of a specific power, but also a metaphor for a deeper, more broad sort of sensitivity or awareness to nature as a whole- Nature and the Land, which contain all secrets. The king is able to hear things "from the wind"- an interesting ability that even traditional Witch Robert Cochrane claimed that the Wise could do- and by doing so, "learn all secrets with ease."

The White Serpent being consumed gives this power. In classical mythology, as well as in Witch traditions from southern Europe, serpents have the power to "lick the ears" of humans, and allow them to understand the speech of animals. But the White Serpent or White Snake Symbol goes much further.

Both the color white and the Serpent show this power to be twofold- the Ancient Power of the Land itself is symbolized by a serpent, and the White Rose is a symbol of Lilith, or the Ancient Concealed Earth and Fate Goddess, in her darker, Underworldly or night aspect; this aspect is the "Kore" or Queen of Elfhame guise, and the dark aspect of Wisdom-the Sophia that descended, and who, as the Elven Queen Below or Secret Presence, was the Mother of Witchdom.

As we will discuss later, there is another angle on the color white- white also refers to the Great Spiritual Lord of Witchery, who also has serpentine forms and to whom serpentine symbols are sacred. As the White Stag and the Great White Serpent or Salmon, He has been a fixture in European Paganism and esoterica for millenia. He, too, in his guise of Master of Animals and the Wild, would have the power to grant the gift of not only deeper awareness, but beast-speech. The Edenic Serpent is likewise a metaphor of his appearance and delivery of the gift of cunning knowledge to infant humankind.

In general, the symbol of the White Serpent can be applied to the Witchmother or the Witchfather; however, in this story, it can also be seen as both and neither- it can represent the great and ominous Mystery of the Land itself, male and female alike- the primordial power that twists and coils in everything, and of which the chthonic Gods partake and mediate. This would be the true Mother-Power, Fate; the eating or consuming of this serpent in a sacramental meal at night is a good metaphor for the initiate merging with the deepest power, from which Wisdom flows.

2. The loss of the queen's ring is an important event, and the symbol of the ring is likewise important. This event had to follow the "awakening" of the servant, because now that he has been made aware of the greater reality, his Fate will no longer allow him to remain a servant. Chaos immediately ensues in his life; the call of the Otherworld. The ring is a symbol of Wisdom- the greatest of Wisdoms- because the roundness has no beginning or end; it is the eternity symbol, the serpent eating its tail.

The circle of the ring is the symbol of Metis- Godly Wisdom. This is the power of the wholeness of all things- the circle of the sun, the circle of the seasons- all metaphors that show that Reality, Nature, this world and all the worlds, are one whole and perfect thing. All things come "back around" in the total fullness of Reality; to be mortal is to exist in the same "great circle" as all other forms of life or orders of existence- the Great Chain or Circle of Fate.

Thus the circle symbolizes not just cycles, but the fact that cycles are not linear- that all things return back on themselves; that "things" are not truly separate from each other, and that the world is not a series of different events, but a great singular event, with many aspects, but still one, whole, perfect and holy singular reality. By sharing reality with the Gods, we are not different from them, ultimately- only relatively. The same can be said for humanity and any other aspect of reality or the world. All is in the circle of reality, and full awareness of this "roundness," or this "fullness" is the key to Divine Wisdom- the Pleroma of the Gnostics, the omniscient awareness of Illumination.

The queen loses her ring, and the servant, now suspected by the king, the dark limiting lord of his own mortal ego, suspects his secret abilities, and threatens his life. The king refuses to be lenient; just like the Hebrew God in the Bible, the servant is a threat to him now, with his new knowledge and Wisdom. Perhaps the king himself took the ring and disposed of it, to accuse his servant- but either way, using his gifts, the servant recovers the ring and proves his innocence.

3. But by using his greater, deeper powers of awareness, and recovering the ring, the servant realizes that he must leave, must grow on to greater things- towards his own full Illumination.

The king tries to seduce the servant into staying, by offering him power and pleasures- but the Wise Servant/Initiate resists and equips himself for a journey, with only the simple tools of a pilgrim or journeyman. The allure of the ego is likewise seductive- to stay within the boundaries of mortality and be a master or king yourself, of all that your ego surveys- but the wise Initiate knows that to uncover the secret of Illumination, the ego must be resisted and sublimated, and a journey of transformation into the unknown must be made. Interestingly, the servant's stated intention is "to see the world"- to expand his horizons, to move into a greater experience of life, outside of the ego-king's halls.

4. The servant rescues some fish who were suffering and dying- out of compassion in his kind heart. By doing so, he allies himself with the powers of the water element. What is interesting to note, as you proceed in reading this essay, is that the tradition revealed in this tale is not a "four element" tradition, but something much older- a "three element" system. The powers of the waters, the land, and the sky will

be encountered in turn by the Initiate, and they will each require a test of his character, and they will each reward him in powerful ways later- allowing him to complete his quest for Illumination.

In this test, which is a test of compassion, we can see that the fish out of water symbolize a greater reality of universal compassion. The simple event of rescuing the fish macrocosmically symbolize the great force of compassion, but also the merging of the Initiate, through his passing of this test, with the powers of watery places and things- which includes all organic life, ultimately.

The Wisdom imparted to the Initiate from these scaly representatives of the water realm seems to say: **Aid others out of kindness, when you are able.** Selflessness is an important part of the native traditions of many parts of Europe, and many Mystery-tests and conditions for initiation.

5. The servant next allies himself to the powers of the Land- aptly symbolized by ants. With his powers of deepened awareness, he hears the complaints of the ant-king, speaking for the powers below and within the Land, and he does the respectful thing, winning the loyalty of the powers in the Land. The ant-king's complaint comes down to us as a great tenet of Wisdom that all Initiates of the Hidden Tradition should hold dear: **Tread with gentleness and respect on the Sacred Land: Within it are great powers, and many orders of being like our own.**

6. Finally coming to a forest or a wood- symbolizing many things, from the "forest" within the deep mind, to the White Wood of the Underworld. Here, the Initiate meets and allies himself not only with the powers of the sky or air- but he finds his own Animal Otherself, or Fetch-beast. In this case, the evidence of the raven being his Fetch-beast will be revealed later in the story- but for now, the ravens also symbolize the powers of the sky, to which the Initiate allies himself. The notion of the shamanic practitioner encountering the spirits of land, sea, and sky, and allying him or herself to them is ancient. Among the Inuit Eskimo people, a shaman named Aua was quoted as saying, at the moment of his Illumination:

"...I could see and hear in a totally different way. I had gained my quameneq ('lightning'), my enlightenment, the shaman-light of brain and body, and this in such a manner that it was not only I who could see through the darkness of life, but the same light also shone out from me, imperceptible to human beings, but visible to all the spirits of earth and sky and sea, and these now came to me and became my helping spirits."

The fact that the servant has to sacrifice his horse is very important. The horse represents his mode of transportation, his means of moving through the world, or the vehicle of his interaction. By sacrificing this sure, strong vehicle, and by sharing it with the ravens, he is bonding himself to them, taking these winged powers as his new mode of experience and transportation- which is the first bit of evidence that these are his Fetch-beasts or his Animal Otherself; however, a greater piece of evidence comes later.

At any rate, in this case, a third piece of timeless Wisdom comes to the forefront: **Selfless Sacrifice aids not just others, but yourself, for all are connected- and what you give up on this day, may be your salvation on another**.

7. Now the servant reaches the Otherworldly location where he catches his first glimpse of the ultimate goal of his journey- his Fetch-mate, or his Fetch-wife, the spirit bride of his soul. Union with this dazzlingly beautiful maiden will be the union of his spirit with his soul, the marriage of the mortal with the immortal and the timeless.

In many of the Grimm Fairy Tales, such as this one, the Fetch-maiden or the Faery Lover is often presented as the daughter of a king, and often sought after by the hero of the tale. In this case, the union with this Otherworldly maiden requires a test- and the cost of failing this test is deadly. All true spiritual attainments are protected by tests and barriers, of very difficult types- but this particular goal- the ultimate Fetch-union, has a deadly cost for failure to achieve it. The reason is simple.

A person who does not achieve the union of soul to spirit during the human life must give their identity soul up to death, eventually. Those who have become consciously aware of the timeless, in the union of spirit to soul, no longer have to suffer through the emotional trauma of "death," nor the loss of memory and gross mental continuity that the experience of death represents for un-initiated people. The mind and soul that are united with and consecrated by spirit undergo a metamorphosis-wherein they enter into a new order of being, an eternal being.

The other men who had lost their lives trying to gain the hand of the king's daughter represent the other "incarnations" or "lives" in which the servant had perhaps once "lived," or failed previous attempts, throughout space and time, in which he had inclined toward the highest union, and failed to attain it.

8. The task to win the king's daughter is to recover a ring- which is an echo of the lost ring motif at the beginning of this tale. This time, however, it represents a deeper Wisdom, the Wisdom needed to go to the penultimate experience.

9. Because of his power over the watery realm, and his allegiance with the spiritual powers of that place, he is able to pass the test; the fish bring him the ring.

10. Unfortunately, the union he seeks with his Fetch-wife turns out to be not that easy- the pure and immortal spiritual bride spurns the mortal soul, for it being "of lesser birth" than herself, and sends him to yet another challenge- a challenge or test that involves the Land, and the scattering of millet all over the ground.

11. Because of his power with the Land and allegiance with the powers in the Land, the intrepid soul is able to pass this test as well, when the spirits of the Land come to his aid.

12. The spirit-bride sets a final task- and the most symbolic of all of them- she sets a condition of great difficulty- that her suitor capture an apple from the Tree of Life- one of the apples of eternity and immortality. Symbolically, the taking of one of these apples and eating it represents the same thing as the union of the soul with the Fetch-bride or spirit.

13. The mortal soul, naturally, does not know where to go to find an aspect of eternity, represented by the apples- so it wanders through the three kingdoms of land, sea, and sky, until it cannot go any further, and comes to rest again in a wood. There, it lies down.

But lo and behold- his aerial allies- symbolized by ravens, bring him one of the apples of eternal life. This is a very important point for many reasons. The mortal soul must achieve union and allegiance with its Fetch-beast, which is the higher power of its soul, before it can achieve union with the Fetch-wife, or the power of spirit. The Fetch-beast makes this union possible- just as the ravens in this tale make it possible by helping the servant to fulfill the last of the conditions he needs for the union.

Notice that the soul itself does not and cannot find the Tree of Life, nor cross the great ocean or dividing Water to reach it- but the Fetch-beast can. The fact that the ravens cross the water on his behalf, to bring his golden apple, and the fact that they make it possible for his union with his Fetch-bride, prove the identity of these animals as his Fetch-beast.

By lying down, the servant is going into a trance, wherein the Fetch-beast "flies forth" or projects itself, to achieve these hallowed goals. Not the human or the soul alone, but the human who has allied him or herself with the powers of the three realms of nature, and awakened within itself the knowledge and activity of the Fetch-beast, can achieve the journey to the Tree of Life, using spiritual insight and power to cross the misty dividing waters between the mortal world and the eternal world where the Tree of Life is found.

Notice, too, that the soul did not even consciously make the journey- that it was largely unconscious when the ravens made their journey- but upon awakening, it discovers that its animal soul has reached out into the depths of the Otherworld to open the way to eternity. It *was* the servant that flew across the dividing waters- but as his Fetch. The two experiences come together, at his awakening. This is not to say that spiritual journeys are all unconscious- far from it. But this symbolizes the reality that the human being alone is not sufficient to deal with the immense realities of the Otherworld. The power of spiritual helpers is required.

Upon returning with the apple, the Fetch-bride and the servant are united. This is symbolized by their sharing of the apple- a common shared meal by which the soul and spirit are made one. And the story says they lived happily to a great age- but the heathen originals of this tale no doubt had them living forever or "to a great age"- the age of the consummation of the world, or eternity.

It all goes together, when you make the greatest of all realizations: **"When I look upon the world, I am not seeing things apart from me; I am seeing what I am**." In this realization, there is no impulse to harm another needlessly; there is a great power in you to preserve the Land and the balance of life.

If you can really do this, truly break the dreamshell of ego and realize every sight, sound, feeling and color as the sights, sounds, feelings, and colors of your greater Self, you gain an "all around sense"- you feel "outside" of your body, outside of limitation; you feel a "ventilating" openness, stretching in all directions, which is the doorway to the Otherworld and to Truth. This is not as easy as just saying "I am not seeing things apart from me, I am seeing what I am"- I wish it were. In reality, it takes a sort of effort, but not strain.

It takes a balanced view, an inner balance that allows you to gently release yourself from the constraints of the effort to maintain a wall between your self and the world you perceive.

Most people don't realize it, but you actually put up an unconscious effort to separate yourself from the world- it is a habitual response that you indulge, anytime you have an experience of any kind; for timeless eons the primordial perception in you- the primordial perception that *is* you- has considered itself as apart from the objects of its perception.

This habit is deeply-rooted and must be un-rooted with time and patience, with effort but not strain- you have to be passive, allow Wisdom to enter you, fill you- a certain calmness, a certain bravery to "let go" and realize that every perception is not "coming at you," but it *is* you. People innately fear the loss of "self" if they do this, but you don't lose Self; you can never lose what is real. What you lose is false self-definitions, and habitual reactions that foster these false definitions.

Living in balance, always open to the ceaseless donation of power that is flowing as an immense spiral from the unseen reaches and depths of reality, is the key to wisdom and peace; you do not create the flow of life and power from the unseen to the seen- you *are* that flow; another part of it; forever.

Open up; receive it consciously, and be a transmitter, a mediator of that power to the rest of the world, without damming the power up in yourself, tangling it in unconsciousness or greed or egocentrism. In this great reality, you only truly have what you give away; by flowing freely like a river, you never cease to be alive and vibrant. This is how the river flows, but never empties; this is how it pours ceaselessly and yet is always a river. To trap the water is to stop flowing, and become a stagnant pool.

We don't die; we can't die because we don't "live" in these bodies. The seat of our true life is everywhere, and everything. What dies was never "you." If you realize this greater Self, you have found wholeness, you have found the primordial man, the Fetch-Master or Mistress; or the True Human Being. When you realize this greater "way of being" while still sharing the lesser way that you grew so accustomed to all your life, one transforms the other, radically, and yet, the other does not vanish.

You then, forever, live in the Diamond Body, the "bone body," the indestructible body of the ever-living; your new path is timeless. You will merge with the spiral of creation which you were always a part of, always an expresser of, to begin with- only now you enjoy it in full consciousness, a rapture, a bond that strikes to the heart of the Mystery of being and consciously births a ceaseless and authenticated whole being or spirit, an effective spirit, a Master-man or Mistress-witch, forever walking in the unseen.

It is for this reason that we wish the greatest blessing and the brightest of Fates upon people with this word: "Wassail"… "Be Whole."

The Master Keys of the Craft:
Four Roads to Mastery

I. **The Path of Initiation: The Fivefold Pattern of the Witching Way**

Most people have the understanding that to claim to belong to a traditional witch "group," one must go through a period of learning, join a group, be vouched for, and be initiated. This is how many modern groups do work.

I think this is a very problematic formula, however, because most people fail to see beyond it. They seek out groups or join them for the sake of membership- but groups don't make witches or mystics; Fate makes witches and mystics.

This standard formula of "joining the group" fails to take into account that the true purpose of "traditional groups" is not to build membership and share rituals. The purpose of a serious spiritual grouping is to achieve Wisdom and Illumination. No wise, thinking person would ever make the claim that Illumination and Wisdom *only* come from membership in a special group.

In truth, Illumination and Wisdom come from the Soul of the World itself, from the unseen worlds, from spiritual beings, from other mysterious forces, and from within. What "groups" do is merely speak a symbolic language, hoping to channel these very things. "Groups" do not and cannot originate these things, nor make them happen in their members with any certainty. Groups may serve some useful purposes, but without members coming to them already aware of the deeper origin of Wisdom, they are doomed to fail as groups, for the same reason exoteric churches all gradually fail.

There is a period of learning involved in becoming a traditional Witch or Mystery Initiate. There are vouches, initiations. But they do not come only from groups. To understand how we all partake of these things, we have to understand the deeper pattern.

The period of learning can occur totally between a person and the Land itself; the group you join are the Pale People, or Hidden People, the dwellers in the Underworld; you are vouched for by your own devotion to the unseen and by your own heart's weight, and the heart of authentic initiation occurs totally within the Underworld, which is simultaneously inside the individual.

Some organizations try to take control of this process, act as "guardians" of it, teachers of it, but I believe that this is haphazard at best; it leads often to a certain abuse of power and a harmful egocentrism that does more harm than good. No group is supposed to be about its members, titles, leaders, or their activities, but about the greater Fate of Illumination. All members of a true grouping of the Old Rite will seek to cast away identity and worldly titles and powers into the great darkness of Wisdom below, and all are submerged in the burning desire for the dark and light Illumination of the Mysteries, and for kinship with the potencies in the Land.

The true "group" is a group of people who know a certain humbleness, and who seek a common spring of eternity, driven by a common thirst- a thirst for the Other and for Illumination, not thirst for temporal powers and offices that are far less. They protect the Land and the true keys to Wisdom because they have given up all for them, and received all back in return, not because they jealously desire to secret up power in some vault.

They know the disastrous consequences of egocentrism- they know how the egocentric, power-hungry human destroys the Land and abuses power and other people; this is why the path is kept shaded with secrecy, and for no other reason. When those of pure heart, ready to cast away all for the Wisdom born of the Underworld and ready to sacrifice for love of the Land show themselves, they are taken into the group and introduced to its Mysteries. There is no other qualification. It is a strange love, a strange desire that the Old Ones use to lure people to the ways of the hidden Craft. Human witches cannot and should not stand in the way of this, for in so doing, they fail in their true role as guardians.

The "outward" initiations that people in groups perform are supposed to be mere representations of a great and timeless pattern of transformation, great and timeless realities that no human being or group can claim a monopoly on, as they underlie all works of art, culture, and inspiration.

The path of Initiation, in traditional folklore, as well as (more generally) in the Western Mystery Tradition, has several stages, that manifest in outward events, but are primarily innerworld realities:

1. The "reaching out" to the powers of the unseen world; the "petition" at the Hollow Hill or the Faery Mound, a stage by which the limitations of the human being are defined through perception and understanding, and the "leap of faith" or the "longing for the beyond" is felt and expressed, from human to what is beyond human; this is the "earth" or Land experience.

2. The "year and a day" period (or a set period of a fixed time) of internal growth, or the "spiritual hermitage," or the trial-time; also, at times, instruction by Otherworldly beings or their representatives; this is the station of the circling airs, that communicate knowledge.

3. The descent into the Cavern of the Black Water and the Two Torches, or the initiatory chamber below, (the chamber or cavern of Enody or Zerinthia) to the source, or to the presence of the Initiatrix in the Innerworld/Underworld, the Pale Woman under the Hill, Queen in the Meadows of Elfhame, who brings about (a normally traumatic) ego death in the candidate, and bestows the Innerworld birth, purification, and regeneration (which at this stage is largely unconscious in immediate depth and effect, but which is necessary to further transformations, and which grows on its own into new, long term understandings).

This represents the first "intrusion" or "appearance" of the outside forces that were called to the initiate in stage one. Their very appearance turns all things "upside down," and destroys and transforms all things. Nothing can ever be the same again after this initial contact with transpersonal forces. This is the "Underworld Initiation" in which old patterns of thinking and living are destroyed and newer, better patterns are regenerated, and the personality of the Initiate is altered forever, and made better, wiser, capable of experiencing life in a new way. This is the descent into the dark waters below.

4. The meeting of the devil or the Otherworldly guardian and the trial, followed by the bestowal of a first stage transformation. This stage is the Fetch-awakening, at the threshold of the soul, wherein the Puckril, the Familiar or "Fetch-beast," is identified or bestowed. This is the merging of the human nature and the animal nature; this is also a further "arrival"

of outside forces that were called by the soul of the initiate. This is the kindling of the Cunning Fire.

5. The meeting with the Fetch-mate, or Otherworldly lover- the Congress of the Incubi/Succubi, the Faery Marriage between the mortal and the immortal, this world and the next, soul and spirit, or the "Wedding Chamber" sacrament of the Gnostics; this is the final culmination of the divine chain of events set into motion by the call of the initiate, the merging and union of the balanced human nature (a balance achieved by the merging with the Puckril) and the divine nature. This is the "invisible Mystery" or the spirit-essence of all.

It is strange but true that even though the Initiate "travels" or journeys to the locations where these forces interact with him or her, their original call set into motion a chain of events that led seemingly inescapably to those beings or forces- and thus, what looks like personal quest is anything but- it is not even a summoning; it is actually those forces coming *to* the initiate.

Only the ego of the outsider or the half-wise views it as effort on the part of the initiate to "reach" them- in reality, when the Initiate travels to reality, reality is traveling to the Initiate.

The Great Forces answer. The purpose of the "time of learning" is to show the Initiate how to be aware of their answer- this is why trance techniques and other consciousness-alteration methods are taught at this time. After that point, everything that happens to the Initiate is in reality an answer from the Otherworld, and this is what the Initiate comes to understand, eventually.

After these five stages are achieved, the Witch or Initiate's "Fate" is transformed; altered into a new path of internal growth that causes an unknowable route into a new condition, beyond this life (and beyond the death of the candidate).

The route of this new condition is the Third Road to Elfland, the destination is Mastery, the Faery/Fetch Metamorphosis or the deathless transformation into the ranks of the Hidden Company, or the Grand Array.

During the remains of an Initiate's life, the affects of these five experiences, and the further attendant transformations, cause Wisdom to blossom in the soul of the candidate (as the soul is now united with the spirit) and it causes the special modes of perception and understanding to open in the candidate (gradually) that are the source of "seership" and other mystical abilities.

"Magical" abilities (and I hate to use that term) are also sometimes gained, though this is a far more poetic idea than the term "magic" expresses. Knowledge and real Wisdom, direct experience of the Unseen world, and the ability to "reach into" the self, or the depths, to directly experience and mediate extra-sensory reality, causes what seem to be like "powers" or abilities to understand and influence some events in life.

But this is only a tiny matter of a greater growth.

The five-fold initiatory pattern leads to internal transformation, a "road change" from the straight road of the common person, moving slowly through Fated time, onto the Crooked Path, or the third hidden road, which is the attainment of a "second destiny" of types. It's very subtle, and does not happen overnight.

This pattern is embedded in the workings of the cosmos itself; we can see it in ourselves and in Nature- the acorn, pulled by the draw of Fate and Nature away from the origin tree falls into the Underworld, where after a time, and when outer forces reach it (light, and water from above), it sprouts and grows into a new being- the fertilization in the seed occurring within, but spurred on by outside forces.

In reality, even the "outside" forces are part of a whole reality, of which the seed may ignorantly think of itself as "apart" from- but the truth is found in a kind of holism. Did the acorn go to the ground, or did the ground go to the acorn? Both occurred. There is only one reality, one system, one chain of Fate. Did the sunlight and water reach the acorn, or did it reach them? Both occurred. Do not let false divisions impede your ability to see the truth of wholeness.

One might wisely then ask- "Did the whole chain begin when an initiate decided to make the original petition to the forces beyond him or herself, or did that decision and petition come from another place make the initiate?"

When you can answer that question, then you will see how Fate calls all things to initiation and transformation, eventually, and without exception.

This entire pattern can be realized through working groups that have the means and understanding to *really* bring about these five transformations, but at heart, all of these transformations (and whatever symbols people use to represent them in the outer world) are not physical, blunt realities; they are internal, Otherworldly Mysteries that emerge through all things.

They come from the unseen. A group is very unique and special indeed if it can really bring about these transformations in a systematic, direct way- most groups cannot, because 99% of people have not gone past the first one or two "steps" on the initiatory path. Most people who call themselves occultists have not even gone past the first.

Luckily, a person can walk this entire path alone. In fact, even before you realize it, you are on this path, whether you belong to a group or to no group.

Groups that tell you otherwise are just trying to get your obedience or money, or both. I'm not saying that a good group of humble, like-minded people, poets and mystics, shouldn't be worked with if you find them- but good luck finding them. The wise would do well to look to themselves, within and beyond, for the emergence of this pattern. The simple act of looking shows that it is occurring.

II. The Secret Under the Mounds: The Origins of the Old Rite, and the True Meaning of Sacrifice

There is a dark red moon in the sky. I have just spent several days out in the woods, walking among hedges and houses, and down long paths of nothing but straw and ponds. I've been speaking with my Puckril, who has made good on his promise to bring me to what I needed to see to understand the Great Inheritance. It's more than I ever could have dreamed. It's also something I could never write about- and luckily, I don't need to. But there is something, one last thing, that I do need to write about. I need to write about the lessons of this red season.

It is August 1, 2004, during the rising of a very red moon. I feel like this communion, this contact, these intuitions, are the culmination of a very long walk, and I speak now words that spring from the Underworld itself. There is no more to say about the "craft" after this; nothing left to learn, only to experience. This is the heart of the true "Old Ways," the secret origin of the craft.

The Funeral Cult

The true Old Ways began in the veneration of the dead. There is no older religion. I have been granted a blessed vision, in the season of Lammas, of the origins of the things I hold so dear and sacred.

Fate was the only power, and is the only power. Great, Dark Fate- She who stands before and beyond all things, and by whose power, everything is constrained to come to pass and to be.

There is nothing greater, not a God nor a man, nothing. There is no older being. Fate is even a poor way to describe this power, for in its totality, it defies our every description or attempt at understanding- but we see its movements in every moment and in every thought. I might say that there is nothing younger than Fate, either, for at every moment it is both the oldest thing in creation, as well as the youngest, newest thing. Its form at every moment is unique and new, but it is still the oldest force.

A young girl once asked me "What is the meaning of "sacrifice?"
I've heard so many answers to that question. Now I know how absurd they all sound, because the people who came up with the answers were distant from the Wisdom that built the burial mounds, and that put the sacrificed humans below the ground.

The deeper sacrifice is not about giving up anything. It isn't about "making something holy" as people have come to think, or even sharing anything. I now know why my most distant ancestors had cults of sacred kingship; I know why sometimes kings had to die; I know where the figure of the "Sacred King" comes from. I know why the ancestors sacrificed people to inter them in the earth, why they buried and worshipped the dead.

And all ancient religions begin here- the worship of the dead. At the time Christianity rose, in the Mediterranean world, magicians believed that invoking the name of dead, executed criminals was powerful, and could bring about great effects. The long-dead ancestors were also worshipped and regularly invoked. This brings us to the true meaning of "sacrifice."

"The Passage Between" and the Key

The Underworld is the realm of Fate, of the dark Mystery that lies beyond life and death- the mysterious place of birth, origins, and regeneration.

The Underworld's dark maw is the darkness of Fate. Fate, the power that holds all things in tight, adamantine bondage- Fate, the power of What Must Be. Without command of Fate, without Fate, where is "magic?" Where is power?

Our ancestors knew the eldest and most powerful of all rites- they knew how to forge a link between the living and the world of the living, and the power of Fate. And that link was achieved through the dead.

When a person dies, and is buried, they "merge" with the Land, and they merge with the powers "below" or "within" the Land. That person "goes" to the Underworld- they are eventually taken "back" into the bosom of the Dark Goddess of the Underworld- a Goddess who, in all ancient Pagan considerations, was associated with Fate.

The dead make the "passage between" the living and the dead, between the living and the power of Fate… Fate, that power of What Must Be.

When the dead make this passage or transition, a temporary phenomenon happens- that "breach" or "entry" or "merging point" or "passage" through the Land swings and flows both ways- but there is more.

The dead eventually become merged with the Mystery, with Fate. But it was shown to me that something else happens- the name and the image of the dead person become keys to "reaching" the power of Fate- Fate which they have merged with.

It's really very simple. Invoking the name of a dead person is the same as invoking the greatest Mystery beyond death- a Mystery that they have gone on to become one with- Fate.

Fate cannot conform to anything we "know"- this great power of powers cannot "look" like anything we could fathom. It is we who need to make images for Fate- and what images have we made? The answer to this whole enigma was sitting right in front of me, all my life.

Fate as a Goddess appears as a pale-faced Woman. Sometimes, She bears a key, as Hekate and Diana do in classical sources. Sometimes, She has a half-rotting face.

The ancestors, as a whole group of powerful beings who embody the Fate of a family, are the Pale People- and the dead and the land-spirits (who are associated with the dead) are always called "white" or "pale" or "wan"… and this leads to a simple conclusion: Fate takes the image of the human dead.

That is why the Goddess of Fate has a pale face and a woman's form- because She appears as a dead woman. Fate takes the form of the dead, those who go to merge with Her.

The dead, the ancestors, and even the slain king make the passage and become keys to the door of the Mystery of What Must Be- and to invoke them after they have merged is the same as invoking Fate, the power that can make anything happen, and without which, nothing can happen.

The dead are keys to the door of Fate- thus, many ancient Goddesses of the Underworld- Funeral Queens- hold keys or are associated with keys in their symbolism. Enody or Hecate comes to mind here.

The Phantom of the Slain

Ancient people needed to contact the other side. They needed the Wisdom of the Underworld- they needed some way to make important changes in their environment and in their lives.

They needed crops to grow. They needed plagues to end. They needed food and animals. They needed guidance. The cult of sacrificed humans, as well as the venerated dead, is based on this- the sacrificed human, laid in the sacred mound, went to merge with the great dark Underworld, and to merge with Fate- and his or her name was invoked and prayed to, at the mound, for needful change- for now, Fate and the Mound-Dead or the Mound King, or the Lady Under the Mound were one; they were the same; to invoke him or her was to bring about What Must Happen.

The deified phantom of the dead person, the sacrifice, remained there, at the point which they merged- the sacred mound or grave or tomb or lake, or wherever their remains were interred- and this place was where the power of the phantom allowed for a "two way flow" or contact with the dark Mystery of Fate, in the beyond-world.

In the British Isles, it was once believed (late in history) that the first person buried in a graveyard had to stay there forever, to act as the guardian of the place. Some Pagans and Christians found a way around this- they buried an animal there first, usually a dog, to be the guardian, so that the subsequent humans could move on. The notion that the dead merge with a Land and form a new relationship with it, as well as acting as a "gatekeeper" within it, are very old.

In Pagan times, divinations were done on the "merging point" or the graves, as well as on grave mounds- and this wasn't just a matter of sacrificed people- the ancestors as a whole were called upon for the same thing- for the ancestors now appeared AS Fate- they were the means by which Fate manifested in human form, just like the sacrificed hero or king.

By calling upon the name of He or She or They who had gone beyond, but who still remained in some fashion to open the ways between, anything was possible. The greatest power in Reality, that of Fate, was available to living humans thanks to the dead, the sacrificed heroes and the ancestors.

But these phantoms didn't last forever- in the case of a sacrificed king or hero- Fate is always changing, spiritual conditions are changing, society is changing, and ancient people thought that the cults of the dead needed to be "upkept" by rituals and commemoration and "feeding" of various kinds- but it seemed to some that more was needed- and in some places, every set amount of years (every seven years, in the Isles, according to hints found in histories and ballads), another person was sacrificed to take up the mantle and perform this sacred function of being the mediator between the human world, and the world of Mystery, Fate, and regeneration.

But this person wasn't killed as who they were; *they were given the name* of the previously sacrificed king or queen. By naming them as the Slain King or Queen, the rite was repeated and the power was renewed.

In this manner, over many years, a powerful name or title was built up for the phantom that was attached to the sacred site- and after a while, the name itself became powerful. This is the birth of the concept of the sacred Sacrificed King. This is the "human" basis for the myth of the dying God.

This is something that you need to understand- the Gods and Goddesses of the craft, the great spirits of our ancestors, were not just Gods and Goddesses, but they were also beings and myth-events sprung from the deeds and sacrifices of human beings.

Poor John Barleycorn

Times changed. Animals became sacrificed in the place of people. This didn't matter, not one bit- for as the ancients believed, even animals were endowed with spirit- even an animal could "merge" in a location if its remains were interred there; even an animal could act as a mediator between the living above and the Mystery below. And even an animal could renew the phantom or power of a sacred place. Its beastly image could serve as the connection between mysterious Fate and the human mind.

And yes- the animal was given the name and the honor of a sacred king before it was killed in his place.

After a long time, the Sacred Kings and Slain Gods became associated with these animals- in the most ancient times, he was probably associated with stags or goats or other horned beasts; hence, now, in mythical memory, he "wears the horns."

In some places, and through even more time, straw men, men made of barley, and corn dollies were created to "be sacrificed" on traditional days, every year.

From human body to animal body to plant body, the Sacred King, the Sacrificed One who, after thousands of years has become a divine and holy power attached to the memory of the Old Ways, has evolved in strange directions.

The Gods of the incoming Indo-Europeans melded in strange ways with these most primal native rituals and beliefs- the All-Father himself became merged with legends of dying and resurrected humans, and other Underworldly dramas.

Human sacrifice no longer occurs, but that means nothing now- the sacrificed Sacred Victim's power is established through thousands of years of veneration and sacred blood. He/She/It has transcended the human ritual of sacrifice, and just the old names, the old images, the old impulses and ideas are enough to invoke and channel this being, and through this being, the power of Fate itself, to bring about *needful* changes.

Praying to your dead grandmother to bring about a change you need is therefore not a lost cause- for once she has merged, she is a powerful image and name by which you can invoke Fate. The same goes for your pet that was killed in an accident. The most powerful place to invoke them is their gravesite, the place they were given to the ground, to merge. If they were burned, bury their ashes in the earth or scatter them on it.

This is the heart, the true meaning of sacrifice. This is the first religion. The true meaning of sacrifice is and was that the dead could create a channel, a pathway between the living and the great powers beyond life, by which change could be brought about.

This was the primal magical spell- the true Old Rite. The dead would "become holy"; they would be "deified" because they would merge with Fate and the great Otherness, and their image and name would become Fate's image and Fate's name, from the perspective of the living.

Times kept changing. This understanding was lost. But guess what? The old names are still powerful, for these sacrifices are still in effect; they resonate in the soul, in lore, in the world itself. Your own dead relatives can become the most powerful allies you have in the craft, for in their names you can do almost anything- if you have a bond with them before and after their death, transition, and merging, and if you maintain it. This is the ancestor cult.

Look at the ballads- while the original ancient names of sacred merged kings and heroes were lost, myth and folklore gave them new ones- John Barleycorn, for instance. Sound harmless? He represents all the sacred kings who died so that the fields could be regenerated. He represents all life renewed by the power below. He is the life in nature, the life of the fields. That name may sound strange, but it is a key to great power, because of its origins.

"Customs" and "traditions" and "folkloric names" are all remains of sacrificial cults and their chthonic heroes and dying/resurrecting Gods and beings that acted as the gateways to death, life, and regeneration, and to whom prayers and needful things were addressed.

People die all the time. So do animals. They all pass below, make the passage, merge, and can be a *key* to the power of Fate if they are venerated and maintained properly- their images, their gravesites, their names, and their memory. If you keep these things alive and fresh, and venerate them, their names will become words of power. It's not really the person or the animal you are invoking, but Fate- in a Mystery, that person or animal merges with Fate, and the lines blur. It *is* them, in a way, but not as we think of them. From the perspective of the living, however, it might as well be.

Look at Jesus, for another example. He was an executed criminal-a dead man- whose name even Pagans invoked for magical spells- see the PGM for more information. A man who was killed and whose name became powerful; a man whose sacrifice was immediately compared to the sacrifice of Pagan sacred kings by both Pagans and the church that sprang up in his name.

While I was writing my notes, after these revelations, I had an epiphany. I remembered something the Bible attributes to Jesus- a quote which says:

"I have been dead, and yet, I live- and I hold the keys to hell and to death."

And suddenly, it all went together for me- the Pagan metaphysic in that statement is as thick as a log. The man who said this is a sacred king (and, knowing what we know of actual biblical scholarship, Jesus himself probably didn't say this- this is no doubt a lift from Paganism which ended up in his mouth- I suspect this statement was originally Mithraic or Dionysian), and listen to what it is saying:

"I have been dead, and yet, I live- the sacred dying/resurrected king or hero has been sacrificed or died, and yet lives on, in the between, in the Underworld, in the new state- and I "hold the keys to hell and to death."

Hold the keys? This is another way of the sacred king saying that he (or they) are the **key**, the being who controls the passage of power between the Underworld (hell) and the world, and who has authority over all change (death). By the name and power of this being, the Underworld is reached, and its powers are mediated, for needful change- "death" being a metaphor for change. But it also means "death" in the sense of the ceasing of life, the birth into the timeless Otherworld.

If Jesus has truly become associated with the dying and resurrected king, then by his name, Fate could be invoked, just as it could by invoking John Barleycorn, or the slain horned one, or Lugh, or Belenus, or the Mound-Dead, or the ancestors, your dead grandfather, or even my own name if I died tomorrow.

Of course, I am not Christian, so while I would extend the possibility that the name of Jesus may have merged with this tradition, or with many native traditions, I still do not use it, because of the stigma attached to it, because of the close-mindedness it has come to represent through the followers of the Christian creed in the modern day. Another reason is because I accept the scholarship that tells us that the "life of Jesus" is not pure history, but a syncretism born from the words of possibly many people, and from many aspects of Pagan mythology, with only a few possible historical events tossed in, and attributed to a semi-historical first-century Hellenized Jewish prophet. Who he really was, we will never know, for no historical records exist to tell us, only the syncretism created hundreds of years after his alleged death by his followers.

But that isn't the point- names have power, and if (as history shows) Jesus took the place of many Pagan dying/resurrected Gods, then over time, his own name could become a part of the Old Rite tradition, albeit a latecomer.

What really matters is whether or not he was a real person- for the name of *any* dead person can do, especially if that dead person is venerated as Jesus became venerated. The trouble is, would the phantom last? Would he need to be refreshed? John Barleycorn does not need to be refreshed, for he has thousands of years of willing sacrifices behind him- and thousands more of symbolic sacrifices and veneration in the form of ale-making, corn dollies, harvest festivals, and even new sacrifices of corn-men today by modern Pagans. And his ballads are still being sung.

Gods of the Dead

Behind this ancient figure of the Barley God is the horned God of the earth, the dying God, The consort of the Earth Mother, and behind that, the humans who died and were placed in the ground to act as keys to the magic that made what the community needed to happen, happen. In the face of that tradition, that primal power, "Jesus" is superfluous.

The horned God is a real divine power, not just humans who became deified- but remember, the Gods are impossible to conceive of. We see them as "humans" because of the deeds of these ancient sacrificial cults!

The Great God of Nature, the masculine force of the Land, is a real being, just like His mother Fate is a real being.

But the God who is the life in the Land is also the life in us- and when a human dies, He dies as well- when crops are cut, He is cut; when an animal falls, He falls.

The sacrificial victim naturally becomes the most moving and powerful, lasting symbol of the dying God, the horned God of Nature. Ancient sacrifices and associations with slain animals got mixed into it all, resulting in the part animal, part human God-image that stands now in the imagination of most Pagans.

And this symbol, this image, is holy, for dozens of reasons which you should be able to easily see now. That image represents sacrifice, needful sacrifice without which we would not be. And from death, life comes again- and the being who holds the keys and guards the portals to the Underworld is the Sacrificed Lord.

It is no mistake that the Goddess of Fate was associated with Earth Goddesses and Death Goddesses- for the Earth is the green gown that Fate wears, the florescence that covers the Underworld or wraps it up This leads to the dead being called by the ancient Greeks "the people of Demeter". In their understanding, the Earth Goddess is also the Goddess of the dead because the dead are within Her.

It is no accident that Queen Persephone was Demeter's daughter. It is also no accident that the Queen of the Dead was pictured as a young maiden- who in her own mythology had to "die." The myth comes from an actual event, the death of a young girl in very ancient times, whose funeral cult was destined to become one of the most enduring on the face of the Earth and to shape the lives of millions.

The image of a young girl is still the image of the Queen of the Underworld to Greek Pagans. And it is not surprising that Demeter and Persephone were seen as Goddesses of Fate- especially Persephone, who had Justice as one of Her Underworldly attendants, as well as Hekate. Now it is easy to see why.

Today, when you sacrifice John Barleycorn, you are stepping out of your own time, and entering into the same archetypal moment of sacrifice, where the human being was killed to merge with the earth under the sacred mound, and by invoking that person, Wisdom, power, good weather, crops, and regeneration could be brought to pass.

By burying or killing your own little straw man on Lammas you are invoking the power that is the key to Fate, that which opens the passages between- and it involves humans who became guardians, who became deified, and it involves the Lord of the Land and the Underworld, and it involves the greatest magic of all.

So some questions remain- how many of these beings remain as phantoms, in their mounds, scattered across the sacred landscapes of Europe? Forgotten, are they still mediating power and regeneration into their Lands? Have they faded? I think most have. But I think some of the forgotten, rotting mounds are still haunted by these powers- and some still function, and others are just asleep, waiting to be awakened by us. Others are long gone.

The name of the sacrificed Lord who is the guard of the Ghost Roads, He who shall come forth again, is the single name to which they all answer.

The dead are the keys to the Fate-door, the Dead-Portals. Old Fate? A pale-faced Lady? A maiden with a key? The Queen of the Underworld? See now, beyond the symbols. These Gods are appearing as dead humans. And death is the door to the powers beyond, and some very brave and holy people made that passage for the rest of us- and by their names, anything can happen, anything can be.

Ask the dying and resurrected King for what you truly wish for- because you have a Fate unfolding, as well. Your every second is Fate. Death, too, is your Fate. But what will death mean? Will you die then, or now? In His great name, you do not need to die as the others die.

The Firebringer has given mankind the power to recognize these things- to invoke Fate, to recognize truth, awareness, and divinity, and Mysteries that remove us from the flow of what seems like helplessness. The

Firebringer also placed his life and power into us, and has undergone death and change. How will you use the Fire to enter the Mystery?

Die tomorrow, and you will go below to merge with Fate. In the darkness of the Great Fate, you will merge with the pool of souls, the dark All; memories and personality will linger as a phantom, but you will undergo the transition into the dream without end, come to truth and cease to be in any way that you think of "yourself" "now." You will have to take one of the roads open to you, based on your Fate, and for most, those roads lead to the final place, where you have to give up and "pay your tithe to hell" as the old ballad says.

But it need not be that way. Ask, now, in the name of the simultaneously dead and living Lord, on Lammas- to extend your life and being into immortality, and the Third Face will open its eyes to you, followed by the fourth path beyond the Hill. You will join the Hidden Company, and nothing will ever be the same. Death will have no power over you. In His name, as the key of the Fate-door, or in the name of your ancestors or dead companions, even death can die.

The Old Rite is about making what we need to happen, happen- even overcoming death. How? The dead who have gone beyond to become the keys.

III. Straw and Twig Body of the Lord of the Land: The Rite of the Wake-Fire and the Funeral Mound

The King is Dead... Long Live the King

White King, Lord of the Land, your body extends as far as my eye can see. Plants grow from you, men and beasts fill your congregations. Your heat touches my face.

The seasons are moving like the stars on the millstone of the sky. Fate is spinning, weaving and unfolding- the Red Day is upon us, followed by the Red Night. I have sworn an oath on your blood to kill you, so that the Old Rite can be accomplished, and all will be renewed.

I have wandered around the Land, through trees and streams, across fields and roads, and collected the parts of your body- dirt for mud; straw for sinews, twigs for bones, stones for organs and adornments, plants for blood and hair, buttons and scraps of cloth for your clothes, and many other things. No matter where I find things, and no matter what I find, from a bird's feather to a kernel of wheat, to a dandelion head, I find a piece of you.

I will make your body from these parts of the Land. This will be you, and I will see your death.

1.

I have stood under a dark sky, facing north, on the edge of a field with a lone standing stone. I have raised my hands to the countless stars of the night, and to the great immensity which stands behind it all. Two roads cross near here, and beyond that, a marsh sinks into the Land.

White Faced Woman with the knotted noose,
Goat-Buck with a Serpent's tongue,
Dish and bowl of the Red Meal Sacrament,
Land that covers all, and births the Puck-child,
In this season be whole and bear to us the blessings
Of the people below.

We have dug a pit into the dark earth south of the stone. The two women that have followed me to this place of sacrifice are coming down the road towards the field.

They are coming closer, their faces painted white. They are coming from the crossroads, each bearing their unique gifts. They are coming down the straight paths, soft dirt underfoot, their eyes fixed on the monolith.

I can hear the first of my female companions call out:

"These are the days of Lammas, the nights of Lammas,
And the Faery folk do ride…"

The other answers her:

"The hunting horses come to the cross!
Bless us, notice us not, horses of the hill,
Brown and white,
We who go to harvest the Good Man's Croft."

They both walk to the edge of the field, watching me silently, as the wind moans with mourning for what is about to take place. A night-bird screams distantly.

2.

There is a large pile of many types of wood here, before the stone. Three dried bones are on top of the pile, waiting for the flame. Sitting next to the dark, waiting bone-fire pile is a kettle of water.

Only the stars and the great stone watch me as I bend over the kettle, and in my mind, I know, I have come to the source of all waters. I touch the water and say in a whisper:

Here is water, blessed by the Old One,
A fertile river of life, a medium of ghosts,
A water that masters every spirit and created thing,
Much grace and vision, from heaven to hell the road
Of the ancient one's spells.

I pick up the kettle and walk around the stone counterclockwise, spilling the water, making the river of time and souls. As I spill the water, I sling out four trickles to each direction, making four roads by which the unseen can approach.

I walk forward, towards the dark and waiting pile of the bone-fire, and hear the steps of the pale-faced women who have joined me, walking up behind me to stare into the dark pile of wood before the stone.

One of them hands me a burning stick of wood, and I thrust it into the kindling below the pile. As it begins to smolder and crackle, I say:

Here is fire, blessed by the Lady under the Land,
Lamp and Light to what is seen and unseen-
Darting spirit and serpent's tongue,
Heat from the Sun and the Land,
A light in every hearth, before the Red Stone,
And burning deep under the Earth.

As I speak, the fire springs up, making the area glow orange and bright- my face is warm, and the white faces of the two women with me suddenly glow. Together, the women say:

Blaze forth, watch-fire and wake-fire upon the Land
Honor to the Great Inheritance.

I look up at the stone and proclaim:

The Hallowed place, ringed by water,
Ringing stone, a consecrate plain,
A field, a meadow above like unto that below,
Like unto the force of the sacred mound-fields,
All within touches all without
And deeper within;
Here is the seat of fire,
A passing place, a joining place of Spirit and Man,
The indestructible circle of Fate.
Let us know what we must know,
Do what we must do.

3.

The first woman walks to the freshly dug pit and drops a broken cup inside. The cup of the Earth's bounty has given much and been broken on the Red Season, for it cannot give forever; it must rest under the white wool of winter soon, before filling with life again.

The second woman walks to the pit and drops a broken knife inside. The plow-man has cut deeply into the earth, the hot edge of summer has cut into the ground, and made red life run freely; now it must end, the power of summer has to be broken. A man with a black face had smashed the cup and knife with heavy blows from a hammer, far from the sacred stone.

The first woman walks to the pit and drops inside it a wooden cross made of bundles of oak and rowan, tied together with Red Thread. The White King who lives in the Land, and who has risen on the Red Night, has to bleed in needful sacrifice for the Land and for all of us.

The first woman then says:

Ancient Providence, Mistress of Corpses,
Concealer of Light, Queen of what must be:
Be not blind nor unmerciful.
About the sacred stone, the work of thy hand is shown.

Dead who live in the Land,
Pale People who offer life,
Keepers of the passages between,
Key holders of the door of Fate
In the sacred field, your power is joined to us
In the name of the phantom of the Slain.
Let us live and love in Wisdom, in day and in darkness.

4.

I sat there, staring at the fire for a bit, before I turned to see my white-faced companions walking towards me, carrying the body of the Lord of the Land. He had been resting on a low mound of earth to the east of the stone; the women had gone to fetch Him.

They paused when they reached the edge of our ring, and held Him up to the stone, and to me. I said the ancient words:

I name thee Cow, and Bull:
All the cattle separately
Their names let them take
As you take this name:

Horse and Mare and Ass,
Dog and Cat and Mouse
All Birds and Serpents.

They carried Him in and handed Him to me. I looked at His body, this living manifestation of the Lord, and walked with Him, making Him to stand, propped up against the stone, facing west.

I closed my eyes and bowed my head and praised and worshipped Him, telling Him my secrets and my desires, and thanking Him for his power and life, and begging his protection and friendship. I gave my heart to Him.

The three of us began treading the mill around the fire and the stone and the body of the Lord. I kept my eyes fixed on the stone, as I treaded slowly then faster, and the Mystery of the roundness of power started to manifest. I could feel the power, and the round walk- how everything that occurs, that comes to be, is round, a great circle. I had a will for this treading- I had to make the body of the Lord of the Land even more alive than it already was. The life under the Land would fill the body of the Lord, channeled up through this great and ancient stone.

In the Mystery of the round circle mill treading, I could do it- my will in the roundness was enough- my intentions, my love for the Lord of this Land.

Around and around I went, my mouth uttering strange and spontaneous sounds. The ever-turning power, and then my eyes locked on the straw and twig body of the Lord of the Land, and I finally had to stop, falling forward on my knees, and throwing my hands out before me, towards the straw and twig body. Through my mind and body, and the Mystery of the roundness, it was done- the Land, fire, mill, intention, love, will,

the straw, the sky, the stars and the fields- all of it flowed together as one and the spirit of the Old One came to rest consciously in the straw and twig body. It all flowed together and opened a door for Him.

I prayed again, to the straw and twig body, my fondest prayer of worship. You are my Lord, the life of the Land- and without You, the farmer does not farm, the hunter does not blow his horn, the tinker does not mend kettles or pots. Men do not love women, nor do women have the strength to weave or birth or love. Men and woman cannot create or destroy, love or hate, without You, lord of life.

5.

I carried the Lord's body to the west, far beyond the offering pit, and laid Him before me. I lifted my knife over the body of the Lord and said:

Horn-crowned King, Life in the Land
Body of straw and branches, eggs and grasses,
Horns and waters,
You will bleed in Needful Sacrifice.

And I plunged the knife into Him over and over again. I hacked His limbs away from his torso, and placed the knife down. I closed my eyes and mourned.

I took out my small wooden flute and played a sad song, a song of death.

I then prayed over His mutilated body:

Mother of All, clothed in a gown of green.
Bearing fruit and plenty,
Holding the dead in your bosom,
Accept this offering.

Grey Hooded Mothers, spinning and quiet
Sweet smell of the Lady lying below
Come, Great Presence, bring forth the Inheritance.
Accept this offering.

I then carried the pieces of His body to the pit and dropped in an arm and a leg. I then carried Him to the north of our water-ringed holy place, and prepared His grave- I dug like wild into the ground, lifted the pieces of His body and placed them in the earth and covered them up. I took many stones and piled them over the grave-site, making His holy cairn, marking His grave. Here is where He would go to merge with the ground, make the passage into the Underworld. Here is the contact point.

I played a funeral dirge on my flute over the cairn. The wake fire was glowing lower now. The white-faced women were weeping, and shaking their tears over His cairn.

6.

I picked up the cup and bowl, and poured wine into the cup, and put a piece of red bread in the bowl. I set them before His cairn, and over the cup, I said:

Mother of the Harvest, Spinning Queen who is clothed with Earth,
Watch over the spirit of the Lord as he walks the Ghost Roads on the
Red Season.
Bless this Cup in your Ineffable Name.

Over the bowl, I said:

Sacrificed Lord, Life in the Land that was cut and hewn and sent
below:
Keeper of the Passage and Key-holder of the Doors of Death,
In your great name and in the blood you shed, all things are possible.
Bless this bread with your Power.

Then, I silently raised the cup to my lips, drank a portion, and ate some bread. I placed the last bread on the ground around the cairn, and poured the rest of the wine on the cairn itself, watching the red run through the stones. The dead below and I were one- I could now pray to the Sacrificed Lord.

7.

And pray I did- that night, before his sacred burial site, I prayed for what I most needed- and in the morning, when the wake fire was burned down, I took its ashes and spread them around the cairn.

Day after day, night after night, I travel to that place and pray at the cairn, for that is the place where he merged with the ground and with Fate- and that is where the contact can be made. Many offerings are left there, many sacred meals eaten and shared there.

In His name, He who has gone below to become the servant of Fate, all things are possible. Fate now appears as He who died for us all, and through Him, What Must Be is made manifest. What I asked for, I received, and one day, He will rise again, renewed.

Next year, on the Red Day, the wake fire will be made before this cairn.

IV. Three Rites of Mastery

The Consecration of the Lord of the House of Fire: The Goat Rite

(Initiation Stream IV. Witch Consecration and Dedication)

In the unlight, make a circle of flour, sand, or branches and twigs, with a triangle within it- the triangle's topmost point should indicate to the east.

Outside of the circle to the east, should be the skull of a goat or an image of a goat drawn in the ground or with chalk, flour, or the like, and one or two candles illuminating it.

Allow a trickle of water to fall from the west, leading up to the western edge of the circle. You should carry an unlit candle or a twig with you at all times during this rite.

Stand a ways to the west of this prepared area, and close your eyes. Meditate on the darkness, just formless, expansive darkness. You must bring to mind a doorway that seems imposing to you- a frightening doorway, threatening and ominous seeming, and even though no two people will have the same image in their heads, all of these doors should have a rough image of a horned man carved or painted on them, his head and face only. He should be leering in a rather disconcerting way.

In your mind's eye, step forward and knock on the door three times, and hear a great hollow booming, echoing behind it, which vibrates in your head and in your bones. Then, watch it open slowly, and feel yourself drawn in, sucked into an even darker void behind it, and feel yourself falling deep, deep within yourself.

As you fall faster into utter darkness, you suddenly feel that you are about to reach the "other side" of this darkness, like something or some barrier you are about to collide with is rushing straight towards you, when BANG! You suddenly hit it and instantaneously go "through" into an infinite void of brilliant light, light of pure brilliant white, so bright that there is nothing else in endless space and time than light, and you plunge into it, feeling the sense of endless expansion, and seeing nothing but pure maximum brilliance. There is no feeling of your body, just pureness of light.

Then, slowly open your eyes, and allow the light to "melt into" your surroundings- see the ritual area you have prepared in the distance, your nighted surroundings; see and know that the light you came into has turned into the setting you now find yourself in, and the light coming from the candles in your prepared area is the same as that light.

Walk to the western edge of the circle, facing east, and cross your hands on your chest, go to one knee, and bow. Bring into your mind the image of the goat-horned spirit of light and occult rites to the east of you, along with the sights and sounds of the ancient one, and say these words:

"I supplicate and invoke
The Lord of the House of Fire and Light
The White body of the King in the Land
Lord and Master, Be kind to me
I share blood and spirit with you;
Be kind to me, and grateful I shall be."

Then, walk around the circle counterclockwise one full time, coming back to the west, and enter the circle from the west, going to the center, and standing there, facing east.

Lift a cup of red wine and say the following words over it:

VINDONUS. MOGONS. VITIRIS. BUCCOS. ANDRAS.

And drink half of it, pouring the rest out over the skull of the goat or onto the image.

Say:

"In the name of the Bucca
Male and Female,
Golden Horns and Fire
Glory of Old
Buccos

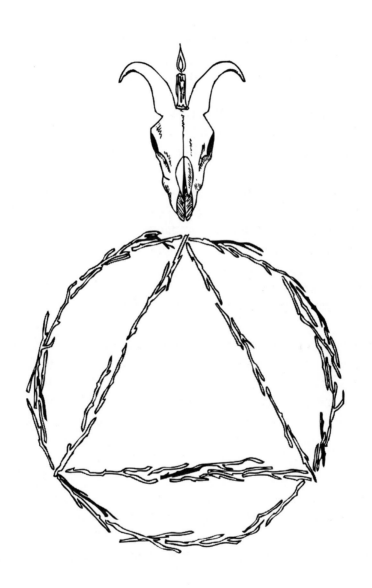

Firebringer
Consecrator
Teacher of Art
Savior

The Dark World's Devil
I am your son (or daughter) and devotee
All-in-between for thee;
On the clear wind of the Great Inheritance
These words echo Above and Below
Let the Pale People of fair Elfland hear me
Let the hordes of black Elfland take note
In the name of the soul of the Old One, see it done."

Then bow once more, and light your unlit candle from the candles that are illuminating the skull or image. If you brought a twig, you have to let it catch on fire and burn long enough to where it has a lasting glowing ember in it, so that you can carry it out, glowing.

Either way, a new flame or ember has to be taken by you from the candles around the image/skull and carried away from the rite.

Leave the area by walking straight east and turning to the right once you are outside of the circle and walking back to the west, going around the southern edge of the circle, and leave the rest of the rite components there until the next day. If you need to go back to blow out the candles, you can. But as far as your own candle or ember goes- preserve it as long as you can, if you can. It represents the light you have gained from the Master.

The Consecration of the Lord of the Funeral Road: The Stag Rite

(Initiation Stream V. Witch Consecration and Dedication)

In the unlight, make a circle of flour, sand, or branches and twigs, with a triangle within it- the triangle's topmost point should indicate to the east.

Outside of the circle to the east should be the skull of a deer or stag (preferably with antlers intact) or an image of the like drawn in the ground, or with flour, or an image otherwise, and one or two candles illuminating it. Allow a trickle of water to fall from the west, leading up to the western edge of the circle. You should carry an unlit candle or a twig with you at all times during this rite.

Stand a ways to the west of this prepared area, and close your eyes. Meditate on the darkness, just formless, expansive darkness. You must bring to mind a doorway that seems imposing to you- a frightening doorway, threatening and ominous seeming, and even though no two people will have the same image in their heads, all of these doors should have a rough image of a horned man carved or painted on them, his head and face only. He should be leering in a rather disconcerting way.

In your mind's eye, step forward and knock on the door three times, and hear a great hollow booming, echoing behind it, which vibrates in your head and in your bones. Then, watch it open slowly, and feel yourself drawn in, sucked into an even darker void behind it, and feel yourself falling deep, deep within yourself.

As you fall faster into utter darkness, you suddenly feel that you are about to reach the "other side" of this darkness, like something or some barrier you are about to collide with is rushing straight towards you, when BANG! You suddenly hit it and instantaneously go "through" into an infinite void of brilliant light, light of pure brilliant white, so bright that there is nothing else in endless space and time than light, and you plunge into it, feeling the sense of endless expansion, and seeing nothing but pure maximum brilliance. There is no feeling of your body, just pureness of light.

Then, slowly open your eyes, and allow the light to "melt into" your surroundings- see the ritual area you have prepared in the distance, your nighted surroundings; see and know that the light you came into has turned into the setting you now find yourself in, and the light coming from the candles in your prepared area is the same as that light.

Walk to the western edge of the circle, facing east, and cross your hands on your chest, go to one knee, and bow. Bring into your mind the image of the stag-antlered King of sorcery and occult rites to the east of you, along with the sights and sounds of the ancient king, and say these words:

"I supplicate and invoke
The Lord of the Unseen Land
Father of the Savior Goat
Lord and Horseman, be kind to me
I share blood and spirit with you;
Be kind to me, and grateful I shall be."

Then, walk around the circle counterclockwise one full time, coming back to the west, and enter the circle from the west, going to the center, and standing there, facing east.

Lift a cup of red wine and say the following words over it:

BUCCOS. ANDRAS. VINDONUS. MOGONS. VITIRIS.

And drink half of it, pouring the rest out over the skull of the deer or stag, or the drawn image.

Say:

"In the name of the Hellekin
Master Invisible, Lord of earth and sky
And the immense regions below
Thorned, Antlered,
Glory of Old.

Vindonus
Fire-Bearer
Horn-Blower
Landwarder
Reverser

The Hell-Track's Master
I am your son (or daughter) and devotee
All-in-between for thee;

On the clear wind of the Great Inheritance
These words echo Above and Below
Let the Pale People of fair Elfland hear me
Let the hordes of black Elfland take note
In the name of the soul of the Old One, see it done."

Then bow once more, and light your unlit candle from the candles that are illuminating the skull, antlers or image. If you brought a twig, you have to let it catch on fire and burn long enough to where it has a lasting glowing ember in it so that you can carry it out, glowing. Either way, a new flame or ember has to be taken by you from the candles around the skull/image, and carried away from the rite.

Leave the area by walking straight east and turning to the right once you are outside of the circle and walking back to the west, going around the southern edge of the circle, and leave the rest of the rite components there until the next day. If you need to go back to blow out the candles, you can. But as far as your own candle or ember goes- preserve it as long as you can, if you can. It represents the light you have gained from the Lord.

The Grand Rite of Elemental Regency

(Cunning Working of Fire for Attained and Dedicated Witches of the House of Buc-Andras)

For this rite, make a circle of flour, sand, or branches and twigs, with a triangle within it- the triangle's topmost point should indicate to the east. To the north of this circle and triangle, the night sky should be visible, with the northern stars clearly visible there. Outside of the circle to the east should be a blazing candle, lantern or lamp of art.

Allow a trickle of water to fall from the west, leading up to the western edge of the circle.

At the south, have a censer with an herb appropriate to the nature of your working, smoldering. The candle, water and censer are of course optional, but the full strength of this rite is greatly aided by their presence.

Begin by going to the west a ways, facing the direction of the working area and closing your eyes.

Meditate on the darkness, just formless, expansive darkness. You must bring to mind a doorway that seems imposing to you- a frightening doorway, threatening and ominous seeming, and even though no two people will have the same image in their heads, all of these doors should have a rough image of a horned man carved or painted on them, his head and face only. He should be leering in a rather disconcerting way.

In your mind's eye, step forward and knock on the door three times, and hear a great hollow booming echoing behind it, which vibrates in your head and in your bones. Then, watch it open slowly, and feel yourself drawn in, sucked into an even darker void behind it, and feel yourself falling deep, deep within yourself.

As you fall faster into utter darkness, you suddenly feel that you are about to reach the "other side" of this darkness, like something or some barrier you are about to collide with is rushing straight towards you, when BANG! You suddenly hit it and instantaneously go "through" into an infinite void of brilliant light, light of pure brilliant white, so bright that there is nothing else in endless space and time than light, and you plunge into it, feeling the sense of endless expansion, and seeing nothing but pure maximum brilliance. There is no feeling of your body, just pureness of light.

Then, slowly open your eyes, and allow the light to "melt into" your surroundings- see the ritual area you have prepared in the distance, your nighted surroundings; see and know that the light you came into has turned into the setting you now find yourself in, and the light coming from the candles in your prepared area is the same as that light.

Walk to the western edge of the circle, facing east, cross your hands on your chest, go to one knee, and bow. Bring into your mind the image of the White Stag-antlered King, or, if you prefer, the Goat-Horned King of Light and Occult Rites to the east of you, along with the sights and sounds of the ancient one, and say these words:

"I supplicate and invoke
The Lord of the House of Fire and Light
The White body of the King in the Land,
Golden Goat (or White Antlered) Lord,
Be kind to me
I share blood and spirit with you;
I am a scion of your house.
Be kind to me."

Then, walk around the circle counterclockwise one full time, coming back to the west, and enter the circle from the west, going to the center, and face east. Then, turn and slowly face north.

Imagine that you have horns, such as those of a goat, or branching antlers like a stag. Imagine a great light welling up from inside you, irradiating you and filling you with warmth.

Say:

"It is not I who undertake this rite,
But the Lord of every hidden power."

Slowly and deliberately hold both of your hands out to the northern sky and say:

"By the Word, I invoke and claim regency over the inconstant airs, forever moving, consenting to the heart."

Let your right hand swing out to reach to the east, and say:

"By the Word, I invoke and claim regency over the royal fires, nurturing and consuming, consenting to the divine spirit."

Let your left hand swing out to reach to the west, and say:

"By the Word, I invoke and claim regency over the fertile waters, life-giving and beguiling, consenting to the dark soul."

Remaining in this "hands out to both sides" stance, let your head tilt forward and say:

"By the Word, I invoke and claim regency over the abundant earth, sustaining and devouring, consenting to the flesh."

Then lift your head again, and say:

"My Words resound above and below, by virtue of
the Great Inheritance
The Invisible Mystery that embraces all
The Invisible Mystery that consecrates all
The Invisible Mystery that fulfills all
It is in this Mystery that I have the Fullness of Being,
Though I comprehend it not."

Stand in this pose, the airs before you and mastered, the fires and waters to your right and left and mastered, and the earth behind you and all around you, mastered by the Word- and the "vertical axis" of the Invisible Mystery coming down to penetrate the cross of the elements- making a three dimensional "hex sign" in you and all about you.

All about you is in your sphere of mastery- all is you- as long as you recognize that it is the Invisible Mystery, the Great Inheritance, that upholds you and the World, the fullness of being, and with awareness and concentration, and slow, deliberate trust in the power of the Word, you can bring reality into manifestation with your mind and speech.

Think of your condition in the rite at this point as being inside a "sphere" which is the size of the whole world- with the vertical axis of the Invisible Mystery coming from "outside" of knowable reality, inter-penetrating it all, and flowing again out of it.

The greatest power is all around us, a part of us, but also separate- and thus beyond knowing in a rational manner. By your will and speech, you will call upon patterns of power that come from beyond the sphere of knowable reality, and call them INTO reality. Bear this in mind, without dwelling on the words; just know this.

The rite continues:

After you have made the declaration of the Great Inheritance, gather your thoughts to what you desire, and say:

"In the Unspeakable Name of all that is seen and unseen, let Fate's threads move with my will!"

<Here insert your intentions, spoken well, poetically, but always specifically.>   Then, chant:

MOGONS…. (while visualizing "being" a serpent")

BUCCOS…… (while visualizing "being" a goat)

VINDONUS…. (while visualizing "being" a dog/hound or a wolf)

BRIMO….. (while visualizing "being" a powerful, snorting bull, or just a formless, terrifying presence below in the dark)

See it Done!
See it Done!
See it DONE!"

As you declare this last "see it done," reach down and destroy the circle and triangle by sweeping your hands on the ground forward and outwards towards the north. You only need to disrupt it right in front of where you stand.

Then leave the area by walking straight east, and turn to the right once you are outside of the circle. Walk back to the west, going around the southern edge of the circle, and leave the rest of the rite components there until later.

What you say in this operation will come to pass.

Your requests should be worded to influence the seeming "developing" of Fate in the world of the senses, or to alter "internal" realities about yourself. Anything is possible. But be cautious in your usage of this rite.

This rite is used for cursing, for transforming the self, for consecrating objects, and for many other things-anything can be accomplished with it.

Ritual Book:
The Craft of the Hidden People

Echoes in the Unseen

The Old Ways teach us that all things are woven together; all things, though seemingly differentiated, are One. In the great tapestry of Fate, the unseen world is not separate from this world of mortals; even though the dim reaches of the netherworld are hidden from the eyes of mortals, they still occupy the same Fate-woven circle of Reality. What occurs in one world "echoes" into the other- and all things that appear in the world of mortals, whether trees, or stones, or animals, or people, are mere appearances of stranger forces.

What you do in this world, occurs in all worlds- thoughts, words, actions, all of them can have great power if you are aware of the subtle connection between what we call "worlds," and your own being- and therefore become able to focus properly, using an arcane "sight" or understanding.

This "sight" is the Witch-sight that we have discussed in detail; this "understanding" is a strange sort of wordless knowledge, a "knowing without knowing." There is a certain condition or "place" a person moves into, where they move in fullness or wholeness, guided by instinct and intuition, or perhaps by the hands of helpers and familiars unseen. All of life becomes a "working" of the unseen world, and the cunning Witch moves with an assurance or faith born in the unseen.

If you were to thrash about in a pool of water, the waves you make would unsettle the entire pool, and you would remain bobbing there in the water- but with study and awareness, you could channel your motions and swim; you could move about at will, using the currents and motions and forces to your will and benefit. When one deals with the unseen world, you must think like this, but you must also realize that the unseen reality is not as clear as a pool of water- it has reaches that require a new sort of sight, and a new sort of "feeling" for dealing with it.

The very point of making "contacts" or spiritual connections with beings in the Underworld or the Unseen is so that they will become your "limbs" and "eyes" in that reality. The forces and currents that you are trying to "channel" and "use," unlike the water in a pool, require a new sort of sense- and a great wordless trust in the powers that you unite with. When you have this connection, you feel it in your bones; you know it without even knowing how, fully.

The information that I am about to give here is never-before seen prose incantations and "ritual directions," given to me from contacts, which literally cause things to happen- they bring about literal journeys into the unseen world, and make other forces unseen move. Through your mind and body, those same powers can cause what seem like "changes" in this world, or seem to influence the unfolding of Fate. These instructions work because they "echo" in the unseen; certain actions and words that encapsulate concepts here are actually causing things to "occur" there- the key to bringing the two "worlds" together is to be consciously aware of what precisely "here" represents what "there." In your conscious awareness, power can move from one world to the next and cause the "magic" to work.

There is no such thing as doing an "accidental" working of any power. It operates on a conscious level, even if the seeds of it, and the keys of it, may be buried deeply in the subconscious, and in the Underworld. Power rises out of the unseen, and your mind and body are channels for it to emerge, in tandem with (hopefully) your will.

However, as we will see, humans are never the power behind "magic" or sorcery- they are the will behind it, and if they are cunning, they know how to gain a "position" and achieve an understanding and condition by which power will respond in conjunction with their will. There is no "working" without the element of will and power- but these are not things that humans themselves can produce in large enough amounts alone- the human contribution is will, and Nature's contribution- the offering of spirits and other natural forces- is power. The Witch is the union point for these two things. We will discuss this soon.

These words and understandings cannot and will not "work" for you, if you have not understood, on some level, all that has been said in this book before this section. The foundational material, from the worldview onward, is crucial.

This final part of the book is a record and "Gramarye" of a system of power-working or magic that underlies the current of the Old Ways. I will first discuss two important things that must be remembered, if and when you ever begin to perform any sort of traditional rite or working, and then I will give a writing concerning "the missing element"- the single vital factor that most people who claim to practice sorcery in the Pagan tradition tend to forget, and which renders their workings mostly ineffectual.

When you have read and understood these two small essays, I will proceed with a description of the "Red Meal" or the Housle, a simple yet powerful rite that I have mentioned many times before. The Red Meal is the act of sharing bread and wine or ale (or some drink) with powers in the unseen world. It is a sacrifice and a sharing, that literally and symbolically brings together the two worlds, and weds your power directly to the powers you are sharing the meal with. It is the basic and most important ritual of the Old Ways and has many levels of meaning and use.

After that, I will discuss the "heart" of the ritual book, the received art of creating the Witch-ring or the "Compass," which is an area of ground wherein actions that occur within "echo" strongly in the fullness of Reality; I will discuss the art of spelling or making "spells" and incantations, as well as singing to or what is now called "invoking" spiritual powers, and then I will discuss a working done at a thorn tree to invoke the powers of the Underworld, and an initiation stream.

Lastly, I will discuss a ritual inspired by ancient rites from Northern England, the "four-sided shrine," and two more operations of great power- the Thorn Tree Door, which is a rite for creating an actual doorway into the unseen, and the Rite of Arriving, which is a ritual for meeting and bonding with local Land powers.

Two Things that Must be Remembered

When doing any kind of craft rite, from a simple Housle or Red Meal, all the way to the greatest of Wisdom or power workings, it is important to keep two simple factors in mind, two understandings that will make any ritual a truly moving and powerful experience. First, always remember that all things are connected, that no two forces or beings are separate within the great body of Nature; therefore, any invocation, any thought or feeling has an affect that is tangible, even across what seem to be vast reaches of space or even time.

If you allow yourself to rest in the secure knowledge that all things are united, and that all motions and events and even words and thoughts echo through an intimate, inter-locked natural system of relationship and Fate, you will be more able to appreciate the affects of your invocations and ritual motions, and more able to "feel" them bringing about the needed and desired transformations on the subtle level. Keeping the understanding of connectivity firmly in mind and trusting it implicitly is the foremost vital thing to bear with you in your rites.

Secondly, when you perform rites and make invocations, or anything, always gently allow yourself to be as deliberate and steady as possible- when I say this, I mean that you should always speak, act, move, and even think with a deliberate, planned out, almost "slow" feel; this is a good way to fall into a deep trance that we like to call "slow time." When you lift a forked wood or a rod or a bowl, when you make invocations, let your every action be as even, steady, and deliberate as possible; these are powerful actions, sacred actions, and deserving of your *every bit* of awareness and attention. When you speak, allow your words to flow steadily and calmly, resonating with deliberate focus.

The mind will try to "speed up" on you, but gently keep it reigned in, and let awareness be deep, steady, and *fully* absorbed in what you are doing, no matter how minor it seems. The power of the rite, the motions, all suddenly increase in amazing ways. Some experienced folk like to get into trances before the start of the rite, but others know another truth: that deliberately and steadily paying full attention to the motions of the rite can itself be a door into the trance, and in this way, some find it easier than "putting on the mantle" before they begin. It is simply another approach to this (or any other) rite. Try both, or use both as you feel the need.

You will discover that these two bits of advice greatly increase any rite's power and affect: the rewarding feeling of any rite is increased when the rite participants are resting in the secure awareness of the interconnectivity of all things, and celebrating every word and motion of a holy rite with the ultimate pure, focused awareness and deliberate steadiness.

The Missing Element

All acts of traditional craft are geomantic, that is to say, Land-based. The Land *is* the mysterious "missing" element that acts as the source of primary power and force to the Old Craft's operations and transformations. This is because the Land itself *is* the Great Queen, the Dame, the living manifest presence of a supreme divine reality, and a being of timeless power and Wisdom.

Forces emerge from within the Land; forces flow through it. It is part of us and we are part of it, inseparable. The Land is the very power that man possesses, as he possesses his own left hand or beating heart. But the Land is the pool of his power; the Land and its interior spaces are the physical manifestation of what has been called the "subconscious" mind or the "collective unconscious." The Land and its dark interior *is* the great well of memory and power and forces that *is* a part of everyone. Your own deepest mind is one and the same with the Land, and the Land is alive. It is full of living forces. Many have wondered where their memories, thoughts, dreams, and deepest mind were to be found- and the answer has always been "right beneath your feet."

When you walk upon the Land, you must pass through the "forehead door," which is a change in awareness of your relationship with the Land- you have to cease to see yourself in terms of separation from the Land, and instead see the Land as the repository of your power, your dreams, your memories, your thoughts, and your life. It is likewise the space that the dead inhabit, adding to the constant murmurings and whispers that run through the ground, the dark spaces beyond, and which meander through your head when you are half awake and half asleep in the twilight.

You and the Land are one. To successfully perform any traditional craft rite, from the Housle or the Red Meal, to the highest operations of power and Wisdom- such as calling forth the ancestors or the sleepers in the dark, or just consciously summoning the might of the Old Ones- you must experience the Land in this way; you must accept the truth of your condition with it, and within it.

But geomancy is the key term here. geomancy (not the divination technique, but a broader term meaning "Land-based craft") is the heart and soul of the true Old Ways, for all powers emerge from the Land.

The forces of the Land emerge in every form imaginable. The flowings of force in the Land emerge in the Landscape and in the unseen roads that crisscross the Landscape. Learning to interact with the alignments and forceful flows of power and manifestation in the ground, and their reflections in the heavens, as well as the invisible realities within that they encapsulate, is the key.

It sounds complex, but it is not; it is a simple shift to feeling yourself as inseparable from the Land, from Nature, and letting- going passive and allowing- the sense of peace and "wholeness" to fill you. The only thing that stands in your way from doing this is your own deeply-seated sense that you are separate; give up on it; let it go. You surrender into a greater way of being.

We must now speak of the roads. The roads are the Straight Tracks; the Ghost Roads; the Owl Lines. They are the flowings of spectral force that manifest in natural and sometimes in human-contrived ways; the boundary between these two can be made thin. Even though we call them Straight Tracks, you must understand something very important- the earth's power does not "well up" in long crisscrossing patterns of lines. It wells up in organic, circular, wave-like patterns, everywhere. It concentrates in certain places.

The "lines" between them are actually human created symbols or concepts that link two or more "upwellings" of force together- and by virtue of the fact that these "lines" connect, using the shortest possible distance, two or more places of power, the lines themselves are useful "pointers" for the inner self and deep mind to "align" on the places of power. Like moths (themselves ancient symbols of the soul) who are drawn to bright lights and flames, a mindstream is drawn from one place of power to another, as though they were torches in the night guiding the mind from one place to the next. Some places of power lead into the Underworld directly, so the departed souls of humans and animals eventually are drawn to them, and find access downward to the source of sources. The journeying soul always follows the shortest possible route- a line- between places of power, and so the "lines" between are called "Ghost Roads."

Where these "lines" meet or have junctions are always special places as well, because these junction points have "great powers" arrayed around them, which can be tapped by a person who orients themselves "between." What begins to happen, naturally, on these "lines," is that innerworldly force starts to take form there- it influences everything, from the growth of certain trees, to the decision on the parts of humans, both in ancient times and now, to build buildings, roads, camps, churches, temples, standing stones, burial mounds, and what have you. These so-called "ley" lines can be found often by looking at survey maps, and looking for tell-tale signs such as these, all lining up.

The Ghost Roads can be indicated by various natural features, or the force in the Land itself can be concentrated and aligned by the use of the water, and the conscious mind of a witch or operant- this is a geomantic Mystery that we must discuss now. Spirits walk roads of water. The living can use water to create lines of spiritual incidence. Of course, there are other meanings to "roads of water"- this can refer to natural waterscapes in the environment.

The Housle, as well as any other effective operation, will utilize the power of the Land, sometimes in the form of the roads. Where these roads and their power are strong, the Old Ones are, or they can be called with ease. Never forget this. The following phenomenon and Land or artifact features should be considered and taken into account anytime you perform a working of traditional craft.

I. THE CROSSED ROADS

This refers to the crossing of any two physical roads in some lonely place. Crossroads were a traditional place for the performance of Witchcraft, as well as sacred since time immemorial to various spirits and divinities who were patrons of the craft, and powers of the Underworld. Few people realize it, but the "crossroads" of classical lore referred not to a "four way" cross where two roads cross, but a "three way" junction where a single road forks.

Any place that two physical roads cross, or where a single road forks, is a spiritually charged place, but the kind of crossroads sought out for the tasks of craft are lonelier, more rural roads, where traffic in the night is nonexistent.

Ironically, the performance of rites at the crossroads is not the main issue at hand. The location where the roads cross is often, but not always, a place of power similar to the hills or trees or stones or the other places we will discuss. A knowledge of where roads cross (for they have an uncanny way of crossing on or near Ghost Roads) is needed for knowing where Ghost Roads may occur within a given region where you may plan to engage in the craft. Look at maps or pay attention to rural crossroads, particularly very old roads or by-ways.

II. TREES

Trees, especially larger, older trees with large root systems, are interfaces of power between this world and the world below. Natural "lines" or alignments of trees often indicate a Trod or Ghost Road; but a lone standing tree of great might or spirit is often a sign of the presence of a track, or an "upwelling." Fungus such as mushrooms that naturally form circles, especially often and in the same region, have a similar force. They can indicate the presence of conjunctions of unseen roads, or simply the lay of a Ghost Road. Stands or copses of trees are likewise to be taken into consideration, as well as stands of woods. Whole forests used to be sacred; the "Bell Trees" may yet exist.

III. THE ANCIENT STONE

Like trees, standing stones, whether lone stones (Godstones or markstones) or circular arrangements of stones, often have a function of showing a road, and all lone stones, especially Godstones, are interface points with the inner reality of the Land, the Underworld or the Otherworld. Circular or other arrangements of stones usually show other complexities. All should be taken into account locally, just like trees or crossroads, or any of the other features mentioned here.

IV. THE HILL

Rises in the Land, especially hills or chains of hills, are indicative of interaction points between the multi-layered reality of the Land, and other forces. Lone hills are chiefly representatives of the mounds of the dead and the passageway below the earth. They are their own special interaction points. Actual burial mounds, constructed long ago (or even recently) are the same- any place human bones or remains, or the remains of dead creatures, has been put in the ground, becomes "thinner"- it becomes an interaction point between two realities.

V. THE BELL AND THE GRAVE

Churches, especially old ones, and gravesites are powerful geomantic locations for many reasons. In the Old World, churches were often placed on Pagan holy sites; graveyards the world over are interaction points between the living and the dead, and these two realities, for a variety of reasons. The main reason for graveyards being so potent is that they contain the remains of the dead, and are places where some of the essence of the dead merged with the ground. They become "interaction" points.

VI. THE WATERS

Natural ponds, lakes, rivers, wells, and streams can all act as Otherworldly interaction points, and can occur parallel or over the Ghost Roads. Ponds, wells, and lakes mostly act as entrances into the deeper reality below the Land; rivers and streams do so as well, but chiefly at their sources. Some of the most ancient and powerful Underworld entrances are ancient lakes and wells.

VII. THE GHOST LIGHT or the KINDLY LIGHT

This is the key to geomancy- the kindly light. This is the Watch-fire or leading fire that is built by the operant, to empower and illuminate the Ghost Roads. When Ghost Roads are to be empowered or tapped for their flows of force, it is the Watch-fire that makes the spirit of the

Land respond. The fire and its light is useless without the mind of the mystic or the cunning one who stands forth, vertical with the ground, and makes the flame and the calls. It is the mind and the human upright body that makes the true "vertical force" that calls the power up.

The fire must be created in harmony with the Ghost Roads of the region! It all has to "line up;" this is to say that the location of the fire is not chosen at random by you- it is determined by the naturally expressed forces of the surrounding countryside. The Land itself shows the interaction points; we must put ourselves in sympathy with it, and we can tap into its power.

You must normally sketch a map of the surrounding countryside and its features, and endeavor to see what the various physical features are trying to say; what patterns do you see? Imagine the lines of the Ghost Roads running to and fro between these various sites- do lines cross in places where there is nothing? This may be where the watch-fire should be. If the Housle is to be done, that is where the flame or the fire of the Housle is to be kindled. If a Compass is to be made, that is where it should be made. The force is there; the Old Ones will respond. You have to do your very best to be in sympathy with the Land's natural powerful places, if at all you can.

Look at the landscape features; look at the crossroads; look at the old church locations and the gravesites. Does a large old stand of trees line up with a hill or a series of hills, and is there a place where two roads cross beyond it all, but still in a relatively straight line? Mark it. Look about. You can begin to see strange symbols and alignments forming in any Land.

You cannot leave out the element of the Land in any operation. I discussed crafting Ghost Roads by using water. It is possible to create sites doing this; but it takes doing.

To begin with, you must work on Saturday, at twilight or dawn, or at the darkest time in the night. You must take water from a river or spring, or from some other natural source, and fill it with force using the later-given invocations of the water.

At the time of your working, you make "trickle roads," or pour the water along the ground between the natural phenomenon (trees, hills, etc.)

that you wish to "align" geomantically. If you create more than one "trickle road" or "water road," then you should be doing it to link the various sites that begin the roads and which are contained on them- and the water roads should cross, so that where they cross, you can create Watch-fires and Compasses.

You should use the water; a large moon is a major asset, though it is not strictly necessary. It would always be better to do this rite in the waxing or full phase of the moon. It also helps (quite a bit) to work this rite near the time of an ancient festival, one in which the Ghost Roads were traditionally trod by the unseen ones- but you must wear some form of protection to do this- normally wearing a shirt or coat or a cloak inside out as you work. The best protection, however, is to be on friendly terms with the powers in your Land, and the powers of the Underworld- something that it takes time, devotion, and regular "inner work" to achieve. Spilling blood from your own left hand and giving oaths of service to the powers of your Land, and the great King and Queen within the Land, are generally the best courses of action.

When you have made the trickle roads of water, go to the location where you planned to have your Watch-fire; most usually near a great tree or stone or on a hill; and if you made or found a series of roads, then try to do it where they meet, and usually near an interaction point- and make the Watch-fire. This is the prayer to be recited over it to give it (and the new roads) force.

First, say the invocation for the fires, given later in this section. Then say:

"Lead, kindly light
Keep Straight on the Way:
The Lady goes as a pale-white malkin
The Lady goes as a pale-white doe;
Wisdom walks the Track!
Be you the flame that lights Her on Her way.

A White Hunter sounds a horn,
With Ratchets all the night;
He moves among the hills
Red Robin all the day.

Fire fills the track!
Be you the flame that lights Him on His Way."

After the flame is blazing, a rite of propitiation for the Land guardians or internal powers of that area should be done in the form of a sacred meal. The subtle art of dealing successfully with Land powers, wards, Wanes, and guardians, is dealt with at length in the essay entitled "Ward and Wane: The Rite of Arriving." Some people like to burn bones inside the fire- the "bone-fire" is not an unheard of thing, and is thought of as an offering to the Greatest Power.

This rite does not need to be performed every time you do a working. If the Ghost Roads that you have connected with were natural, that is, not crafted by the trickle-roads of water, it seldom needs to be repeated. If you created the alignments, you should repeat this rite seasonally. But otherwise, you may work in the area, doing any operation of traditional craft, with greater force. At any rate, regardless of what you do, the Land is the missing element from most operations, and the most necessary element to any work. Do not forget this.

The Red Meal: The Housle, or the Sacrament of Bread and Wine

The Red Meal or the Housle is the traditional craft rite par excellence. In its simplicity and power, it makes the central statement of the entire traditional metaphysic: that the seen and the unseen worlds are one, and by the vehicle of the meal itself, they are mentally and physically made so.

The Red Meal is called so by virtue of the fact that the dead were believed to eat "red food"- and it is worth noting that apples in the northern reaches were seen as food for the dead, just as the pomegranate was seen as food for the dead in the south, and the pomegranate, like some species of apple, is a very red food- the edible seeds inside are blood red. Red is the color of life force, and the idea that the dead ate pomegranate or "the apples of Dame Hel" in the Underworld leads to the idea that the dead are receiving nourishment that will regenerate them.

To eat the "Red Meal" is to place yourself, a living person above ground, in the same "space" as the dead below ground, and merge with their Underworldly condition.

The Red Meal is, ideally, red; what I mean by that is, you should try to use dark breads and red wine. This carries the symbolism mentioned before, but it also represents the sacrifice of animal or human flesh from ancient times- the red bread representing freshly killed meat, and the red wine representing blood.

Actual live sacrifices are not normally carried out anymore, for a variety of reasons. The power of sacrifice is fully mediated and called forth by the symbolic bread and wine, so killing is actually quite unnecessary; the spiritual fulfillment and bond created by the Red Meal is every bit as strong as the ancient act of live sacrifice.

Underworldly or Otherworldly forces are called upon to send their power into the body of the bread and into the liquid of the wine, and when they are consumed, that power enters into the people who are partaking of this most ancient sacrament. This is directly in line with the logic of ancient sacrifice, by which the God or Gods were called upon to bless the animal being offered, which was then butchered at an altar or in a holy place, and whose body was roasted and shared by the gathering, and whose blood was sprinkled on the gathered, and on the altar. The act of sacrifice was called "Blot" by the northern heathens, and it simply means "Blood" and a "blessing," or a "Bletsian" literally meant to be "sprinkled with blood."

The act of the Red Meal, today, embodies the ancient act of sacrifice totally, as the body and blood, or bread and wine, is blessed, divided, shared, and the wine is used to anoint the body and sacred items or to consecrate a place. Then, the portion that was not eaten or drunk is given directly to the earth itself- and this portion is absorbed into the Land, to move into the Underworld/Otherworld, and be consumed by the powers that the Red Meal was dedicated to.

When this happens, not only have the participants been blessed by taking physical food and drink into their bodies which was blessed with the power or powers of Otherworldly beings, but the beings themselves also "eat" a portion, forming a perfect link with the human participants- for the time of the Red Meal, and ever after, the participants are literally one with the powers unseen, through the vehicle of the meal. This is why the Red Meal has more than just a worshipful purpose- this is how it can magnify and empower sorcerous workings; after sharing the meal with powers in the unseen, you are one with them, and your incantations or spells are *their* words and spells, as well.

The meal shows a spiritual, ongoing reality, though expressed in serial time- the union of the seen with the unseen. It consciously awakens the participants to the reality of their oneness with the unseen, and acts as a direct channel for power to enter them, and for their power to enter the unseen. The Red Meal is a two-way flow; it causes deep spiritual transformations, and reaffirms our ties and bonds with the spiritual powers that rule over the Old Ways, and with our ancestors and other powers that are our patrons in the unseen.

Any spiritual power or powers can be called upon to bless and share the Red Meal with you- normally it is done for the White King or the Witchmother, or for both of them, and in the case of both, he is called to bless the bread and she the wine. If only one is called, both bread and wine are blessed in the name of that one. If the ancestral powers or the Pale People are called, they, too, can bless the bread and wine- our

Germanic ancestors called this form of the sacrifice an "Alfablot" or an "Elf-blot"- An "Elf-blood," the Elves being the same as the Faeries or the Feeorin, or the Sidhe people in the hollow hills. Alfablots were actually done at burial mounds, to underscore this fact.

Any power can be called upon, from the Pale People as a whole, to the spirit of a particular dead person, to the spirit of an oak tree that the Red Meal is performed in front of. Your familiar spirit or Fetch-beast, or your Fetch-mate can be called upon to bless and share the Red Meal, and the union created with them through this act is very powerful, and it leads to further meeting and internal experiences with them. The Red Meal is first and foremost an act of worship and attunement- but as we shall see later, it has a sort of "practical" usage as well, in the art of power-working.

The local Land-powers are often honored using the Red Meal, and it is a handy way of gaining familiarity with them, and gaining their trust, if they are at all friendly or willing to give trust.

Remember- through your mind and body, intent and word and motion, the unseen powers are called and mediated into the body of the bread and wine, thus making it their true appearance and the vehicle of their entry and blessing into people and the Land; a perfect circle that begins and ends in the Land.

Concerning the Use of the Bell

As with many callings or invocations to powers in the unseen world, a bell is used during the Red Meal. If you don't have a bell, anything that makes a good, sounding noise can be used- a flute, a horn, a drum, or even a sharp hand-clap; but the bell is traditional and was taught to me. As I discuss the secret to using the bell for any invocation here, bear in mind that this applies to any device or action that makes a good, sharp or resounding noise.

It is said, "The bell is ringing to the ears of spirits." This statement may sound a bit funny at first, because spirits don't have ears as humans do. However, this short statement is communicating something else entirely- the sound of the bell ringing, and slowly fading, is reaching the spirits or beings that are being invoked.

The bell "echoes" both in this world and in the unseen. When you ring the bell during the Red Meal, before the invocations, or when you use a bell in any other rite, you have to be aware that as it rings, and as it echoes and resonates and slowly fades out, the "sound" is traveling all the way to the "ears" of the spirit you are calling- you have to internally know that this is the case, visualize (without seeing anything) the "power" of the sound "fading" out, and yet, know that it is "being absorbed" into the unseen world, and ringing there as well, traveling all the way to the awareness of the spiritual power that you are calling. The bell's sound, and its fading, is the physical "bridge" that connects your invocation and will to the spirit's attention.

Of course, just words can do this; you need no resonating sound beforehand. But it is better, stronger, if you have one. Some people just stomp or tap the ground/floor three times before the Red Meal (or any rite) to "get the attention" of the beings below. That is a variant on this bell technique described here.

We will discuss verbal invocations soon, but it should be mentioned here that the bell (or horn or flute or whatever) can be used as a powerful form of "wordless invocation"- if your mind and heart is fixed firmly on the power you wish to contact, the sound of the bell fading and flying to their awareness can actually "invoke" them well enough. It is simply a more advanced, yet organically simple, technique. In the end, invocation is about awakening the attentions of omni-aware Otherworldly powers. If the sound of a bell (or whatever) can make you feel that you have their attention, it has succeeded as an invocation.

The Meal

I am going to now give the passages and basic outline of the Red Meal, and be warned: this outline will contain instructions for ritual motions that are unfamiliar to you. Ignore them for now, as they will be explained in the coming pages.

The Red Meal is best performed outdoors, near a place of power-especially in front of a huge old tree of some kind, preferably one with a big root system. If it has to be done indoors, that is fine, but the end of the rite requires you to give the remains of the meal to the ground, so you will have to go outside to do that, or at least, go outside later, after the rite is over, to deposit the offerings on to the earth or into a body of water somewhere.

1. Walk a counterclockwise circle or semi-circle around the place where you will be doing the Red Meal. You should say the "Spell of the Road" as you do so.

2. Perform the spell for the water and make the four roads, and then do the spell for the fire.

3. Ring the bell- ringing its sound to the ears of the powers you are sharing the Red Meal with. If this is all the invocation you need, then continue. If not, then invoke them, using your own words, or with one of the invocation techniques we will discuss later.

4. Say the blessing for the bread, with your left hand held over it:

"Here is bread, the life of the Earth,
Blessed to give us life and strength.
I consecrate it in the name of_____
With my left hand I bless it
With my left hand I shall eat it."

5. Ring the bell again (you don't have to re-invoke if you already succeeded at that), and say for the wine, while lifting the cup:

"Here is wine, filling the cup with abundance
I consecrate it in the name of _____
With my left hand I lift it,
With my left hand I shall drink it."

Holding the cup in your left hand still, bring it near your lips, and say

"I drink this cup in my Lady's name: She shall gather me home again."

Then drink a little. Everyone who shares from the cup should say the same, holding the cup with their left hand, before they drink.

After you (or everyone gathered) has shared from the cup, everyone should eat a piece of the bread- tear or cut it apart, making enough pieces for everyone.

As you bring the piece of bread, held with your left hand, near your lips, you should say:

"I eat this bread in the unknown name, for fear and care, and want of Him."

Then eat.

The rest of the wine should be poured into the same bowl or dish containing the remains of the bread, mixing the two together, and each person who is at the gathering should dip their finger in the mixture and anoint their head with it. If the area that the Red Meal is being performed in needs to be consecrated or blessed, the wine inside the bowl can be sprinkled around it, and objects can likewise be blessed with the same sprinkling.

When that is done, the bowl with the remainder of the bread and wine should be held up by the person leading the Red Meal. He or she says the **Declaration of Giving**:

"As some is taken, so is this given
By the sons and daughters of the family of the Old Faith
I give it to the Ground (1)
I give it to the Pale People below (2)
That above and below will become one (3)
For what is taken is truly given
And what is given is truly taken
The day and night are wed
As the living and the dead.
Here is shown a Mystery."

Notes to this declaration:

1. If you are indoors, you say "I give it to the ground," and after the rite, you bring it outside. If you are outside on a field or meadow, you say "I give it to the ground" or "I give it to the Land." If you are before a huge old oak tree, you say "I give it to the roots" or "I give it to the tree;" if you are at a body of water, you say "I give it to the stream" or "I give it to the lake," or whatever. If you are making the offering at a stone, like an ancient standing stone, or an offering-stone, you say "I give it to the stone"… just use common sense here. No matter what, the Red Meal's remains *have* to reach the earth, the Land or the water, in some way. That is how they will "pass below and within" to reach the powers and "complete the circle" of the meal. This is a tithe to the Underworld.

2. The standard declaration says "I give it to the Pale People below"- but if you wish, you can declare that you are giving it to any power- if the Red Meal was done for a deceased relative, you can say that you give it to that person; if it was done as a devotion to the White Lord of Elfhame, you can say "I give it to Lord Vindonus" or "I give it to the Old One;" it can be given to any power- "I give it to my familiar spirit" is also an option. But remember, even if you did the Red Meal for a relative or for a certain power or powers, you can still say "I give it to the Pale People below" here- it's just a matter of how you feel, how inclusive you want to feel.

3. The standard "request" for the meal is that the powers in the Unseen make you whole- that "above and below," or, in other words, "this world and the unseen world" become one- the basic message of the Red Meal. However, this meal can be used for specific purposes that go beyond that, and turn this offering into a form of magic. To make an example, imagine that you did the Red Meal outside before an oak tree, to the White Horned King specifically, to have him send you a dream of guidance, to help you through a difficult situation. You could say, in the declaration: "As some is taken, so is this given, by this son of the family of the old faith… I give it to the roots of this tree, I give it to the Horned Master, that he might send dreams to guide me, in my time of need… for what is taken is truly given, etc." But the "standard form" of the Red Meal merely requests that above and below be made as one.

After the declaration is made, the bowl or plate containing the remaining mixed bread and wine is poured onto the ground, or onto the roots, or the stone, or into the water, wherever. That is the end of the rite.

Killing the Red Meal

There is one more variant on the Red Meal that has to be discussed- the darkest version, called the "Killing of the Red Meal." It is done exactly like the Red Meal as described above, with one change- a knife or small reaping hook is required, and the person blessing the bread and the wine has to symbolically "kill" the bread and "slit the throat" of the cup that is used to hold the wine.

This variant is used only in one rite that I know of, and which I will give later in this ritual book. You may use it at other times, when you are especially focused on the theme of sacrifice, such as around Lammas-time, or other harvest times.

To perform this variant, after you have said the blessing over the bread, you put the bowl or plate down (or have someone else hold it, or hold it in your right hand) and take the bladed implement in your left hand, and say:

"With my left hand I take its life and give it to
_____" (whatever power or powers)

Then you cut the bread up.

Then you proceed to the wine. After you have said the blessing over the wine, you take the bladed implement in your left hand and hold the cup in your right, or have someone else hold it, and you say:

"With my left hand I take its life and give it to
_____ "

Then you slide the blade over the cup, across the top of it, and immediately tip the cup to the side, letting a little wine splatter to the ground, or into a waiting dish if you are indoors. This represents the initial spray of blood from the throat of a sacrificed animal.

Then you put the bladed implement down, take the cup in your left hand, and proceed as normal with the rest of the Red Meal.

The Witch-Ring: Drawing the Witches' Compass

Before I proceed into this very important section of the Ritual Book, I have to make it very clear that the traditional craft is a highly simple, earthy and organic spiritual art. Do not ever feel too constrained by what you read here- while the system that is written here is perfect as it is written, it is also highly adaptable.

The Compass or the "Ring of Art," is a ritually created working area, specifically used for what some call "magic," or for power-working. It is not a space designed to "protect" the people inside from hostile powers; it has a far more sublime use and far deeper symbolism. The roundness of it symbolizes the "circle of Fate," the adamantine circle of all reality, and the power of circling, repetition, eternity. But beyond that, the Witch-Compass is an attempt to create a miniature world or a microcosm which is linked to the "greater" world or the macrocosm, and thus it becomes a circular area wherein ritual actions and motions can be performed, such that they "echo" into greater reality.

The real symbolism of such a "ring" is that of a meeting place- it is a place where the unseen world meets with and unites with the seen world. Its design and construction is based on the circular places of power, like nemetons, groves, or even (perhaps) megalithic stone circles- many of which were surrounded with ditches of water.

Indo-European Pagans did not build the "stone circles" in Europe, nor did they religiously tend to use them- they preferred their own groves, nemetons, and temples. But many groves and other sacred areas of the Indo-European peoples were also surrounded by ropes hanging from posts driven into the ground around the area, or ditches full of water. Something was used to delineate the area from the rest of the world, to make it a place of special "meetings" and unions and communication with the unseen world.

The Compass, attested to from history and traditional lore, may well be a descendent of the same notion. At any rate, it is mostly used today for works of magical intent, for any action performed within it carries an echo that is believed to affect the outer world as well, because inner and outer, as we have seen, are intimately spiritually joined, and that union can be consciously experienced on many levels, using many ritual actions.

What I discovered when I learned about the inner workings of the Witch-ring or Compass was that it had another level of operation that most people never considered- it was itself a physical representation of the descent into the Underworld. When the Compass is done properly, it is a great invocation of "reversal" and "turning inward" or "going left" or "going below"- spiritually and literally speaking, the Compass occupies both space in this world and "space" in the Underworld. This is its highest and deepest symbolism and use; it creates a literal Otherworldly place, an Underworldly location, where the powers that live in the Land and in us can be approached with ease. It is an uncanny but powerful place and occurrence.

What I have to offer you here are actual incantations and instructions for creating a compass that I received from contacts. I will give these instructions in the following manner:

First will come the outline of how to draw the Witch-ring or the Compass. Then I will give the six actual pieces of "received" prose, followed by my personally written "variants" to them. Next will come my notes and analysis on the "received" prose, discussing the symbolism or metaphysical meaning and value, and how it is used. Then I will discuss alternate methods of using these six "pieces."

As a final note- remember that any of the names given in previous chapters for the Witchfather and the Witchmother can be used in the place of "devil" or "Lady" in the "received" or basic form of any of these spells or prose, whether it be in the Compass drawing, or in the section on spellwork. These prose pieces are meant to be used according to your own needs and particularities; as long as the symbolism and intent stays intact, they work.

The Witches' Compass is made in the following six steps:

1. The "Going Forth" declaration is made
2. The Spell of the Road is done.
3. The Spell for the Water is done, and the Four Roads are made.
4. The Spell for the Fire is done.

5. The River's Edge incantations are made (if needed)
6. The Ring of Art invocation is done.

I. The "Going Forth" Declaration

"I come hither, west of the bridge to Hell, a holy stone, a holy tree, a holy well, where the good folk dwell, north of hedges and comforting bells, I come hither, from the world I leave behind. In the name of the Devil and his Dame I come, bearing the wand that is a flying steed. In my left hand I bear it, and a mark. As a tree I ride, as a dead man I ride, I take the witch road into far deep Lands where the pale people hie."

Variant:

I come hither, west of the bridge to the Unworld, a holy stone, a holy tree, a holy well, where the good folk dwell, north of roads and man-haunted dells, I come hither, from the world I leave behind. In the name of the Old One and his Lady I come, bearing the stave that is a flying steed- in my left hand I bear it, and a mark. As a tree I go, as a dead man/woman I go, I take the leftward road into far deep Lands where the pale people dwell."

Analysis and Ritual Action:

The declaration is the beginning of the drawing of the Compass- and as you can see, it is also the beginning, verbally stated, of a journey or voyage into the Underworld. It is an invocation of the "Leftward Road," or the road that goes against the sun, to the left, counterclockwise, or widdershins, and therefore goes against the flow of life- in other words, towards death, towards the within, and into the reversed world, or the Underworld. The Witch is going into the presence of Dame Hell herself, and the Master of the Dead.

The Witch is declaring that he or she is going into the "far deep Lands" where the Pale People come, or live. The Witch precedes this by describing the directions to that place- the Witch has gone "west of the bridge to Hell, a holy stone, a holy tree, a holy well, where the good folk dwell." This means that the witch has walked a little west of a place that was traditionally seen as an entrance into the Underworld, before making this declaration. They also mention that they have gone "north of hedges and comforting bells," in other words, north of mankind's familiar habitations. North is the cold, dark direction, the direction of Queen Hel and her covered, hidden realm, a forbidding direction that only the brave will walk, just as west is the traditional direction that the "misty waters" that separate this world from the unseen world are found in.

"I come here, from the world I leave behind," the Witch then says, affirming that they are consciously leaving the world of men behind, and putting themselves into a state of mind ready to receive the wordless and boundless Mysteries of the Otherness.

"In the name of the Devil and his Dame I come…" the Witch says; of course, as my contacts mentioned, "the Devil" in this case is a reference to the Master of the Underworld, either the Witchfather or true Master who acted as the guide of souls into Underworld, or the King of Faery/Elfhame, the white and ancient one who rules over the transitions from our state to the Otherness. As you can see from my variant, any name for either of these beings mentioned in part one of this book can be used in place of "the Devil," or, if you wish, you can just use the "Devil," so long as you realize you are invoking a being who is certainly not the Christian anti-God. The Witch is blessing his or her expected journey in the name of the Lord and Lady of the Underworld with this line.

"Bearing the wand that is a flying steed- in my left hand I bear it and a mark." By saying this, the Witch affirms that he or she is a member of the Witch-cultus, for these things- the wand that is a flying steed, held in the left hand, and the mark on the left hand- are signs of the Witch, and of the Witches' power to "fly" into the unseen reality, that is, to engage in transvection, or spiritually journeying beyond the boundaries of the body-mind center- "carrying over" the awareness into the fullness of things, and into the Otherworld. It is the riding-pole, and the virtue of the spiritual powers and allies who empower the Witch, that do the "carrying over."

The flying-wand is a particularly important part of this invocation, because it has been held since time immemorial that Witchcraft included the power to fly through the air with old Gods and spirits and to enter caves, go down into mountains, or cross dividing hedges and rivers into another world, where the Sabbat was held. Flying "wild rades" and the like, led by heathen Gods and Goddesses, are very common, and most records indicate that the witch used some sort of steed, whether a broom or a stick of wood, or some other plant-stem or shaft, or an animal. This can clearly tie into the "riding poles" that are dressed up like horses and used for spiritual journeys by the shamans of the Altaic peoples.

When making this declaration, the person doing so should have a stick of some kind, or a long wand, or a stang or a broom, or a forked piece of wood, all of which should be at least 4 to 5 feet long, and it should be held in the left hand. It is a powerful symbol for what is about to occur. In Gerald Gardner's book "High Magic's Aid," which is rumored to contain the traditional teachings of a coven of witches operating in Southern England, it is mentioned that witches had to walk or go to the Sabbat with a stick between their legs, and if I recall correctly, the book describes this as a fertility rite, which honored the Master of the Sabbat. If this was a traditional teaching that Gardner received, then it fits in well with the idea we are discussing now.

The mark on the left hand is nothing more than a scar, left after blood was released from the left hand during an initiation, which we will discuss soon. This scar was believed by some to be in a certain place on the left hand- normally on one of the fingers. This scar is a sign that the person is initiated into the sorcerous Mysteries of the Old Ways.

"As a tree I ride, as a dead man I ride…"- the Witch begins to identify him or herself with the World Tree, or the center of all things, which touches all places and realities, and with a dead person, a person already "reversed" and merged with all.

This declaration should be made first, before the rest of the Compass drawing proceeds.

II. The Spell of the Road

"The Left-way road I walk, the crooked road amid the sky and earth I take, going down and within and around, a road to hell and heaven forsake. I draw a compass round and walk the road to Wormsel."

I come hither : West of the bridge to hell :
A holy stone, A holy tree, A holy well

Variants:

"The Left-way road I walk, the crooked road amid the sky and earth I take, going down and within and around, a road to the deep and sunlight forsake; I make the black sun road and walk the way to the Unworld."

"The Left-way road I walk, the crooked road amid the sky and earth I take, going down and within and around, a road into the deep and the living world forsake, I draw a leftwards ring and walk the road to Elfhame."

Analysis and Ritual Action:

At this point, the Witch making the Compass walks in a counterclockwise circle around the area that will be the Compass. As they walk, they say this "Spell of the Road"- which describes the path, and which, through the word, the intent, and the power of the leftwards or counter clockwise motion, invokes the power of "Otherness," in the inner world.

Walking in a circular, leftwards manner causes a netherworldly "echo"- what occurs in the unseen world simultaneously with your leftwards walk is nothing short of a kind of invocation of "inwardness"- and this simple motion is the key to many journeys towards the Mysteries beyond.

The leftwards road, the road leading within, is called "the crooked road" on account of its constant turning- the opposite of the straight road, where what is coming can be easily seen. This road is a road of Mystery, of uncertainty, but it leads to the heart of all things, to the depths. It is the same road walked by the dead, though they are compelled by a hard Fate that generally prevents their return. All who walk this road go "down and within and around," spiraling downward. This is a "road to hell and heaven forsake"- in other words, a road to the unseen, which forces those who walk to say goodbye (temporarily) to the outer world of consensual reality.

It is also called "the black sun road" on account of it being a left-way road, going against the normal path of the sun, the bright "white sun" road of fire, life, and clockwise movement.

"Wormsel" apparently comes from "Wyrmsele," which means "Wyrm's Hall," a reference to the serpent-choked hall of Queen Hel, but also a reference in general to the halls of the Underworld, within the coils of the serpent-power in the Land. "Elfhame" and the "Unworld" or any name for the unseen world can be used in its place.

As the person making this road chants, they should drag their riding stick (or whatever they used) on the ground, marking out the ring. This Spell of the Road makes any area that it surrounds symbolically (and, in the Innerworld, literally) a meadow of the Underworld, for once you step off the left-way road, you are in the Underworld; so being inside the circle so created is the same as being in the depths of the earth, in the interior of the Land, even though you, the Witch, are still alive and conscious- you have gone, alive and conscious, into the Land of the Dead or the unseen world, and can now become a "union" point between the seen and the unseen, and commune with unseen powers.

III. The Spell for the Water and the Four Roads

(I have gone to the source of all waters.)

"Here is water, blessed by the Devil, a river of fertile life, a medium of ghosts, a water that masters every spirit and created thing, much grace and vision, and from heaven to hell the road of the Master's spells."

Variant:

(I have gone to the source of all waters.)

Here is water, blessed by the Old One, a fertile river of life, a medium of ghosts, a water that is a bridge of passage for every spirit, a water that nourishes every living thing; a water of mastery over all- much power, much vision, and from the heights to the depths, the road of the spells of the boundary-keeper and the boundary-crosser.

Analysis and Ritual Action:

There should be a bowl or cup or some other vessel of water waiting for you inside the Compass area, and you should be facing north, as most people inside of Compasses orient themselves north. You look into the water, and *think* to yourself "I have gone to the source of all waters." Then, lightly touching the surface of the water with your fingers, you *say* the rest- the spell for the water. Then dip your fingers again and anoint your forehead with the water, and the foreheads of everyone present. This is cleansing and "the devil's baptism" as it were- a devotion to the White King of Elfhame. Some people put a small pinch of salt in the water before doing the spell on it. This is not necessary, but is sometimes done.

Then, you take the water container, and walk around your Compass again counterclockwise, pouring the water around it. You are making the "river of souls" or the "river of time," the classical Styx, or the "misty waters" that separate this world from the next. As you come to a cardinal direction, a "water road" has to be made, by making a straight line of water extending out a few inches towards that direction, and when you are finished, you will have surrounded the area totally with water, and made four "water roads." Return to the center and face north; always orient yourself northward in a Compass.

By going downwards on the left-way path, you have gone into the Underworld, from where all waters of the upper earth have their ultimate origin. Water is in fact a symbol of the Underworld, and this spell describes well the power and function of the water.

The container holding the water should be waiting for you at the center of the Compass, and when you go to it, and think the first part of this spell, you should recall that you have gone to the source of all- not just water. The water is blessed by the Old One, because just as He rises from the primordial womb-waters (just like we do), He also uses them consciously to His will, as we will see.

The waters are called "fertile river of life," because the Underworld is the ultimate source of life, and the waters are life-giving, all over the earth and under it. They are teeming with life and without water, nothing would live. Our bodies are mostly water. They are called "medium of ghosts," because the waters of the Underworld are packed with the Pale People- the water, as I said, is a symbol of the unseen world because the unseen world is at the heart of all things just as water is at the heart of all living things, and the unseen world acts as the unseen "medium" of the transmission of power, the unseen roads that ghosts and spirits walk- and this brings us to another important point.

Spirits are said to walk "roads of water"- water is the symbolic (and actual) agent of the motion and transmission of spiritual beings and power. By making the four "water roads," you have made Ghost Roads by which spirits can approach you in your Compass- and this is an important element to any successful spell-working! Water is the "boundary" element as well; one does not make the transition into the Underworld or into the unseen world, without the misty and flowing transmission-medium of the fluid world, of the dark water. Chaos and the darkness of the Underworld are always associated with water, which is the womb-element of all, from which all forms rise.

The water is finally said to master every spirit and created thing- to be endowed with much grace and vision, and from heaven to hell (or the heights and the depths) to be the road of the Master's spells.

It is all of these things- its power is the ultimate power of origins, and all things rely on it and return to it; it is endowed with the ultimate Mystery, and is the means of arriving at the ultimate Mystery, and it is the medium of psychism and visions, when pulled and warped by the moon's attraction. From the heights to the depths, meaning anywhere in reality, it is the "road," the agent, that transmits the power of the Master- His spells- and the Master here refers to the Witchfather, as well as the human witch.

IV. The Spell for the Fire

(I have passed below, here is the light beneath the Land, shade light, the light of Wormsel, Enody's dim dwelling.)

"Here is fire, blessed by the Lady, lamp and light to what is seen and unseen, darting spirit and serpents tongue; heat from the sun and

the Land, a star come down from heaven, in the living body forever from her blessed bounty, a light in every hearth, and burning deep under earth."

Variant:

(I have passed below, into the deep, and here is the light within the Land.)

"Here is fire, blessed by the Mothers, given of the maiden, lamp and light to what is seen and unseen, swift spirit and serpent's tongue, heat of life from the sun and the Land, a star fallen from the sky, living in the body- the warmth of Her blessed bounty, a light in every hearth, and deep below the earth."

Analysis and Ritual Action:

A bonfire or a candle has to be lit now at the center of the Compass. If you have no fire of any kind, the hand has to be held over the "forehead door" or on the forehead, so that you can feel the heat in your own body, as you say the Spell of the Fire, because your own body's fire can (and does) act as an equivalent- the same fire in you is the fire that burns in bonfires or candles.

A person must think the part of the spell in parenthesis, and say the rest aloud, while gazing into the fire or holding the hands out over it (or putting the left hand on the forehead).

This is the "watchfire" of legend and lore, the guiding light for the powers in the unseen, and, when inside the Compass, it is the "Fetch-light" or the Light in the Land- the power and "clear light" or white light of the Underworld. It is also the presence of the Lady, or the daughter of the Great Mother- the fire Goddess, the spirit that is the manifestation of all the mothers and powers of nurturing and fertility, and occult Mystery.

The fire is associated in the spell with the "serpent's tongue," linking it to the Master as the teacher and awakener of mankind- and it is linked to the fire in the sky (the sun) and the fires in the Land- and it goes further to mention that the same fires are in the stars, and reiterates the old

Here is fire : Great inheritance :
Lamp and Light to what is seen and unseen

belief that the "stuff of man" is the same as the "stuff of the stars." The connection between the living body, the hearth, and the fires under the earth completes the circle of living fires.

"Enody" seems to be "Enodia," another name for Hekate.

Once the Spell of the Fire is done in the Compass, the two elements- water and fire, have been called to complete the Compass. Water represents the Underworld and the dark Mystery of origins, and fire represents the emergence of life and form and "order"- the dawn of creation and the processes of the world. Together, they are the strong negative and positive poles of all life and creation, the "fire and ice" of the primal world in northern Heathenism.

V. River's Edge Incantations

(ring bell)

"Here on the river's edge (or the compass rim) I place the _____, with my left hand I place it, in the Devil's Name and the name of his Lady."

Variant:

(ring bell)

"Here on the river's edge I place the_____. With the hand of otherness I place it, in the Old One's name and in the name of His Lady."

Analysis and Ritual Action:

There is no "calling of the quarters" as it is commonly said or understood, in traditional craft as I have found it and experienced it. However, each cardinal direction does indeed have links with various powers, spirits, symbols, forces, and concepts.

Even though it is not strictly necessary, the "true Compass" includes items placed around it that are in harmony with the traditional force and symbolism of the various directions. Having an item or two on the "River's Edge" to each direction makes the compass most powerful for craft workings, but it does not need them. In most workings, you can (and usually will) place just one or two items, in sympathy with the direction that most links to your working.

These items, animals, and other things are listed here below, along with a "secret" craft name for most of them. If you wish to place one or more, when you go to place it, you place it in the proper direction, at the edge of your Compass, with your left hand, and you say the "secret name" in conjunction with the given incantation.

For example, if you were going to place one of the traditional implements of the east- a blacksmith's hammer and tongs- on the eastward edge of your Compass, you would see in the list for the "eastward Compass" that "hammer and tongs" are "secretly" referred to as "Blacksmith's Trade."

So, you'd say, after ringing the bell and placing the hammer and tongs on the eastern rim:

"Here on the river's edge I place the Blacksmith's Trade; with my left hand I place it, in the Old One's Name and the name of His Lady."

To make another example, if you were going to place a sprig of some evergreen to the North of your Compass, you would ring the bell, place it at the north edge of the Compass, and say:

"Here on the river's edge I place the ever-living bough; with my left hand I place it, in the Old One's Name and the name of His Lady."

Placing these items is all the "quarter calling" you'll ever need, for these items all mediate and symbolize the totality of that direction. For most acts of basic craft, you won't use many, usually just one or two- the "riding pole" that you used to make the declaration and the Spell of the Road is an implement associated with the north- and unless you had other plans for it, it can be stuck in the earth, standing in the north, or laid on the northern realm with this incantation. Never overdo it; normally, when I work, I put my riding pole and a hound's skull on the northern rim of my Compass, and that's it; sometimes my pole and an owl's wing.

I only really make it a point to place symbolic objects to each direction when I am doing a very strong working, or make it a point to bring some specific item for a specific direction when it will call upon some important power that is needed in my working- spells of fertility and romance, for instance, (which as we shall see) are linked with the south, and the rose- few workings of this "southward" or Venusian nature should lack the element of the rose, or other items that channel and mediate the power of the southward ways. Always place the objects counterclockwise, starting with the north, if you have any to place.

Here are the four "tables" for the items that are empowered with meaning to the four directions of the Compass. The corresponding "secret name" is given in bold after each item that has a secret name- if the item doesn't have a "secret name," it is simply called what it is called. Many animal parts are listed in these tables; do not ever kill or harm an animal to get its parts- it is always better for Fate to give them to you, by finding them in nature or buying them from somewhere.

NORTHWARD

The north of the Compass is the direction of winter, midnight, and Elfhame or the Underworld. It is the direction of the stars, the night sky, and the winds, and the "third way" or the transcendent Mystery, and of Fate. Its powers are strong in curses, initiations, and Saturnian workings. The Dark Master of the Underworld and the Queen of the Underworld/Old Fate are the chief powers, and the items, symbols and beasts here are especially tied to their power.

Implements of the Northward Compass

Forked Stick or Stang: **Branching Staff**
Grave Earth
Skull: **Head of Man**
Antler: **Antler Bone**
Stag skull: **White One, King Below**

Bone: **Fleshless Bone**

A Hound's skull, teeth, or bones: **Ratchet's skull, Ratchet's teeth, Ratchet's bone**

Any evergreen bough: **Ever-living bough**

Elder: **Old Mother**

Raven's skull or feathers: **Very black one, Very dark one**

Owl's skull or feathers: **Howlet skull, Howlet wing**

Goose skull or feathers

Bull's skull or horn

Goat's skull: **Black king below**

Toad's corpse or skull: **Toad's boon**

Serpent: **Old Sorcerer**

Riding pole

Horse's skull: **Hell-steed** (only placed if the working is a curse)

Broom

EASTWARD

The east of the Compass is the direction tied to springtime, dawn, and mastery or realization. It is the direction of the awakened mind. It is the direction most associated with the holy fire that the Master bestowed on mankind at the beginning, fire in general, and the sun. It is the direction of new life, and (along with the south) the direction that is associated with fertility and the awakening of lust and sexuality, though the actual consummation of sexual lust is fully realized in the south. Its powers are strong in workings for craft-skill, skill at work, intelligence, mental power in the sense of scholarship or rhetoric and manipulation, new life, insight, and protecting children in birth. It is the direction for solar and Mercurial workings. The Master as teacher and lord of light, and the feminine spirit of the fire dominate this direction, and the items, symbols, and beasts here are especially tied to their power.

Implements of the Eastward Compass

Fire (even the fire that you lit at the center, if it can be moved, can be placed east, if you choose): **Holy flame, burning fire, Light**

Knife or Sword: **Artavus**

Goat skull: **Virile king, secret Master, Buxen king**
Hammer and tongs (either or both): **Blacksmith's Trade**
Hare's skull or bones: **Malkin's head, Malkin's speed**
Serpent: **Cunning Sorcerer**
Raven: **Very black one, Very dark one**
Birch: **Mother Tree**
Badger skull or hide or bones: **Old Brock**
Fox's skull or bones

SOUTHWARD

The south of the Compass is the direction of summer, midday, and the upper-earth or the world of humans and animals. It is the direction associated with the fertile fields and the Land. Its powers are strong in workings for fertility, growth, and attraction, and all Venusian and Martial workings. The Horned Master of the Forest and the Land, and the Earth Mother/Rose Queen are the chief powers, and the items, symbols, and beasts here are especially tied to their power.

Implements of the Southward Compass

Phallic stone: **Godstone**
Oak stave or branch: **Jove's wood**
Wooden phallus: **King's life**
Oak twig with leaves: **Oaken chaplet**
Antler: **Antler bone**
Hare's skull or bone: **Malkin's head or Malkin's speed**
Cow or Bull skulls or horns
Stag skulls or bones: **White One**
Broom (can be placed at this direction as well)
Swine skulls or bones
Horse skulls or bones or horseshoes: **Queen's mount, King's strength**
The Cup and Bowl used in Red meals: **Housle cup/Housle bowl**
Rose: **Loving rose** (dead roses are placed north, and used for curses against relationships, and are called **Hateful rose.**)

WESTWARD

The west of the Compass is the direction of autumn, dusk, and the misty waters or "World River" or river of time and death (also called "the one-strand river") that separates this world from the unseen. It is the direction associated with the waters and mists or fogs, and the moon. Its powers are strong in workings for Wisdom, transition, sacrifice, dreams, and psychism, and all lunar workings. The Horned Master as the White Stag, guide of the dead to the Underworld and the Lord under the Mound, and the ancestral powers (the clan mothers or the Three Hooded Mothers) are the chief powers, and the items, symbols, and beasts here are especially tied to their power.

Implements of the Westward Compass

Cup, chalice, or cauldron: **Abundant cup, abundant vessel**
Horn-cup
Mirror: **Reflecting glass**
Scythe or Reaping Hook: **Lady's slender reaping hook**
Bell: **Sounding bell**
Apple: **food of the dead**
Cat's skull or bones
Cup or Bowl used in the Red Meal (can also be placed here, instead of south)
Toad: **Toad's boon**
Goose skulls or bones or feathers
Stag skulls or bones: **White One**
Any creature that lives in water

How the Compass is especially used for "magical" workings will be discussed in the next section, on spelling and incantations. For now, we have to return to the final element of the Compass-drawing, the "Ring of Art Invocation."

VI. The Ring of Art Invocation

"Master, I reverse myself, move within and down below, on the left-way road, the ring of art is the crown of the grave-mound, a consecrated field across the water, a world in reflection, a stone, a reddened ground with a seat of fire, a door, a bridge to God and dead, Fate's adamant circle."

Variant:

"(O Master, Old One, Lady, see) The Hallowed place, ringed by water, ringed by stone, a consecrate plain, a field, a meadow, like unto the sacred mound-fields, temples, all within touches all without and deeper within- here is a sacred seat of fire, a passing place between spirit and man, the indestructible circle of Fate."

Analysis and Ritual Action:

This is the final declaration that states, definitively, that you are standing in a place that is sharing the same potency and power of any sacred place of the traditional way- the Compass is done, and it is compared to the "crown of the grave mound" or an interface point between this world and unseen- it is called what it is, a consecrate ground across the waters- a reference to the old heathen sacred place as well as the Otherworld that waits across the River of Time or the misty border. It is called "a world in reflection," underscoring its connection with the world outside- the "reddened ground" is another way of saying "ground filled with numinous force." The Compass is called what it is- Fate's adamant or indestructible circle, the circle that contains all.

After this point, the Compass is done. Always remember that these six steps are not long or complicated, and considering you don't even need to build or make an actual fire, all you really need, at bare minimum to make a Compass, is yourself; a riding pole, stang, broom, or forked stick/staff of some kind; and a tiny bottle or bowl/cup of water.

That would be minimal, but enough to do the declaration, the spell of the road and marking out the Compass, the spell for the water and the baptism, as well as creating the border and the four roads; your own body heat can be the fire, and the riding-pole can be placed on the northern "River's Edge"- and the bowl or cup or water can be placed on the west, if you wanted, or left in the center at your feet, all followed by this final declaration. That would be the bare minimum Compass, and would not take long to make. Of course, in ideal circumstances, you'd have an actual fire and maybe one or two implements to add power and definition to your Compass. There is a certain art to this, and it should be done with taste and an eye to aesthetic.

What really "makes" the Compass is your awareness of the symbolism, the motions, and what it all means. Never forget that since you face north always in a Compass, the items placed there (if you place any) become representations of the powers of the Underworld- especially the chief powers, namely the King of Elfhame and the Queen of the Dead- the stang, or the forked staff/riding pole, particularly becomes almost an idol or "stand in" for Him, with the suggestion of "horns" on the ends of these staffs- and other items represent these powers as well. The hound's skull is the physical appearance of His Underworldly hounds, but it also overlaps with the Lady of the Underworld as well, for dogs have a way of barking and going crazy at night when She rises to the earth and walks about. The Elder-branches or twigs or berries, or the owl skulls or feathers, or the feathers of geese, and the horse's skull especially represent the Queen of the Underworld, but all items generally represent the Underworldly pair.

The Art of Spell-making, Invocation and Incantations

Invoking and Calling the Old Powers

In the section entitled **"Two Things that Must be Remembered,"** you were treated to the secret of invocation- all things are united, and every thought, word, and deed on your part makes "ripples" in the united chain of Reality and Fate.

The powers of the unseen world are already (usually) infinitely more aware of the Truth or aware of Reality- things as they are- than mortals could ever be, especially the powers the Witch has traffic with- the Master, the dark and omniscient Mother of All who embodies Fate and the divinized dead; but any power of ancient times that was described by the ancestors as a "Goddess" or a "God"- a being invoked, normally to receive prayers or sacrifices, likely already has the power to be quite aware of what you are doing and saying at any time- inside or outside of your Compass.

Invocations do work better inside the Compass Round- but they work anywhere, at any time, if you are aware of the fact that: 1. your words, thoughts, and actions "ripple out" across the entire universe, 2. the spiritual powers unseen are ever aware of what you are doing, and what everyone else is doing. Have total certain trust in that.

The last element that you have to bring to invocation is just your ability to be clear and open, to receive or sense the "presence" of the being invoked, which will move into contact with your spirit, as you invoke- not that it wasn't already; in the unseen world, a "placeless place," things don't have to physically "be" somewhere as we know it- but awareness still changes, and a being can be "brought into" your conscious and aware mindstream and your ability to feel and interact on many levels; this is how spirits "come" to you when invoked- or when they are compelled to or choose to for some other reason. Just take a care to remember that when you feel like your invocation is to "bring a spirit's presence into your awareness," in reality, it is bringing your *attention, consciousness, and awareness to them.*

Dreams and visions are the two most likely places for beings in the unseen world to appear, though intuitive sensing of spiritual approach and presence is totally common. You must make an effort to acquaint yourself with the symbols and beasts and other aspects of Reality that resonate with the power of the beings you intend to invoke, and alongside that, you must be open to what you personally experience of them while in deep trance states or Fetch-flight, and recall the way they appeared to you, if needs be, when you are calling or invoking them. You have to have an all-around "feeling" of them, both on the level of name and symbol, but also on non-verbal levels- pure intuitive sense.

The most simple manner of invocation is a matter of changing your awareness, to be more open and in touch with the fullness of Reality, and then slowly, steadily (even silently, in your heart and mind, if you choose), saying the name of the being invoked, with full attention and centeredness. Repeat the name; three or seven repetitions is traditional and powerful- but the reality is that only a name and an open heart and mind is needed.

The element of the bell can be added- the ringing of the "sounding bell" or any resounding element such as a horn, flute, drum, or the like. I personally like to use the bell, or other more poetically appropriate methods when calling the White King in the Land, such as a blast from a hunting horn- the blast that carries to His ears in the unseen- because it adds not only a powerful "sonic" beginning to the invocation, but it also seems to formalize the occasion.

You do what you have to do, bearing in mind what I have said, and your invocation ends when you sense and feel the attentions of the being invoked- and you have to have faith in their power to be infinitely aware of you, even if you are having trouble feeling the presence in your own awareness- though if you practice the "Witch-sight" clarity technique often, you will never have this problem; you will become aware of their subtle presences- or not so subtle- all the time.

Even though the above methods are more than sufficient for invoking, there is a bit more I have to share- received methods and forms for doing so. These can be used if you desire something a bit more formal.

Invocation:

"Master
I invoke you with words of worship,
Leftwards I say them
I beg you to rise here and notice my art
I call on you as an invoker would call,
As a conjurer
A doer of sorcery and cunning witch
Bound by oath and pact, by blood and Fate, to you
Hie hither and notice my art."

Variant:

"Old One (or whatever spirit)
I call to you with words of worship
Into the otherness I say them
Rise and circle here in answer to my call
I call on you as the wise would
As a chanter of spells, a singer of old songs
As a keeper of memory, a human born of trees
And of the ground
I honor my oath and pact with you
In blood and Fate we are one
Come forth and attend my working here."

Necromantic Variant:

"(name of spirit or power)
I invoke you with words of power and worship
Leftwards I say them
I beg you to rise here, and notice these rites
By the power of the East, and the crossroads,
I call on you as an invoker would call
A conjurer of the dead, a diviner,
A man of sorcery and cunning witch
By oath and pact sworn to the Ruler of the world

And they who have power in the Infernal world
Hie hither (come forth) from the Unseen, constrained here."

Analysis and Ritual Action:

This invocation form is meant to be used to call any and all spiritual powers. For the basic "invocation form," you replace the name "Master" or "Old One" with the name of the power you are trying to invoke. It is meant to be repeated, three or seven times.

There is one change that has to be made if you are invoking beings that are nature spirits or the dead- in other words, spirits or powers that are not the Witchmother or the Witchfather- you would say this (and I will use the example of invoking the spirit of an oak tree)"

**"Old Oak
I invoke you with words of worship,
Leftwards I say them
I beg you to turn here and notice my art
I call on you as an invoker would call,
As a conjurer
A doer of sorcery and cunning witch
Bound by oath and pact, by blood and Fate, to you and your Masters
Hie hither and notice my art."**

There is a lot of talk about being "bound by oath and pact, blood and Fate" in these invocations- the beings invoked are asked to see that the invoker bears these four bonds which unite them to the beings called. When we cover the section (next) on initiation and induction, you will discover why this is so important- and why these invocations don't work as perfectly or fully as they should until you have actually taken the "oath and pact" and shed your blood, sharing it with the powers, so that you are bonded to them, and able to wield these invocations with the right and authority born of these things.

It is precisely the fact that you are "bound by oath and pact, blood and Fate" to the "Masters" (the Great Queen and the White King) of the powers of Nature and the dead that gives you the authority to summon them in this manner. When it comes to invoking the greatest ones, it is your oaths and pact, and your blood shed in initiation, that gives you the ability to call them with these particular words- Fate, the fourth aspect of the bond, is there for all, because the fact that anyone would find these words or say them is already evidence that Fate has brought them into contact and into involvement.

Spell-working and Incantations

Making spells is the heart of the "magical" art as most people understand it- the means of "getting things to happen" by asking or willing things to occur in conjunction with the powers you have invoked, or "receiving gifts" from powers that you invoke.

Spell-working is not complex. The only thing you need to do for a proper "spelling" or working is create a Compass Round, as best you can. The nature of your working can help to dictate the time of day or night, as well as what you will use in the creation of the Compass- always have at least one of the implements of the direction that is most in sympathy with your working there.

The next thing you have to do is invoke the powers that are most needful for your working, once you have created your Compass and are standing inside it, using any invocation method you like.

I find that it helps to do several Red Meals specifically for those powers in the days leading up to the actual working, or in the time right before it, if the working is sudden. This creates an initial strong connection between you and those powers, and insures strong contact during the work. It makes you one with Them, and your words and deeds become their words and deeds- no mortal makes powerful magics unaided.

The Red Meals can actually be used within a working- and I have done so to great effect.

The center of all spell-working is the "petition," where you ask the invoked powers for precisely what you need. We will discuss the "petition charm" next. After the petition charm is done, if you wish to share a Red Meal with the invoked powers, and give the remains of the Red Meal to the direction in sympathy with your working, you would actually be making a wonderfully powerful addition- the craft-equivalent of Pagans making sacrifices in the old days in times of need. But this, as I said, is not necessary.

The last thing you have to do, to end any spell-working, is to run *clockwise* around your Compass one time, and leap out of it, but leap out in the direction that is in sympathy to your working. This is very important. For example, if you were doing a very dark, Saturnian curse against deserving enemies, you would run around your Compass once and leap out to the north; a working to get yourself pregnant, or increase your own personal fertility would be a leap out to the south. This is a symbolic return to this world, suddenly reversing the reversal you did to get into the Underworld- it is symbolic of your spell-work, the wish or intention you fixed through your spell, suddenly flying up out of the unseen and into the seen world, where it then goes to accomplish its will by becoming a part of manifest Fate.

Now, we must discuss the Petition Charm and the "parchment" technique.

The Petition Charm:

"Master,
I bring you offerings: With my left hand I bring them
I pledge myself to you and your ways
I ask for _____ in return, as Fate would have it.
My will and your power bind it so.
I ask for_____ in return, as Fate would have it.
And Fate now has it."

Variant:

This variant is for use when you are making a petition from a spirit of nature or a "lesser" spirit of that type- not what was once called a "God" or a master-spirit of the craft, in other words. I give this variant using the example of the spirit of an oak tree:

"Old Oak
I bring you offerings
With my left hand I bring them
I pledge myself to your honor and protection
I beg_____ in return, as Fate would have it
My will and your power bind it so.
I beg_____ in return, as Fate would have it
And Fate now has it."

Analysis and Ritual Action:

Like the other rote forms, the names of the beings being petitioned with this charm should be changed to correspond to the being you are actually speaking to.

This one simple charm actually conceals the secret of the truth of power-working or spell-working in traditional craft. Follow me through it:

The being you are making the petition to has already been invoked. You are now telling this honored guest and power that you have brought it offerings- and with your left hand you have brought them. This is an important preliminary, because you don't get anything for nothing- no matter what it is you are bringing, you are showing a willingness and a seriousness to give of yourself to the working.

One of the best reasons for doing a Red Meal during spell working is because the bread and wine acts well as the offering that you are "bringing with your left hand." Of course, anything can be- many Witches use a lock of their hair, or something else small and precious to them- so long as the "given" item, if it is hair, or a piece of jewelry, or whatever, is destroyed or buried or "given" in such a manner that it is never reclaimed again.

However, the "parchment" that we are about to discuss- a petition that is actually written on physical paper and burned at the end of the spell- can act as the "offering," making it twice as useful, as we will see.

The pledge that you make next is to reaffirm your connections to the master-spirits, and perhaps a gentle reminder to them that you have a pact with them, a pact we shall discuss in the next section on initiation and induction.

The next three lines are very important, and must be studied closely to understand why and how the "magic" of it all works:

"I ask for _____ in return, as Fate would have it.
My will and your power bind it so.
I ask for_____ in return, as Fate would have it."

Obviously, you are meant to "fill in the blank" here with what you need from the working, but you append it with "as Fate would have it"- which is a way of stating that you are willing to realize that Fate Herself may have a different take on the means in which this working will "play out." I wish for so-and-so, as Fate would have it; you are essentially introducing a wish as a strand of Fate into the greater tapestry, "as Fate would have it"- to be shaped and formed as Fate will shape it and form it. No single magical working can be greater than the Force of Fate as a totality; the answer to this dilemma lies in the next line of the charm:

"My will and your power bind it so."

This is the key. You, as the human operant, bring the element of will- what you will to happen- but the power you have invoked will provide the power that makes Fate alter and warp, as She will. Your spell is a union between your will and another power in the unseen world- this world and the unseen being united to a purpose. It is not so much your human power that moves Fate, for the human being as we know him or her is very limited, a tiny strand in Fate- but the unseen powers, especially the Master Spirits, are massively powerful in the totality of Fate. To this power, you can bring your will. The human being becomes a conduit for greater powers.

Why should these powers respond? Because, (and again) as you will see in the next section on initiation, they are engaged in a two-way pact with you, after you have undergone a true initiation. Without initiation, without a true pledge and bond on your part to them- and without your full heart's devotion to the powers unseen and the Old Ways, there is not much hope of them giving so much of themselves to your work, unless they choose to for their own unguessable reasons.

Then, you repeat your desire, again giving the proper respect to Fate.

You end by saying, "And Fate now has it"- indeed She does; the occurrence of any moment, and the content of the moment, is Fate's manifestation, and as soon as the moment occurs, it is part of the past- Fate "has" it now, as an eternal part of the weave of things, influencing the moments that rise afterwards. Just stating the Petition charm puts your working in Fate's hands, in the weave, and begins influencing things. Working the craft is all Fated- your craft workings are all parts of Fate's omnipresent unfolding. You aren't doing the craft as much as it is doing you- literally. In this way, remember- it all expresses what must be, through you and your rites. One might call it "effortless effort," when you think about it. Just let go and be fully honest to how you feel at any moment.

The Petition Charm as a whole is repeated three or seven times. If all you had to do with your working was create a Compass, invoke the needful powers, and make the petition and perhaps share a Red Meal with them, then the work is over; at this point you'd run or dart around the Compass once clockwise and hop out to the direction most aligned with your work, and it is done.

What is required of you is to understand and experience the rich and deep symbolism of all that you have done; you have made a journey figuratively and literally into the Unseen world, to the depths, crossed the river of dread, entered into the spiritual dimension at the heart of things, asked the powers there for changes, then suddenly shot back to the "surface" world, emerging reborn into the light of space and time, transformed, and having trembled the webs of Fate.

The Parchment Variant

Instead of just stating out loud in a Petition Charm what you want or need, you can also write it down on clean paper, before the working, and carry it with you into the Compass.

This is the "parchment" technique, and it has other uses- the parchment or paper that you carry rolled or folded up with you, can be the "offering" you bring when you state, "I bring you offerings, with my left hand I bring them" in the Petition Charm.

When you make the Petition Charm, you should be holding the parchment in your left hand, and instead of having to state out loud what your purpose for the petition is, you can just say, "I beg that what is written on this paper come to pass, in return, as Fate would have it."

When the petition is over, the parchment has to be burned from either the Watch-fire at the middle of your Compass, or the flame of an eastern light, if you have one. It has to burn, however, normally left to burn in the direction in sympathy to your working.

When writing the parchment, be very specific- you are doing a literal "spell"- spelling out what you desire, arranging symbols and letters in the shape of your desire or will. Also, it helps to draw symbols of your own power or spiritual connections on the paper, even over the words that you wrote, if you need to.

Sometimes, people will do Red Meals and other petitions to spirits to send them dreams of what they need to see or know to make an especially difficult spell work- and then, those symbols or visions given in dreams are drawn on a parchment, along with the request, before they are burned- this is how many workings can become one great working. Very powerful workings will last days or weeks- and contain the use of many Red Meals and "secondary spell workings" leading up to a main one.

Do recall that compasses are not needed for all "magical" work- but they make them a hundred times more powerful. A person can simply walk into the woods, invoke some spirit or power and burn a petition or make a verbal petition, then perhaps have a Red Meal there, dedicated to them and your intentions, and walk away considering the task done, but this is not nearly as powerful. But then, not all workings need so much power.

As a final note, when you make spells or workings, do so with a poet's soul. What you request, say, write, and all the implements you use or do not use, should all be chosen to make an event that is both eldritch and beautiful- never, never overdo it. It should be focused, and powerful. A true working is always a mystical event.

There is much talk about the moral and ethical considerations regarding curses, but the reality of the entire matter is very simple: in traditional Paganism and craft, nothing is more important than the Land, and the family, friends, and loved ones of the Witch or Pagan. When something threatens those things, there is no ethical or moral problem with spinning the most black-hearted curses to settle the situation. Beyond that, if a person were to use the powers to curse and manipulate based on their own egocentric needs or desires, that is a matter for the person's conscience. It is just as unethical or immoral to curse or manipulate for selfish ends as it is to lie to someone, cheat them in business, or steal from them.

A person who comes to the Old Ways to learn power for selfish ends was a poor example of a human being long before they ever applied to learn witchcraft. They will get their just desserts, just as all people will- in the system of Fate, in the ruthless power of Truth, you can rest assured that all accounts are settled, and everyone gets the devil- or the sunlight- that they deserve.

Making Objects "Red"

The spell-working instructions can be used to "consecrate" items, or endow them with certain powers, given to them by the powers you invoke. This is the "enchanting" or "ensorceling" of items, and it can be very useful; however, it has its limits.

Have the item or object you wish to be endowed with whatever virtue in the Compass with you, or just on the ground before you if you aren't using a Compass. Compass Rounds are almost always good for this sort of work, however.

Invoke the powers you will ask for this working, and make the petition, stating precisely what it is you desire that the item become endowed with. But a time limit must be placed on the working- the item can be "endowed" or "made red" for seven minutes, seven days, seven months, or seven years- any multiple of seven- but it loses this virtue at the end of this time, and the working must be repeated to recreate it.

The shorter the time, the stronger the "reddening" will be- the longer, the weaker. Items thus enchanted are meant to be aids in some manner to you- the best examples I've ever heard of were small mirrors being blessed and empowered in the Master's name to "reflect back" wicked spirits and spells from hurting the person carrying the mirror. Another common working of this type is to endow a vessel or cup with the power to give visions or prophetic dreams to a person who drinks water from them before going to sleep. This is how charms and talismans are made to "give luck" or protection or whatever to the person who carries them, and anything can be enchanted in such a way- jewelry, folded up parchment in bags, whatever.

When the petition for the empowerment of the item or talisman is made, you *must* perform a Red Meal, and then use the wine at the end to anoint the item- this is literally how it is "made red." If you are using a Compass, take the item with you when you run once clockwise at the end, and leap out to a direction in sympathy with the purpose of the charmed item.

There is a deep "sympathetic" stream of sorcery that is as old as the hills, and which always manages to make itself known in the craft- and even though I do not intend to discuss sympathetic magic in detail, its workings are easy to understand and create- when within the Compass, anything you do "echoes" out into the greater world- so making sympathetic images (or dolls or poppets) and carrying them into Compasses, where you then "do" actions to them, causes those actions to "echo out"- but first, those images or dolls or poppets should be created as carefully and as fully as you can to mimic the intended subject of the working.

Then, before they are used, they are "baptized" in the Compass with the water you did the Spell of the Water on, and when baptized, they are "named," and then displayed to the four directions, with their name being announced. After you have done your work on the image, carry it with you as you make the clockwise darting run and leap outwards to the proper direction.

The Ash-Protection Charm

The Compass is not primarily used for "protection," but spiritually speaking, it is protective in ways; when you stand inside one, your own natural desire to be safe and free of the molestation of your enemies or baneful forces is naturally magnified and reflected into the "outer world"- and invoked spirits, if you ask them, will watch over or protect you, especially ancestral powers, or local powers that you make generous offerings to. But there are ways to add a stronger element of protection to your Compass Rounds.

You have to get an ash twig or stick, and enchant it or "make it red" with the power to protect anyone or anything that it draws a circle around.

Once you have done that, when you make your Compasses, use the stick to trace the Compass boundary after the Spell for the Fire, but before the River's Edge incantations.

As you trace, say this:

"I circle myself with a rod of Ash, against sore and bite, against all dread and dreadful ones; I circle myself against the horror that is hateful to all, and all evil that enters this Land."

You don't have to be in a Compass to do this. Once you have the ash-rod enchanted, you can do it anytime, by just drawing the circle around yourself and saying the charm.

Exorcising the Restless Dead

Sometimes, the dead do not rest lightly. A tale from Wales reveals both a haunting by restless dead, who are incidentally described as "elves," and the means by which an old Witch-woman on the edge of the wood of Coedygadfa rid the locals of the menace of these phantoms.

In 1244, near the town of Rhewl, the forces of Henry III slaughtered an army of men loyal to Prince Llywelyn. The phantoms of the slain began to plague the local villagers, taking the form of "little elves"- and coming out of the wood of Coedygadfa- a name that means "Wood of the Battle." An old woman living on the edge of that wood knew a charm to keep these phantoms at bay, or drive them away- a charm that had to be carried out at dusk- a "between" time that makes contact with spiritual powers easier.

At dusk, she would venture into the woods with a stout stick and a frying-pan full of cooked and scorched rabbit and frog-legs- the smell of which was reminiscent of burning bodies on the battlefield. It is said that "this smell, which was a horrible reminder to the dead of their mortal ends, sent the elf-like spectres cowering back under the ground."

This is a very important point to ponder- the restless dead are "dispelled" by reminders of their deaths, or by making them aware that they have died. The "stout stick" was more than a means of protection; it was the wand of her craft- the emblem of her authority in the unseen world, but also of her ability to pass into the unseen at will.

The two animals used to simulate the smell of burning flesh- rabbits and toads or frogs- both have symbolic power; the rabbits of the Goddess of life and death, and of life in general, and the frogs of the passage west across the waters that divide this world from the unseen. The rabbit resonates with the power of the east and the Hyldor or Fire-Queen, and the frog or toad with the west, the waters, the twilight, the ghost-passage.

Naturally, anything that simulated the smell of burning flesh could have been, or can be used, if the phantoms are of those who died in fire or in violence that involved fire or smoke, like battles, vehicle accidents, or even gunshots and the like.

The general smell of decay is enough to "wake" the awareness of the dead to their Fate.

In many places, such as Wales, it is believed that if people hide things before they die, and never have a chance to retrieve them, they run a high chance of being bound to the earth, until the items they hid are uncovered and exposed to direct sunlight outdoors, thus revealing them. This is another important fact to remember and take into account, if you ever encounter such a situation.

The Thorn Tree by the Crossroads

This somewhat dark but powerful working makes use of the power of the thorn tree- a gateway tree between this world and the Underworld- and the nearby presence of crossed roads, to invoke the powers of the Pale People and the other powers of the deep world to aid the petitioner.

It is a simpler working- no Compass is required, nor really any implements- but it does require a good bit of fortitude, because it requires you to steadily pray and invoke the powers below for an hour at least, and if possible, all night.

At night, go to a thorn tree near a crossroads- and if you have no such place, you can create the crossroads using the "trickle roads" technique discussed elsewhere in this gramarye.

When you go to the thorn tree, kneel under it, and begin invoking- begging more like- the powers below to aid you in what you need. You must continue this for at least an hour, but the more time you spend the better. The sort of trance that arises from this potent work is profound- after a while, the power of the time and place will become joined with your one-pointedness of mind and your words, and "overflow" you, making you sense them. Of course, doing Red Meals before this work helps, and it should, like all other works of craft, never be done in a place where you are a "stranger"- you should perform the "Rite of Arriving" (discussed last in this section) to acquaint yourself with the powers in this place before you try it.

I give below some sample "rotes" that you can start by saying, but as time passes, say what your heart feels- only remember to continually put emphasis on the fact that you are calling the "Pale people deep in the Land" and mention the nature of their "perpetual" and "timeless" existence and power.

**"Pale People deep in the Land,
Who dwell in perpetuity,
Be kind to me."**

"Powers below,
Those restful,
And those untimely gone into the earth,
Powers of the deep, who dwell in perpetuity,
Deeper powers of hard Fate, Hear me!
Be kind!

Powers timeless, Pale people, answer to me…"

The Induction Charm and the Initiation (Initiation Stream I.)

This initiation is the key to gaining the bond between the Powers and the Witch who wishes to access the workings described in this book on a deeper level.

This is the "pact" you must take with the Old Powers, from the Master-spirits, all the way to the Powers of the Land, and even the spiritual guardians of plants and beasts. It is not hard to perform, but it is lasting and binding, and if any hint of insincerity is in your heart when you perform this rite, it will not work. There is no "getting out" of this oath and pact, and it should never be taken lightly.

You should do it around one of the old holy or hidden festival days of the Old Ways- especially around Hallows Eve or the Twelve Nights of Yule. But the tide of Lammas is a good time as well, underscoring the sacrifice of one way of life and the birth of a new.

It should be done at night, or at dusk, and the workings of it are simple-days before, you should have been doing various devotions, trance works, internal communions, even walking the Left-way road if you can, to communicate your intentions. You should have mastered the understandings given in this whole work; nothing written anywhere in this book should hold any sort of vagueness for you. You should have performed the "Rite of Arriving," given later, if you can. There should really be no "if you can"- effort is always rewarded. Open yourself, go simply; be aware, be clear. The fire of love that burns in your heart for the Old Ways and the Land and the Old Powers is what draws you to this pact.

You begin by making a Compass round, as well and as perfectly as you can- for the initiation, it should, if possible, have at least one implement to each direction.

You then invoke the Witchmother and Witchfather, and, before you make the oath, you strip bare and put on new clothes. The old clothes should be clothes that you have worn often, which you will never wear again- they must be burned later. After you have changed, you pierce one of the fingers of your left hand, letting several drops of blood fall onto the bare earth. This is very important.

Then you say:

"Old One, Veiled Queen, I shed my blood for you.
An oath on the Land, an oath to life and to spirit-
Masters of the world, of fire and weaving
Of beasts and forests, fens, sky, human desires and destinies,
Powers inside the Land,
Hear an oath, sealed by blood and by blood carried into the Land:

In the name of the Pale Woman below the Hill,
Youthfully dead and ever-living, I am bound to your Wisdom and power.

Great oak, birch, elder, thorn, holly, ash,
Growing creatures of green coat and root,
Spirits who guard you and carry forth your lives,
By pact and oath I am sealed to you as friend,
Brother (or sister) and pupil, guardian and receiver.

Owl, hound, wolf and fox, badger and toad and bull,
Goose and raven, serpent and hare, horse,
Swine and stag,
Beasts of the Land and air, and unseen places,
By pact and oath I am sealed to you as friend,
Brother (or sister) and pupil, guardian and receiver.

I shed my blood for you;
From my left hand I shed it,
I bind myself to the Land and your spirit.

Support me, protect me,
Shelter me on the Witching way
The hidden road to Wisdom.
Let your power answer to my will,
In the holy meadow, the Ring of Art,
In my days and nights,
As my power will answer to your will

And rely on you.
Speak to me in vision,
Do not abandon me to the grave,
Nor hand me over to Hard Fate utterly,
Nor those whom my love protects.

Bestow on me the birth of Mastery, birth to the Deathless,
And ever your ways and will I will keep and honor.
I am named_____, singer and invoker of powers and Wisdom."

Then you must immediately do the Red Meal. After that, run around the
Compass once clockwise, and leap out to the east. This is rebirth into
your life as a Witch.

Analysis:

There are a few parts of this Induction Charm that need to be examined,
to understand the implications of this oath.

You begin by calling upon the Master-spirits of all things, and the people
inside the Land- and you ask them to "hear an oath, sealed by blood and
by blood carried into the Land"- the blood you shed is literally carrying
your life-force and the spiritual essence of you into the Land, to where
you physically merge with these powers, and the essence of your oath
goes with it. You now share blood with these powers, not just spiritual
oneness. You become a blood member of their Otherworldly "house."
This is why this oath is so serious and unbreakable.

In the name of Old Fate, the "Pale Woman under the hill," you then call
upon all of the powers of green growing things, and beasts- and to both,
you say this:

"By pact and oath I am sealed to you as friend,
Brother (or sister) and pupil, guardian and receiver."

This is a strong contract, for you are telling the spiritual powers of all
trees and plants, and all animals, that you will be their friend, their brother
or sister, their pupil (willing to learn from them) but most importantly,
their "Guardian" and "receiver".

To be a guardian of plants and animals means that you will not stand by while animals or plants or trees are needlessly or wantonly destroyed. You cannot expect their powers to respond to you, or empower you, if you call yourself their friend and guardian, but pay no attention to what becomes of them in the world around you. It means doing *whatever you can*- if you see little kids tearing up plants or flowers needlessly, gently ask them not to and encourage them to admire these things and let these beautiful things do what Nature has intended them to do. If you see people tormenting an animal, ask them why, and do what you can to stop it. Report them to the authorities if they are being cruel to animals.

Give as little money as you can to industries that are cruel to animals, and if you can, stop supporting factory farms. Give donations to environmental groups that try to save forests or preserve animal habitats. Try to find homes for homeless animals, and do not bring animals to "kill" shelters where they will be killed if not adopted within a week or two- seek out "no kill" humane shelters.

But aside from the title "guardian," you have also given yourself the title of "receiver"- this means that you are in a two-way contract- as you give your effort, these animals will also give to you, and you will receive. "What you receive" covers everything, from their flesh as food when you need it, all the way to their enjoyment, guidance and company. This is a two-way contract. You will receive the flesh and bodies of plants and animals to sustain you; spirits will guide and protect you; it is a full contract.

With your blood and words, you are binding yourself by oath and pact, blood and Fate, to the Land and to all beings within it, or on it. This is important, for this is the way of power- living creatures and plants mediate power to us everyday, and with deeper awareness, they will open up to you.

Your oath is also to the "Powers inside the Land"- referring to both the ancestral stream of your own dead kin, and to the dead in general, but also to the Land-spirits, the powers of natural places. This is a "faery oath"- in the most inclusive meaning of the word- an oath which places taboos upon you. You will not knowingly pollute or fill the natural world with anything that you know will despoil it, that will destroy the Land or degrade it- you will not destroy or move nor help another to destroy or move standing stones, the remains of stone age tumuli or other ancient monuments that are gateways into the Land, into the unseen.

You will not defile or destroy or deface burial mounds; you will not despoil graves except to take a little earth for needful things. If you take from the Land, or from any sacred place, you will take only tiny amounts and leave behind something of yourself- blood, hair, nails, offerings of ale or beer, or something valuable to you. You will not wantonly destroy natural areas, in form or function, nor encourage others to do the same, for any reason beyond saving a life. Remember these things, like you remember your oath to the powers of green growing things and beasts- because to break them may spell the end of whatever power you have received "back" in your contract.

Continuing on, you address the Powers you are making this oath to- animal spirits and plants, but chiefly to the Great Queen and the Old One or the White King, you say:

"Support me, protect me,
Shelter me on the Witching way
The hidden road to Wisdom.
Let your power answer to my will,
In the holy meadow, the Ring of Art,
In my days and nights,
As my power will answer to your will
And rely on you."

Here is where you enter into the binding part of the contract- in exchange for their support, protection and shelter on the witching road to Wisdom, and in exchange for THEIR power answering to YOUR will, during petitions wherever you happen to be- in the Compass or just anywhere in your "days and nights", you swear that YOUR power will answer to THEIR will- and rely on them.

This is very important, because it is the balance. A day will come, perhaps many days, when their wills will command, and your power, your essential power and life as a person, will have to obey. Even your death may be their will. You agree beforehand that you will willingly

join your power to their will, whatever it may be.
Your further ask them to

"Speak to me in vision,
Do not abandon me to the grave,
Nor hand me over to Hard Fate utterly,
Nor those whom my love protects."

This is important, for dreams of them, and dreams from them, will usually start in the nights following a successful and "accepted" initiation rite. But you go further- considering Wisdom and Truth are the only "salvation" worth seeking, you ask your new patrons to never abandon you to the grave- meaning that you will rely on them to see to it that you have found the Wisdom you need before you go below the earth, to death. If they should require your death for some reason, you trust that they will not abandon you to "Hard Fate utterly"- meaning not give you up fully to the powers of death and dissolution. If you keep up your end of the pact, the powers will see after you, in life or death.

And on the tail of that, you ask that this same protection be extended to "those whom my love protects"- those whom you love become protected as well. This is a great gift, and all the more reason for you to uphold your end of the pact, with no reservations. Broadly speaking, what you will "uphold" is a life of protecting the Land that you have become one with, and the creatures who dwell on it and within it, and you will uphold the values expressed in the Hidden Tradition- the belief in the sacredness of life, and the central importance of Truth, chief among those.

This moving oath is ended with the initiate swearing him or herself to them once more, and taking a new name to be used in the Witching way- the name that spirits and beings in the unseen will know you by.

The Four-Sided Shrine and the Offering Well

This rite to Vindonus, the White Stag-King, is inspired by ancient rites done in northern England. This working would ideally create a permanent working spot or shrine, but it can be done without making it permanent- but if you can, you should. This working is tied in strongly to the creation of a holy place of types, a "four-sided shrine."

Draw a good-sized circle on the bare earth, leaving an "opening" on the east rim of the circle, and when you are done with that, mark out a rectangle inside. The rectangle should have its two long sides facing east and west. Do not use metal implements to do this.

Hammer a white stake into the middle of the "west long side" of the rectangle. Hammer a white stake into the ground on the east rim of the circle, in the middle of the entrance gap you left. Hammer these stakes down as deep as you can, till their tops are pretty much even with the ground. These stakes have to be wooden, and should be oak or ash or hazel wood.

Take white stones and start placing them all along the circle's rim, if you can, making a perfect circle lined with stones, with a doorway to the east.

Inside the southern rim of the circle, and outside the southern "short" side of the rectangle, dig an offering pit of good depth. The first thing that should be dropped into this pit is a stick upon which you carve an image of a stag, as crudely or finely as you can. Have it prepared, to place in the pit when it is dug. I personally make this carving after I have done a Red Meal to Vindonus, the White Lord in the Land, a day before the beginning of the construction of this shrine.

Inside the rectangle, along the western edge of the western long side, write the word DEO in the ground and draw a serpent in front of it. Every time you use this shrine, you should redraw the rectangle and the word "DEO" and the serpent, or any other thing that is easily swept away by wind and time.

Make a spot in the center of the rectangle for a fire-pit or a place for a candle.

To consecrate this built "shrine" for its first use, or for any use, you begin by walking in from the east, through the entrance, and into the center of the rectangle, and always face west. Using this "shrine" as a ritual area, you should always face west. There should be an earthenware or wooden bowl of water there at the center of your rectangle waiting for you.

Touch that water lightly and say:

"Here is water, blessed by Vindonus, a fertile river of life, a medium of ghosts, a water that is a bridge of passage for every spirit, a water that nourishes every living thing; a water of mastery over all- much power, much vision, and from the heights to the depths, the road of the spells of the boundary-keeper and the boundary-crosser."

Then anoint yourself with it, and carry it around the circle counterclockwise, pouring it on the stones, and making the four roads to the cardinal directions.

Return to the center and light the fire, saying

"Here is fire, blessed by the Mothers, given of the maiden, lamp and light to what is seen and unseen, swift spirit and serpent's tongue, heat of life from the Sun and the Land, a star fallen from the sky, living in the body- the warmth of Her blessed bounty, a light in every hearth, and deep below the Earth."

If you have a stag's skull or horns, you may put them to the west of the circle, inside the circle but outside of the rectangle. Say "I place this in the name of Vindonus, the White Stag- with my left hand I place it." If you have a hound's skull or skulls, it or they can be placed to the north, saying "I place this (these) in the name of Vindonus, leader of the hunt- with my left hand I place it (them)." These are really the only other items you should use to "place around" this circle.

When all that is done, say:

"Great Vindonus, see the Hallowed place, ringed by water, ringed by stone, a consecrate plain, a field, a meadow, like unto the sacred mound-fields, temples, all within touches all without and deeper within- here is a sacred seat of fire, a passing place between spirit and man, the indestructible circle of Fate."

Then bow once to the west. After that, you can work.

This shrine can be used for any working- but any Red Meal here should use the "killing" variant of the red meal, always. All Red Meals done here should have their remains poured into the pit dug in the south. If you make petitions here with parchment, they should be burned and the ashes put into the pit, or they should be tossed into the pit while burning.

Any offering brought to Vindonus here should be deposited in that pit, NEVER to be touched again. It is useful to take sticks or flat pieces of wood, and carve requests to Vindos-Vindonus on them, and your own name, as well as your thanks and promises to do more Red Meals and offerings to him in exchange for your favors being answered, and use them in petition rites, dumping them in the pit as well, burned or unburned.

After you have the shrine "set up," if you desire it to be a permanent area, you can return to it without doing all the other ritual motions- just coming into it, making sure the words and lines in the earth are still visible (some people just bite the bullet and carve the word DEO and the serpent on a rock and stick it in the west of the rectangle, and line the rectangle with rock too) and then anointing yourself with some water and lighting a fire, or resting for a moment with your hand on your forehead, as a fire invocation, then continuing with prayers, invocations, or whatever. It is very flexible. You can meld it with the other rites and understandings given in this ritual book.

The "Two Trees" working for entering the Spirit World (Thorn Tree Door)

I was taught this rite from two sources: one was a gentleman that I worked with in 1994, who demonstrated this to me in person, an experience that really drove home how effective this rite is when done properly.

The second source was from an unidentified spiritual being that walked me through it in a dream, only a short time ago, in response to a change that occurred in my own life.

This rite is for creating a "door" and actually physically entering the Otherworld.

So many methods for Otherworldly visits or contacts involve "inner journeying" through meditation or visualization; this is the only technique I have ever come across for actually, physically journeying or moving through the environment of the physical world, and ending up in an "Otherworld" condition.

I should be fair and say that this rite is for creating a broadly defined internal state, a state that you physically walk to transition into or "enter," and thereby make yourself mentally and spiritually open to the presence and contacts of unseen presences or beings.

Unlike "internal" visualizations, this rite keeps you up, awake, and moving, running, or walking the whole time, and in a very different condition than you are used to. The character of the entire "other" reality has a chance to manifest itself. It is a moving experience if done fully to the letter.

There is a touch of danger involved in this process, I admit- though not the "soul stealing" kind of danger that the less experienced and more immature occultists often whine about. The danger in this working stems from a kind of disorientation or confusion that can occur, and the fear or mistakes that it can cause.

This rite can only be done outdoors, and it requires the presence of two trees, in close proximity to each other. Traditionally, they should be thorn trees. But I first saw this technique done with oaks, and it was quite powerful.

You will need a good, quiet, isolated or disturbance-free place; a forest or an abandoned field is best. This technique also works within cities (like on huge campuses or empty parks with lots of hedges and trees), but not nearly as well as in rural locations. Besides, this rite has to be done at night, and city parks at night are not really safe.

The two trees will act as your door, but only after you have done the rite. The use of two trees as a "doorway" point is apparently very old in the British tradition. I have come across mention

of it in places as far apart as the poetry of Yeats, relevant mythology, and the writings of the Matthews, who mention a visionary form of this technique as being "very old."

You will need a bowl and a cup, some water and some bread, and two candles that can be shielded, like put inside of clear cups or candle-holders, to be protected from wind. You will also need a goose feather. If you happen to be a person who has identified with your Fetch-beast, and that beast happens to be a bird, a feather from the bird of your Fetch-form can be used in the place of a goose feather.

This rite can only be done at night. If that night happens to be on of the hidden festival nights, or a holy night, or the night of a full moon, all the better. If the night happens to be very misty or foggy, that is even stronger. If it is all three, this rite would operate at a purely mythical level of strength, to the cunning person who applied themselves to it with true dedication and desire.

Failing all the above times, any night can be used. But you will discover the effectiveness of this rite increasing and decreasing at times. What matters most is that you find a place with two trees that are far from where you will be disturbed, and that it is night-time.

You begin by sitting in front of your two trees, and blessing the water and the bread (in the cup and bowl) and consuming them partly in a modified Red Meal rite. This rite should be simple and powerful. Light one of the candles and use it in the Red Meal- you don't have to make the spell of the road or the blessing of the water, or make the four water roads. You just have to sit before your trees, and light the candle, bless the bread and water (with the blessings given below) and eat and drink one half of both.

This candle that you use has to be lit with firm intention to part the ways between the two worlds with its heat and light, but there is more to it.

The flame of the candle has to be thought of as a beacon of types, to act as a guide for those who are unseen and those who are traveling the unseen ways, but you have to look at the flame as though it were some sort of "meeting point" where both worlds meet, and the means by which they penetrate each other. In some way, the tiny flame is a door, as well, an Otherworldly presence whose very existence causes "locations" to meld and overlap and inter-relate somehow.

In short, you are lighting this flame with the intention of going "through" the door in the air or through the trees, and into the Otherworld.

Thorn Door Red Meal Blessings

Use these following invocations to light the candle and to bless the bread and water.

1. "Come forth, fire, seen and unseen
Source of flame and fire, illuminate the dark world:
Reveal the way beyond.
Burn here: Be the light that marks the way."

2.

"Elfin Queen Under the ground
Behold, a vessel of water
May it be a water that divides the quick from the dead
Bless it with your hand, and I shall drink,
And bring me to that distant Land."

3.

"**Giver of Light, deliverer of man**
Who walks the roads east and west
Who goes below, and rises above
Who makes the crossroads open
See the ancient covenant,
Body as bread, and bread as body
Bless it with your hand."

You must now take what is left of the water only- and pour it, slowly, from the right tree, to the left, making a boundary line. As you pour it, make a short invocation to the Pale People merged with the Land, or the dead, followed by an invocation to Queen Hel or the Queen of Elfhame

These invocations have to be stated slowly, clearly, with all awareness. They "liven" the door.

You then light the second candle from the first one, and place one candle near the left end of the line of water you made, and the other near the right end of it, thus illuminating your doorway. You then take the other half of the bread that you didn't eat, and either put it in your pocket or carry it with you. You must now walk away from the lit doorway you just made, and walk a good long distance. You have to walk, with the door behind you, far enough away that you can't see it anymore. The trick here is to walk in a great big counterclockwise circle, which will of course end up back at the door.

As you find yourself approaching the lit doorway again you should be holding your feather in your right hand and the bread in your left. You have to keep your mind on the **fact** that when you cross through that door you just made, over that water, that you are going, literally, into the Otherworld.

As you get near the door, before you step across, you hurl the bread through ahead of you. That must be done before you step across. Then, you go on through.

Now, from this point, you must not put down the feather. You have passed through into the Otherworld. From the point of your passage through the Two Trees door, to the time that you return to our world, you must be *totally* aware of anything and everything that happens to you- full sensory awareness. What you see or hear or encounter is no longer just an average, everyday encounter- it is an Otherworldly encounter.

If you find something on the ground, something unusual, you may or may not take it back with you. But no matter what you do, you must always realize that it was something that you brought back from another world.

As you wander through the world on the other side of the door, you should do it in a large clockwise pattern. In much the same way you made a huge counterclockwise walk to get to the door, as you wander through the environment on the other side of the door, you should do so in a huge semi-clockwise manner, before reaching the door, and leaving.

You can take all the time you need, but you have to return before the candles go out. Some people don't like to go too far from the candle light, preferring to keep them in sight, even if at a distance. They are the guiding light back home.

You are in a special mental and physical condition when you are on the other side of the door- you have opened yourself to the Otherworld, and symbolically and actually (on the mental and spiritual level) entered it.

Animals or even people that you meet may not be what they seem. The man who showed me this rite in '94 used it as an initiatory rite, as well as a means of divination. If a person is fortunate enough, this rite can be used to find Fetch-beasts, but only if done in a very remote area. I personally don't suggest this rite for discovering the identity of the Fetch-beast, however, I do suggest that this rite can be done in conjunction with other rites to find it.

Everything that you experience on the "other side" of these doors is significant. If Otherworldly beings wanted to manifest to you, they could do so easier, in many ways, while you were on the "far side" of the trees.

Rites that are done on the "other side" are likewise more powerful, as you will discover if you try them.

If the doorway marking candles should be out when you return, that is not a good sign. What you must do in this situation is pick up the bread that you cast through the doorway when you entered, and carry it with you across the threshold again. That will suffice.

If the candles are still lit when you arrive to return into our world, all is well. Just leave the bread where it is on the Otherworld side, and walk on through, and collect the candles and leave. The rite is over.

If the candles are out, and the bread is gone too, that is a VERY bad sign- you must simply exit the Otherworld through the door, and come back and repeat the rite the very next night- and instead of wandering around in the Otherworld the next time you do it, just make a quick clockwise circle and pass back out. Until you have done this, you are considered to be "still there," and in at least a bit of danger.

If you ever drop the feather while in the "Otherworld," that is not a good sign. You must do the rite again the next night, in the same manner as if you had returned to find the candles out and the bread gone.

Since moving through this "door" puts you in closer, (some would say direct) contact with the Otherworld reality, the most moving use of this rite I have ever seen was a necromantic one- a dear friend had died recently (only a week before), and a person I knew did this rite, entered the Otherworld-condition, and sat out there, opening themselves in meditation to the dead one, to contact them. It wasn't long before they experienced the presence of this departed person. This rite is an excellent gateway rite to putting yourself closer to them.

I will be the first to say- in all the years I have practiced the craft, few experiences have been as uncanny as the ones I have had using this rite, at night, in some very lonely places. These sort of rites are useful for putting yourself in the proper states for contact across the strange spaces that keep us so perceptually separate from extra-sensory reality.

I think that this rite can be used to great effect, on certain times, at powerful locations, like grave-mounds and the like: the stories of "doors" opening on certain nights are not just mere folkloric superstition. Naturally, a person needs to be careful and protected when doing such things.

Notes:

1. You can use only one "door marking" candle if you want- the one you used in the Housle or Red Meal. Place it right in the center of the door. I suggest that you use two.

2. If you don't want to carry the feather all the time, you can affix it to the end of a cord that you loop around your neck. That way, even if it comes out of your hand, it will still not fall to the ground, just hang there around your neck.

The Rite of Arriving: Guardianship and the Old Persuasion

You arrive at the hill, the field, or the wood, and so this is called the Rite of Arriving, the Rite of the Ward. You travel to your working place... leaving behind what is familiar to you. This rite is for communing with the Genius Loci, the spirit of a place.

Each of us is ultimately a Mystery, an immortal power rooted in and inseparable from the dark Source Herself. Each individual is deriving its sense and basis of true "self" from Her, and even the will to be...and places are no different. Here is the Mystery within the body of the Green Gown: beyond the Land-Mother is the mysterious Queen of Fate. This is the "Mystery in the green."

Every place is also a reflection of Her, a part of the Green Gown's weave. Every place is also drenched with Her awareness and life.

Thus, it has worked out, from the distant beginning, the truth of animism, first uttered from the lips of the first wise- those primal shamans and seers...all things are "alive"; all places and things have a "spirit." This we can see and experience. The secret is in the reality of your essential being's involvement with Nature and with every hill and ford. You cannot separate the human awareness, mind, and being from the chain of forces that give rise to that which is.

After centuries of contact with men, animals and local flora, the spirit of the place builds a character, its own being becomes involved with humans, becomes influenced by the minds and dreams and events that saturate it, just as people's personalities, feelings, and thoughts are affected on a deep level by the spiritual climate and powers that fill the places where they dwell. This "power of the place" often appears in mythology as a woman (the White Lady), or the warding clan or village Goddess that co-inhabits the Land that she appears on- these are manifestations of the Mystery in the Land itself; the guardian of that place. Sometimes, there is more than one. Other times, the guardian is the presence of a very massive stretch of Land.

Sometimes this guardian can seem to be male, but this is a matter of the seeing person's own intuition. One I have known called itself "spirit of this earth," and it seemed to cover nearly all of a parish, and the Lands our river drained. It was powerful, patient and inquisitive. In truth, I've never "spoken" to a more curious spirit in regards to who I was and what I was doing. I saw it make a very old oak tree totally collapse and destroy two telephone poles, within an hour after I asked it for some visible sign of its presence, to convince myself that I wasn't dreaming up my contact with it, so be careful in your dealings.

The spirits of the Land are called the Hidden People, the Strangers, or the Huldafolk. The powers in the Land were the first Gods that men adored, when ancient people were closer to the potencies of Nature, and had awe and true respect for them. They lived by their blessings of corn, health and game. The heart and soul of the old craft is about the sacramental relationship of man to Nature, which is a divine reality itself. The white powers still exist in the Land, and they exist all about us. They can be dangerous to men, sometimes for seemingly no reason; others can harm by causing accidents in a place, or nightmares, or drive away intruders with unexplainable feelings of dread. Truly wicked or malicious Strangers are sometimes called the "Red Men;" they are the giants of old lore, the chaotic powers that strain against the world-order. The lesson is plain: not all places want people.

The Feeorin, or those hidden folk who dwell below the Land (the post-mortem and pre-birth powers of men and beasts), can emerge in natural places, and often do, but do not confuse them with pure Land spirits. Sometimes, the overlap between them is enormous, enough to make them seem one and the same. In many ways, the Feeorin are such a part of the inner reality of the Land that they are seen as Land spirits. Sometimes a place is even warded by Feeorin. But the manifest activity of the Feeorin in natural locations is almost always tied to temporal cycles; the spirits of a place are the non-human powers that manifest there always. In the end, there are no real clear-cut rules for the spiritual forces in the body of Nature; the boundaries between the Land powers and the Feeorin are always vague.

The following ritual is designed to help establish contact with the guardians of Places. If they are there with any great awareness, and undisturbed, they usually are all-knowing and nearly all-powerful when it comes to their areas, and tend to be very protective.

If you have ever been alone in the woods somewhere, and for no reason experienced a feeling of dread that made you leave, or want to leave, you may have just been "kicked out" of the area by a guardian or the local powers. In our practice, we will not do rituals of any kind in an area without first going to a large Tree (preferably oak or thorn: the tree acts as an interface between the above-Land world and the unseen dimension below and within the Land) in that area, with a wooden bowl of milk, and offering the milk, as well as making a watch fire (described in this ritual book). We say to the guardian(s):

"To the Hidden Ones (or hidden powers) of this Land, Who watch from Below: To the Ward of this place, We make this offering and give you honor and good faith; From you we make bidding to join in the adoration of the Old Ways of our blood herein. You know us by our oaths, and what we love- let us seek Wisdom here."

The Red Meal can be used, utilizing just the milk, for this purpose. For the next while, we wait and watch for any sign of the guardian's acceptance/ refusal. Watch animals carefully, for local animals, especially birds, are often linked with the Wanes, and act as outgrowths of their power.

Listen for winds, listen for any sudden noises or strange sights. No sign is a good sign, in case you see nothing. But your chances of seeing "nothing" in a natural area is not good; all places are full of motion and life. More than anything, you must feel the presence in the place. "Feeling" the place will speak volumes, but you must have no expectations one way or the other as to what you will experience. Go open and free. Sometimes, people will like to do a Compass Round and take the Left-way road at a place to meet the powers therein; that is a more complex way, but just as powerful, if not more so.

Be aware that guardians are not always just the spirit of the natural place: the departed powers of people can become guardians, if they choose or are compelled to merge with a location, as can animals, who in the past were sometimes ritually killed or buried for the purpose. This is especially true for houses and villages. Other spirits and powers can become guardians for many reasons. I suggest you look into Stewart's "Underworld Initiation" for the best insights into the concept of Guardianship.

A Note on Guardians

Why are they "guarding" a place? "Guardianship" doesn't mean that a spirit or power is standing there like a sentinel. "Guardianship" indicates a state of being in which a being, either living or dead, whether it be a human, animal or deity, is "merged" with the inner reality of that place, becoming an innerworldly mediator, ensuring that the proper transfer of power is maintained in an area (the transfer of power from life to death, from form to form, from world to world) and that nothing wrongly or radically disrupts it.

They also are ensuring that the form of the area only changes naturally, or in accordance with respect, and that the environment and those who are dependent on the environment stay intact as well.

Finally, there is a duty of guardianship that ensures that defacement of the area and irreverent behavior or occurrences do not take place within. The guardians or Wards, as they are called, can cause "accidents" to occur, can cause fires or saturate places with feelings of dread; these are their usual tools of defense. Also, those who disrupt the unified power of areas with maliciousness can find themselves trapped in a sequence of events leading to their own misfortune- a self-created sequence of powers that compels them to be merged with the disrupted forces before and after their own bodily deaths; they could find themselves transformed into a power or spirit, bound to ward a place until the power flows harmoniously again.

All of life is a great cause-and-effect participation, a weave of many types of power exchange, countless changes and interlinked events. Never forget that the existence before, within and beyond what we call "life" is exactly the same, though expressed on other levels of awareness. Consequence, in the greatest sense, is something that must always be considered by the wise. There were times in the distant past, when certain people or families were appointed guardians of special locations or holy places. We in the present day can still join in this tradition by adopting places and making sure that they remain undefiled and clean, and treating them with reverence.

With time, and with the acceptance of that place's guardians, they can become powerful locations for the practices of the old faith. But be warned: this is not an undertaking to go into lightly. When you devote yourself to an area, it isn't supposed to be just for a couple of months or even years. Try to make it a lifetime commitment, or even an after-life commitment, because the powers you involve yourself with may require that. At that point, you will begin to grasp at the seriousness of guardianship.

The Rite of Arriving

Just making some pesky little offering and pledging to respect the work-site is not quite enough. It is required that working group members (particularly the leadership or people gifted at consciously experiencing extra-sensory reality) spend time getting to know the guardians or Wards of their area. Once, when I had to live in a city, I started this process from my front yard, and finally made strong contact at a city park, so living in a city is no excuse not to try. The Wane spirit here happens to have a city on its "back," but that doesn't mean that it's not there. Remember, cities are natural places, too.

How do you spend time "getting to know" them? Let me warn you: in many cases, we are not on our ancestor's ground. Be respectful. If you are in the US, and you are of non-native American descent, then you are probably standing on ground that your ancestors took by force, or other less honorable methods.

The local spirits may reject you outright, or if you are polite, they may accept you. It may take weeks or months to get into good rapport with them. One thing is for certain: your effectiveness in ritual and rite will be driven down low if the local guardians or Land spirits resist you. So get on their good side, if possible. If you plan on working near ancient Native American holy sites, be especially careful. I'd suggest that you didn't.

The Rite of Arriving can be done however you like, so long as you have the following "ingredients:"

1.) A libation of milk or ale, to be poured on the ground or at the location.

2.) A Watch-fire. This can be a small built fire, or even a candle. But, when you light it, you must light it with will and intent...you must have the intention to light it, as a sign that "I'm here, ready to talk, let this flame illuminate me, make me visible, guide you to me, keep us warm." Lighting a fire with will and temperance "feeds the Wanes and raises the Feeorin." This signal-fire, when lit with intent, is the key to communing with the powers of a Land. When you light any ritual fire, you have to do it with expectation of power; you have to reverently light it, knowing that by doing so you ARE creating a space and a beacon to which powers can and will be attracted. You have to feel that you are creating and coming into a mystical place. Without this knowledge and acceptance, you can consecrate no fire or anything else.

3.) An emotional link to the place and the guardian. You have to desire the communion, desire to learn about the place, to get Otherworldly insight into the place. You need the desire to be accepted at that place. The powers there act as mediators, and you must desire to know the inner nature of the place, and to experience it, and to demonstrate it, which is what "ritual" at a natural location (particularly a sacred place) really is.

4.) Symbolic Nakedness. You must learn to become symbolically "naked;" in other words, to have the trust, simplicity, openness, and willingness to be receptive and learn that a youthful child possesses. Your self-assured, "educated" adult self cannot do this. Become the "naked" child again, confronting the Mystery of the wide world, and really listen.

5.) The Words of Power. These words are "Here I am; grow forth, Hidden Ones, and witness my art. Come to the Watch-fire. I pray you teach me." End your invocations to the guardians with those words, introduce yourself by name and your mother's name. Again, you can use the Left-way road to make contact; this was the older way, and is still just as appropriate.

Never forget that the key to authentic, genuine experiences when communing with these powers is to have a good passivity in regards to what you will "see;" harbor no expectations and stay clear and open to what is there.

* * *

As far as the Rite of Arriving, that's it. Other than that, just make sure this rite is done alone, and at night. Go to them. They won't generally come to you- until they know you, that is.

And, one more piece of advice: All Land spirits/guardians around the world have one thing in common, and we happen to share this commonality- we have the same mother and Queen. The true Queen below and within, the Veiled One- She is Queen of the Land powers as well as humans. If you love Her, follow Her, respect Her, they will know it, and probably react better to you. Also, The guardians/Land spirits will all respond to Her name, and the name of Old Fate, and react to your using it. They know what the real power is; they exist in it. It is hard to separate the two from each other.

She is essentially "the supreme being" to them, as She is to all things. One can easily see how closely related "Land spirits" and the "Earth Mother" concept would have to be. Many Land powers are direct manifestations of Her, especially the ones that appear as dark, stately women, or women clad in white or on horses.

List of Essential Books and Works

If you are interested in traditional Paganism, and related scholarship involving folklore, esoterica, and studies of antique religions, supernaturalism, and older worldviews, I can suggest no better books than these- these are the books that have been my companions and friends throughout my own spiritual quest.

From these books, and from these authors, I have gained some of my most important understandings and insights, all of which were keys to my eventual discovery and realization of my personal path to the Old Ways. These books were essential to the writing of the book you now hold. Please look these books up and acquire them, because these works by talented and insightful people are true treasures, invaluable dispensers of knowledge that unlocks doors in the mind… doors to deeper places.

"Call of the Horned Piper" by Nigel Jackson
"Masks of Misrule" by Nigel Jackson
"The Compleat Vampyre" by Nigel Jackson
"The Pillars of Tubal Cain" by Nigel Jackson and Michael Howard
"In the Dark Places of Wisdom" by Peter Kingsley
"Reality" by Peter Kingsley
'The Myth of the Eternal Return" by Mircea Eliade
"The Underworld Initiation" by RJ Stewart
"The Living World of Faery" by RJ Stewart
"Power Within the Land" by RJ Stewart
"Celtic Gods, Celtic Goddesses" by RJ Stewart
"The Western Way, Vol.1: The Native Tradition" by Caitlin and John Matthews
"The Celtic Spirit" by Caitlin Matthews
"Haunted Clwyd" by Richard HolLand
"The Crooked Scythe" by George Ewart Evans
"Confessions of a Pagan Nun" by Kate Horsley
"Pagan Celtic Britain" by Anne Ross
"Witchdom of the True" by Edred Thorsson
"British Fairy Origins" by Lewis Spence
"Twilight of the Celtic Gods" by David Clarke and Andy Roberts

"Hero Tales from the British Isles" by Barbara Leonie Picard

"The Mabinogion" trans. by Lady Charlotte Guest

"Celtic Britain and Ireland" by Lloyd and Jennifer Lang

"The Age of Stonehenge" by Colin Burgess

"The Way of Wyrd" by Brian Bates

"The Real Middle Earth" by Brian Bates

"The Inner Mysteries of the Goths" by Nigel Pennick

"Ecstasies: Deciphering the Witches Sabbath" by Carlo Ginzburg

"Practical Magic in the Northern Tradition" by Nigel Pennick

"The Triumph of the Moon" by Ronald Hutton

"The Sacred Ring" by Michael Howard

"Leechcraft" by Stephen Pollington

"By Standing Stone and Elder Tree" by William Gray

"Myths of the Norsemen" by H.A. Guerber

"Grimm's Complete Fairy Tales"

"Celtic Myths and Legends" by T.W. Rolleston

"The Norse Myths" by Kevin Crossley-HolLand

"The Elements of Earth Mysteries" by Philip Heselton

"Witches, Werewolves, and Fairies" by Claude Lecouteux

"Witchcraft: A Tradition Renewed" by Evan Jones

"The Roebuck in the Thicket" by Evan Jones

"Dionysos" by Carl Kerenyi

"Eleusis" by Carl Kerenyi

"The Gods of the Greeks" by Carl Kerenyi

"Prometheus" by Carl Kerenyi

"The Spiral Dance" by R. Garcia Y Robertson

"The Great Mother" by Erich Neumann

"Shadow and Evil in Fairytales" by M.L. von Franz

"The Way of the Shaman" by Michael Harner

"Fire in the Head" by Tom Cowan

'The Red-Haired Girl from the Bog" by Patricia Monaghan

"Light from the Shadows" by Gwyn

"Mastering Witchcraft" by Paul Huson

"A Celtic Book of Days" by Sarah Costley and Charles Kightley

"Mysterium Coniunctionis" by Carl Jung

"The Golden Ass" by Apuleius

"The Oxford Dictionary of English Folklore" by J. Simpson and S. Roud

"An Encyclopedia of Fairies" by Katharine Briggs

"The Vanishing People" by Katharine Briggs

"The Knots of Death" by Alby Stone
"The Bleeding Lance" by Alby Stone
"A Splendid Pillar" by Alby Stone
"Ymir's Flesh" by Alby Stone
"Straight Track Crooked Path" by Alby Stone

"The Knots of Death," by Alby Stone which was quoted in this work, was first published in The Cauldron 65, Summer 1992. To see more works by Alby Stone, please visit this website:

http://www.hoap.co.uk/stone.htm

Index

A

Adam 23, 196, 217
Aelda 122
Aleithea 121
alfablot 56
alfar 56
ancestor 49, 53, 76, 350
Ancient White One 39
Andras 90
Andred 110
animism 48
animist 48
Annwn 92, 95, 97, 120
Aphrodite 119
Apollo 97, 98, 201
Apollon 60, 61, 97
Arawn 97, 100
Asgard 120
Ash 6, 23, 324
Ash-Protection Charm 324
Awen 143
Azael 90

B

Ballad of Tam Lin 6, 182, 187, 192, 200, 201
Beauty 5, 70, 71, 72
blessing 137, 154, 225, 284, 285, 287, 290, 295, 340, 341
Bloodmother 39
Blot 284
Bone fire 282
Brahman 29
Briggs, Katherine 131, 194
Brigid 119, 120, 124
Britain 35, 71, 93, 94, 97, 121, 143, 353, 354

C

Cailleach 116, 118, 120, 121, 124
Callirius 100
Candlemas 172
Capax Dei 155
Cauldron 96, 355
Celts 44, 50, 54, 57, 60, 64, 97, 120, 124

chaos 76, 143, 152
Christianity 13, 21, 25, 26, 29, 89, 236
clairvoyance 135
Coedygadfa 325
Compass 6, 92, 273, 280, 291, 292, 294, 296, 298, 300, 306, 307, 308, 309, 310, 312, 316, 317, 322, 323, 324, 333, 348
Conal Cernac 90
cosmos 46, 70, 73, 74, 76, 93, 119, 137, 209, 233
Crooked Path 5, 165, 233, 355
Cunning 89, 111, 153, 154, 155, 156, 174, 217, 231, 279, 308
Cunning Fire 111, 231
Cunning Serpent 89, 155, 156
curse 27, 29, 57, 154, 198, 199, 307, 317, 322
Cwn Annwn 92

D

Dagda 97
Daimon 46, 49, 54, 57, 61
Dame Dark 111
Dame Venus 112, 122, 124
Demeter 56, 114, 143, 245
Deus 61
Devil 89, 93, 204, 231, 292, 294, 295, 299, 304
Diamond Body 225
Diana 237
Dionysos 61, 354
Dises 50
Distaff Line 64
Divine Child 150, 152, 155
Double 5, 46, 80
Druid 141

E

Earth 23, 51, 52, 56, 65, 74, 100, 110, 112, 114, 116, 118, 121, 126, 127, 128, 217, 244, 245, 250, 251, 255, 284, 287, 299, 302, 306, 308, 311, 334, 336, 352, 354
Earth Goddess 112, 114, 116, 245
Eddas 51
Eildon Thorn 180
Eleusis 114, 143, 354
Elf 17, 56, 285
Elfhame 36, 39, 110, 111, 115, 126, 127, 128, 171, 180, 193, 194, 198, 217, 231, 289, 295, 298, 299, 300, 306, 311, 342
Elfland 122, 193, 196, 199, 200, 201, 232
Ellhorn 110
Ellorn 110
Enody 231, 238, 301, 304

ensorceling 322
Enthusiasmos 61
Eros 71
Etruscan 119
Eumenides 114
Eve 23, 192, 196, 217, 329
Exorcising the Restless Dead 6
extra-sensory reality 24, 233, 344, 350

F

Fae 54, 126
Faery Marriage 232
Faery Mound 231
Faery Rade 126, 192
Feeorin 54, 126, 181, 285, 347, 351
fertility 23, 93, 129, 201, 296, 302, 306, 307, 308, 317
fetch 10, 27, 172, 215, 231, 251, 302, 340, 343
Fetch-beast 165, 285
Finn Macool 95, 96
Fintan 66, 96
Freedom 77, 78, 79, 82, 83, 84, 87
Frey 93, 125
Freya 119, 120, 125
Frigga 120
Fullness 37, 40
fundamentalist 25
Funeral Cult 6, 235
Fylgja 49

G

genuine experience 38, 140, 173
Germania 23
Germanic 44, 59, 64, 70, 115, 120, 198, 285
Ghost Roads 212, 246, 255, 276, 277, 278, 279, 280, 281, 282
Ghost Tree 5, 135
Gnostics 217, 219, 232
God 5, 27, 38, 39, 49, 54, 59, 60, 61, 62, 69, 76, 89, 93, 94, 97, 98, 100, 112, 114, 124, 135, 142, 145, 185, 196, 217, 219, 240, 244, 245, 283, 312
Gods 6, 15, 24, 27, 28, 29, 30, 31, 40, 41, 47, 49, 51, 54, 55, 56, 57, 58, 59, 61, 70, 78, 79, 110, 111, 112, 114, 115, 120, 121, 141, 142, 150, 151, 152, 153, 154, 155, 162, 164, 182, 196, 197, 202, 218, 219, 240, 241, 242, 244, 246, 283, 295, 296, 347, 353, 354
Godstone 69, 308
God of Light 60, 61, 97
Going Forth 6, 292, 294
Grand Array 128, 158, 166, 232
Grand Seal 79, 92, 141

Great God 61, 94, 97, 244
Great Inheritance 62, 92, 235, 250
Great One 43, 98, 100, 120
Great Queen 5, 39, 70, 71, 95, 100, 119, 120, 122, 275, 315, 333
Greece 66, 117, 118, 143, 201, 206, 245
Greek 44, 50, 57, 60, 97, 114, 117, 118, 119, 121, 195, 245
Greencoaties 129
Grey women 128
Guardian 6, 193, 204, 207, 208, 209, 231, 331, 332, 346, 348
Gwyn 95, 96, 97, 100, 354

H

Hades 55, 56
Hecate 114, 238
Hel 110, 115, 116, 117, 118, 119, 120, 122, 283, 295, 299, 342
Henry III 325
Hermes 55
Hestia 119
Hidden Folk 128
Hindu 29
Hissing of the Serpent 5, 139, 140, 153
Hob-th'rus 90
Holda 116
Hooded Ones 74
Horned One 10, 89, 96, 98, 165, 243
Horn Child 61, 71, 150, 155
Horseman 90
Housle 6, 159, 166, 168, 273, 275, 277, 280, 283, 308, 345
Hudec, Ivan 51
Hulda 116
Huldafolk 115, 347
Hyldor 110, 115, 122, 325
Hyldor Queen 122

I

Imbas 143
immortal 30, 31, 37, 42, 48, 54, 57, 59, 60, 62, 66, 143, 154, 158, 193, 200, 222,
    232, 346
Incubation 157
Incubi 232
Indestructible Life 71
Indo-European 23, 45, 94, 96, 111, 117, 118, 120, 121, 291
Induction Charm 6, 329
Infinite 28
Initiation 6, 38, 166, 195, 229, 230, 231, 329, 348, 353
Invocation 6, 310, 312, 314
Ireland 10, 11, 35, 66, 121, 143, 194, 354

Irish 57, 95, 96, 118, 194
Islam 29

J

Jesus 243, 244
John Barleycorn 6, 240, 242, 243, 244, 245
journey 13, 53, 55, 58, 128, 138, 160, 167, 196, 219, 221, 223, 294, 295, 320
journeying 35, 165, 276, 295, 339
Judeo-Christian 22, 27, 29
Justice 114, 181, 245
Justified Ones 38

K

Kalypso 116
Kerenyi, Carl 51, 354
King of Faery 100, 295
King of the Woodland 100
Kingsley, Peter 97, 119, 151, 353
Kolyo 96, 112, 116, 117, 118, 119, 120, 121, 122, 128
Kore 56, 114, 116, 124, 143, 217

L

Lancashire 126
Land-based 35, 129, 164
LeCouteux, Claude 44
Left-way road 165, 296, 298, 329, 348, 351
Lethe 56
life force 45, 46, 51, 54, 55, 56, 184, 283
Lord of the World 92, 97
Love 31, 53, 54, 56, 57, 71, 72, 119, 194, 199, 200, 230
Lugh 60, 97, 243

M

Mabon 71, 143, 145, 150
Magna Mater 114
Malkin 281, 308
manifestation 15, 24, 36, 48, 50, 57, 60, 70, 71, 74, 75, 94, 110, 119, 122, 252, 275, 276, 302, 320
Master 5, 6, 38, 39, 79, 80, 85, 89, 90, 92, 93, 95, 97, 98, 100, 126, 128, 138, 153, 158, 165, 166, 168, 216, 218, 224, 225, 227, 289, 294, 295, 296, 299, 301, 302, 306, 307, 308, 309, 310, 312, 314, 315, 317, 319, 323, 329, 331
Master-souls 38
Master Men 5, 38, 126, 128, 158
Master Puck 90
Matriarch 5, 110, 166
Matrones 50

Matthews, Caitlin 66, 353
meadows of Elfhame 126
meditation 156, 339, 344
Meister Eckhart 142
Mithraic 243
Modron 110
Mogontia 98, 100
Mound 3, 6, 118, 231, 238, 243, 246, 248, 309
murder 30, 182, 184, 185, 246, 283, 338
Muslim 29
Mysteries 5, 59, 60, 61, 62, 68, 69, 114, 121, 143, 230, 354

N

Naming 144
Nature 14, 15, 22, 23, 38, 40, 41, 43, 46, 54, 65, 69, 71, 72, 73, 74, 75, 89, 90, 92,
         93, 94, 100, 110, 118, 121, 135, 137, 143, 145, 148, 157, 158, 162, 200, 206,
         209, 217, 218, 233, 242, 244, 245, 272, 276, 315, 332, 346, 347
neo-pagan 198
neo-pagans 25, 27
Night 111, 155, 248, 251, 281
Nine Nights 63
Nornir 50, 74, 118
Norns 50, 74, 118
Norse 49, 50, 117, 118, 119, 120, 124, 354

O

Odin 117, 118, 120
Old Fate 39, 51, 68, 78, 95, 96, 110, 111, 116, 118, 122, 124, 182, 246, 306, 331,
         352
Old One 89, 92, 166, 249, 254, 289, 294, 299, 300, 304, 305, 310, 314, 315, 330,
         333
Old Persuasion 6, 165, 346
Old Rite 6, 230, 235, 242, 244, 247, 248
Old Ways 5, 6, 10, 11, 13, 14, 31, 35, 36, 39, 41, 64, 66, 71, 80, 89, 131, 132, 137,
         138, 166, 175, 177, 182, 235, 241, 271, 272, 273, 276, 284, 296, 319, 322,
         329, 348, 353
Ondred 110
oneiric 167, 173, 174
Otherworld 24, 31, 36, 39, 50, 57, 58, 70, 96, 111, 128, 137, 142, 165, 181, 182,
         184, 194, 195, 198, 201, 202, 203, 207, 218, 223, 224, 232, 278, 284, 310,
         339, 341, 342, 343, 344

P

Pale People 5, 97, 111, 126, 128, 129, 181, 229, 251, 284, 285, 288, 289, 301, 327,
         342
Pale Woman lying below the Land 110
Pandora 23

paradox 43, 77, 78, 81, 197, 202
Parmenides 119, 120
Pereplut 54
Persephone 114, 116, 119, 143, 195, 245
Pouck 90
Pripelaga 51
Psyche 55, 56
Psychopomp 55
Puckril 165, 166, 170, 171, 231, 232, 235
Pwyll 95, 100, 120

Q

Queen Hel 110, 116, 295, 299, 342
Queen of Elfhame 39, 110, 115, 126, 128, 171, 180, 193, 194, 198, 217, 342
Queen of Faery 110, 198
Queen of Hell 110
Queen of the Dead 111, 112, 120, 199, 245, 311

R

rebirth 24, 35, 41, 44, 54, 56, 57, 63, 64, 65, 66, 77, 126, 127, 183, 185, 193, 195,
    197, 198, 200, 331
Red Meal 6, 159, 168, 248, 273, 275, 283, 284, 285, 286, 287, 288, 289, 290, 309,
    316, 320, 321, 323, 331, 335, 338, 340, 341, 345, 348
Red Thread 5, 62, 63, 79
regeneration 36, 56, 63, 111, 112, 120, 201, 202, 231, 236, 240, 242, 246
renewal 36, 203
Rhiannon 100, 120
Rigantona 100, 120
Ring of Art 6, 291, 293, 309, 310, 330, 333
Ring of Art invocation 293, 309
Roodmas 172
Rose Queen 112, 122, 124, 308
Rozenhitsye 50

S

Sabbat 139, 172, 295, 296
Sabbats 172
Sacrament of Bread and Wine 6, 283
Sacred fire 69
Sacred King 61, 241
Sacred Meal 282
sacrifice 117, 180, 184, 193, 194, 195, 197, 198, 201, 202, 221, 230, 235, 236, 238,
    241, 243, 245, 249, 251, 273, 283, 284, 285, 309, 329
Salmon of Knowledge 96
salvation history 24
Sator 90
science 25, 26, 27, 74

secret name of God 124
Serpent in the Land 5, 139, 140, 159
Seven Year Tithe to Hell 6, 201
shimmering 165, 172
Sidh-folk 111
Sidhe 54, 126, 127, 285
Silvanus 98, 100
Slavic 44, 50, 53, 54, 60, 61
soul 10, 15, 27, 31, 32, 41, 44, 45, 46, 47, 48, 53, 54, 55, 58, 63, 65, 66, 67, 68, 80, 110, 121, 124, 126, 141, 143, 152, 162, 177, 183, 185, 194, 197, 204, 221, 222, 223, 231, 232, 242, 276, 321, 339, 347
Spell of the Road 6, 287, 292, 296, 299
Spence, Lewis 127, 353
spirit 10, 13, 14, 15, 21, 27, 45, 46, 47, 48, 49, 50, 51, 52, 53, 54, 55, 57, 58, 60, 61, 62, 64, 67, 75, 89, 92, 114, 115, 121, 122, 125, 127, 157, 165, 166, 197, 200, 223, 225, 232, 240, 249, 250, 254, 255, 278, 279, 285, 286, 289, 299, 301, 302, 307, 310, 312, 314, 315, 317, 321, 330, 336, 338, 346, 347, 348, 349, 350
Stang 95, 306, 311
Stone, Alby 116, 118, 355
Succubi 232
Supreme Being 61, 112, 121
Svarog 61

T

Tam Lin 6, 182, 187, 189, 190, 191, 192, 193, 194, 195, 196, 197, 198, 199, 200, 201
Tao 50
Termagant 61
The Cruel Mother 178
The False Knight on the Road 6, 204
The Path of Initiation 6, 229, 230
The Rite of Arriving 6, 282, 346, 350
The Strangers 5, 129
The Tale of the White Serpent 6, 213
Thirteenth Hour 38
Thomas the Rhymer 171, 180, 196
Thorn 6, 180, 273, 327, 339, 341
Thorn Tree by the Crossroads 6, 327
Thorn Tree Door 273, 339
Tir nan oc 57
Tiwaz 61
Trance 5, 133, 135, 138, 153, 154, 155, 167, 274
Treading the Mill 168
True Beings 39, 76, 78, 79, 153, 158
Truth 5, 6, 23, 24, 30, 31, 37, 41, 42, 58, 68, 70, 71, 72, 73, 77, 78, 79, 80, 84, 87, 90, 121, 137, 142, 143, 144, 145, 149, 152, 181, 182, 185, 198, 205, 206, 207, 208, 209, 210, 211, 212, 224, 312, 322, 334

Tuirigin 66, 67
Tyr 61

U

Underworld 36, 39, 43, 51, 53, 54, 55, 56, 57, 59, 63, 65, 69, 71, 92, 94, 95, 97, 100,
110, 111, 112, 114, 115, 116, 119, 120, 121, 122, 126, 127, 128, 129, 130,
137, 139, 152, 162, 165, 180, 181, 183, 192, 193, 194, 195, 196, 197, 198,
199, 200, 201, 206, 220, 229, 230, 231, 235, 236, 238, 243, 245, 246, 255,
271, 272, 276, 277, 278, 279, 281, 284, 289, 292, 294, 295, 299, 300, 301,
306, 309, 311, 317, 327, 348, 353
Urd 74, 79, 118
Uroboric Darkness 95

V

Veiled One 112, 116, 128, 158
Veles 60, 61
Vindonnus 97, 98
Vindonus 98, 100, 289, 335, 336, 338

W

Wales 65, 90, 93, 95, 100, 325, 326
Ward 282, 346, 348, 350
Wassail 225
Western Isles 57
White horned king 94
White King 39, 100, 139, 165, 248, 284, 300, 313, 315, 333
White Lady 65, 95, 121, 346
White Stag 96, 100, 309, 335, 336
White Tree 5, 69, 135
White Under-Wood 36
Wholeness 6, 36, 40, 50, 128, 137, 154, 157, 225
Widdershins Walk 5, 139, 165, 166, 167, 168, 172, 173, 174
wisdom 11, 16, 24, 26, 27, 28, 29, 30, 36, 37, 38, 39, 41, 43, 44, 56, 57, 58, 59, 60,
64, 67, 68, 73, 76, 78, 79, 82, 83, 85, 101, 110, 121, 128, 129, 142, 164, 166,
171, 179, 183, 185, 196, 204, 208, 213, 216, 217, 219, 221, 222, 224, 230,
236, 238, 246, 251, 273, 275, 330, 331, 334, 348
Wisdom-Metamorphosis 38
Witch-Ring 6, 273, 291
Witchmother 5, 39, 110, 139, 284, 292
Woden 23, 60, 61, 70, 97, 117, 120, 198
Word of Creation 92
worldview 13, 21, 22, 23, 24, 25, 26, 27, 28, 29, 31, 35, 36, 62, 68, 85, 137, 164,
166, 272
Wormsel 296, 299, 301
Wyrd 31, 68, 70, 74, 75, 76, 354

Y

Yarilo 61
Yarthkins 129
year and a day 201, 231
Ygdrasil 70
Young Puck 5, 142

Z

Zerinthia 231
Zeus 56, 61, 121

About the Author

Robin Artisson is a proponent of Land-centered traditional Paganism and a believer in the Wisdom to be found encoded in the symbolism of folklore, mythology, and in traditional stories and ballads. He is the coordinator of the Owlblink Bookcrafting Company and the founder of the Hollow Hill Fellowship. Robin loves Owls.

For more information, see:

www.robinartisson.com

Lightning Source UK Ltd.
Milton Keynes UK
25 June 2010

156110UK00001B/97/P